Regent's Stu
General Editor: 1

Flickering Images

Theology and Film in Dialogue

Regent's Study Guides

Flickering Images

Theology and Film in Dialogue

edited by
Anthony J. Clarke
Paul S. Fiddes

Foreword by David Coffey

Regent's Park College, Oxford
with
Smyth & Helwys Publishing, Inc.
Macon, Georgia

© 2005
Published by Regent's Park College, Oxford OX1 2LB, UK
in association with Smyth & Helwys Publishing, 6316 Peake Road,
Macon, GA 31210, USA

The paper used in this publication meets the minimum
requirements of American National Standard for Information
Sciences—Permanence of Paper for Printed Library Materials.
ANSI Z39.48–1984 (alk. paper)

Flickering Images: Theology and Film in Dialogue

Library of Congress Cataloging-in-Publication Data

Flickering images / [edited by] Paul S. Fiddes & Anthony J. Clarke.
p. cm. (Regent's study guides; 12)
Includes bibliographical references and index.
ISBN (USA) 1-57312-458-3 (pbk. : alk. paper)
ISBN (UK) 0-9539746-1-81.
Motion pictures--Moral and ethical aspects.
I. Fiddes, Paul S.
II. Clarke, Anthony John.
III. Series.

PN1995.5F555 2005
261.5'7--dc22

2005021591

Contents

Foreword..ix
David Coffey

Notes on Contributors xiii

Acknowledgements xvii

1. Introduction 1

Part One: Methods

2. Movies and Meaning: 7
   An Introduction to Reading Films
   Robert Ellis

3. Understanding Films: Reading in the Gaps....................25
   Steve Nolan

4. Transcending the Cave: Fantasy Film 49
   as Spiritual and Philosophical Reflection
   Léonie Caldecott

5. Gaining Fresh Insights: Film and 59
   Theological Reflection in a Pastoral Setting
   Anthony Clarke

Part Two: Reflections

6. Virtual Literalism: *Big Fish* 83
   David Sutcliffe

7. When Text Becomes Voice: *You've Got Mail* 97
   Paul Fiddes

8. Bucking the System: *One Flew Over the Cuckoo's Nest* 113
   Nicholas Wood

9. Taking the Waves by 'Surprise': 123
   Master and Commander
   Sally Bedborough

10. Pondering Providence: *Sliding Doors* 137
    Robert Ellis

11. Fatherhood, Fate and Faith: *The Terminator* Series 149
    Simon Carver

12. All-Consuming Holiday Snaps: *Open Water*...............................163
    Tim Bradshaw

13. Finding God in the Holocaust: *Schindler's List* 175
    John Weaver

14. The Grace of the Valar: *The Lord of the Rings* 193
    Stratford Caldecott

15. The Trouble with Paradise: *Pleasantville* 207
    Chris Holmwood

16. Interpreting the Gospel: *The Passion of the Christ* 217
    Steve Holmes

Part Three: Resources
John Weaver and Larry Kreitzer

Introduction to Part 3..231

17. *The Mission*: Some Missiological 233
    Dilemmas Portrayed

18. *Blade Runner*: On the Definition of Humanity 241

19. *Witness*: 'In the World, but not of the World' 247

20. *Amadeus*: The Destructiveness of an 251
    All-Consuming Jealousy

21. *Gandhi*: The Strength of Weakness..255

22. *The Killing Fields*: The Extreme Limits 263
    of Friendship

23. *The Color Purple*: Breaking Through 271
    the Barriers of Prejudice and Violence

24. *1984*: Controlling the Past and 279
    Determining the Future

25. *Cry Freedom!*: Living with Apartheid 287

26. *Bridget Jones's Diary*: Self-Image and Self-Worth.....................295

27. *Saving Private Ryan*: The Value of a Single Life 303

Index of Films 309

Foreword
David Coffey, President of the Baptist World Alliance

As I sat in a cinema on Saturday mornings in the 1950s and watched the weekly episode of *Jessie James*, I confess there was very little theological reflection as Frank and Jesse James robbed banks and performed railroad hold-ups.

Deeper thinking was stirring when I saw *Bridge over the River Kwai* (1957), *Ben Hur* (1959) and *Lawrence of Arabia* (1962). But a true dialogue between film and theology probably began with *Becket* (1964) and *A Man for all Seasons* (1966), and the rest is a personal history of flickering images.

I was reared in a Christian climate which saw Hollywood and Ealing Studios as a threat to discipleship and some of my respected Christian mentors, to whom I owe so much, would have agreed with the theological perceptions of Herbert Miles who declared movies were 'the organ of the devil and the moral cancer of civilisation'.[1] With hindsight, in my early years as a Christian there was an absence of any dialogue between cinema-going and Christian discipleship. You went for light entertainment to see Doris Day in *The Glass Bottom Boat* (1966) – and I can still hum the theme tune – and for escapism to *The Ipcress File* (1965) – and I preferred Len Deighton's book. But it was never with an expectation that a visit to the cinema might be a divine encounter or that a movie scene could be a sign of God's active presence in his creation. Paintings and art galleries – yes; films and cinemas – no. I was awaiting that C. S. Lewis experience of the 'baptism of the imagination' that enables a way of seeing and is fostered by a discipline of looking and listening, reflecting and evaluating.

This evaluation of film is best done in community and I am grateful for being a member of a film group for the past fourteen years and for the companionship of a group of friends with whom I can enjoy, reflect and think. As a group we have come to appreciate the distinction that Robert K. Johnston makes between the analytical and the revelatory in films.[2] A true dialogue between film and theology will analyse critically the metaphors and messages of the film maker. Is Oliver Stone's *JFK* (1991) a spectacular re-enactment of the greatest controversy of the 20th century or an irresponsible piece of revisionism? Is Mel Gibson portraying in *Braveheart* (1995) the Christian virtues of courage and self-sacrifice or is the film a revenge fantasy? Have the brothers Larry and Andy Wachowski provided in *The Matrix* (1999) a new contextualisation of the gospel in the main story line or are the points of connection too tenuous to be taken seriously? Is *Johnny English* (2003) a hilarious spoof spy thriller or a sign of the coarsening and vulgarization of our culture?

The revelatory experience will be more personal. There is ample evidence of film-goers experiencing transcendent moments and glimpses of divine insights through a film. It is reported that following the release of Spielberg's *Saving Private Ryan* (1998), young people in their twenties were challenged freshly about the morality of war and sought out veteran soldiers in their seventies to thank them for the heroic sacrifices they had made in the Second World War.

I can remember sitting in a Melbourne cinema and experiencing an overwhelming stillness of spirit as I watched the endless litany of names scrolling through at the end of *Cry Freedom* (1987). I cried as I allowed the injustice of the Steve Biko story to wash over my mind and heart and this film came back to me when many years later I stood outside the prison cell on Robben Island which had been occupied by Nelson Mandela. I was numbed by the capital punishment scenes in *The Green Mile* (1999) and was made to review my thinking on restorative justice. I thought the scene in *The Man Who Sued God* (2001), where Steve Myers (played by Billy Connolly) sits in an empty church and gazes at the figure of Christ on the cross, was a deeply compelling image without words and, for me, the heart of the film.

I am glad that such a book as this has been written and I look forward to using it as a creative companion for my occasional visits to the cinema. As one of the characters says in the film *Grand Canyon* (1991), 'everything you need to know about life is in the movies'. Not totally true - but it *is* a great starting point.

Epiphany 2005

Notes

[1] Herbert Miles, *Movies and Morals* (Grand Rapids: Zondervan, 1947), p. 20.

[2] Robert K. Johnston, *Reel Spirituality: Theology and Film in Dialogue* (Grand Rapids: Baker Academic, 2000), p. 154, and more extensively chapter 8.

Notes on Contributors

Sally Bedborough, having trained for Baptist Ministry at Regent's Park College, Oxford, is now minister at Hill Street Baptist Church in Poole, Dorset and a team chaplain at Poole Hospital.

Timothy Bradshaw is an Anglican priest, who has served in churches in Hackney and Bristol, and most recently in Oxford. He has been a tutor at Trinity College, Bristol and is now Senior Tutor and Fellow in Christian Doctrine at Regent's Park College, Oxford. His books include *Trinity and Ontology* (1988), *The Olive Branch: An Evangelical Anglican Doctrine of the Church* (1992) and *Praying as Believing* (1998).

Léonie Caldecott is associate director of the G. K. Chesterton Institute for Faith & Culture and co-editor of the Institute's journal *Second Spring*. After winning the Catherine Packenham Award she earlier worked as a journalist, writing for the *Guardian*, *The New York Times Book Review*, *Over 21* and a variety of other publications. She is a regular contributor to *The Chesterton Review*, *Touchstone* and *The Catholic Herald*.

Stratford Caldecott is the Oxford director of the G. K. Chesterton Institute for Faith & Culture, which is based at Seton Hall University in New Jersey. His books include *An Appeal to the New Age* (1992) and *Secret Fire: the Spiritual Vision of J.R.R. Tolkien* (2003).

Simon Carver trained for Baptist ministry at Regent's Park College, Oxford, and has been minister of New Road Baptist Church, Oxford for over ten years. He is also Associate Chaplain at Regent's Park College.

Anthony Clarke is Tutor in Community Learning at Regent's Park College, Oxford and editor of the Theological Journal *Regent's Reviews*. He is a Baptist minister who has served churches in Essex and Oxford. His books include *A Cry in the Darkness. The Forsakenness of Jesus in Scripture, Theology and Experience* (2002).

David Coffey, a Baptist minister, is General Secretary of the Baptist Union of Great Britain, Moderator of the Free Churches, a Co-President of Churches Together in England and, from July 2005, President of the Baptist World Alliance. He has published *Build That Bridge: Conflict and Resolution in the Church* (1986) and the Crossway Bible Guide to *Romans* (2000).

Robert Ellis, after taking his doctorate in Theology at Oxford, was minister of Baptist churches in Milton Keynes and Bristol. He has taught at Bristol Baptist College and is currently Director of Pastoral Studies at Regent's Park College, Oxford. He has published *Answering God. Towards a Theology of Intercession* (2005).

Paul S. Fiddes, a Baptist minister, is Professor of Systematic Theology in the University of Oxford and Principal of Regent's Park College, Oxford. His books include *The Creative Suffering of God* (1988), *Past Event and Present Salvation* (1989), *Freedom and Limit: A Dialogue between Literature and Christian Doctrine* (1991), *The Promised End. Eschatology in Theology and Literature* (2000), *Participating in God. A Pastoral Doctrine of the Trinity* (2000) and *Tracks and Traces. Baptist Identity in Church and Theology* (2003).

Steve Holmes has taught at Spurgeon's College and King's College, London as well as being minister of a Baptist church in London. He is currently Lecturer in Theology at St Mary's College, St Andrew's University. His books include *God of Grace and God of Glory: An Account of the Theology of Jonathan Edwards* (2000) and *Listening to the Past: The Place of Tradition in Theology* (2002).

Chris Holmwood is Assistant Head at Shenley Brook End Secondary School, Milton Keynes. He studied English at Regent's Park College, Oxford and as a former Head of English in schools he speaks at national conferences on teaching English, especially Shakespeare.

Larry Kreitzer, a Baptist minister, is Fellow and Tutor in New Testament at Regent's Park College. He is also a University Research Lecturer within the Faculty of Theology in the University of Oxford. His many books include several in the area of film and theology: *New Testament Images in Fiction and Film* (1993), *Old Testament Images in Fiction and Film* (1994), *Pauline Images in Fiction and Film: On Reversing the Hermeneutical Flow* (1999), and *Gospel Images in Fiction and Film: On Reversing the Hermeneutical Flow* (2002). His books on the New Testament include *Jesus and God in Paul's Eschatology* (1987), *The Gospel According to John* (1990) and *The Epistle to the Ephesians* (1997).

Steve Nolan is currently chaplain at the Princess Alice Hospice in Esher, Surrey. He is a Baptist minister who has previously served at Kingsbury Baptist Church, London. His doctorate, through the University of Manchester, was entitled *Faithful Representations: an application of 1970s Lacanian film theory to the study of liturgical subjectivity.*

David Sutcliffe, having trained for Baptist Ministry at the Northern Baptist College, Manchester, is minister of Milford Baptist Church, near Godalming, Surrey.

John Weaver is Principal of the South Wales Baptist College, Cardiff and Dean of the Faculty of Theology, Cardiff University. Previously he was minister of Highfield Baptist Church, Rushden, Northamptonshire and Director of Pastoral Studies at Regent's Park College, Oxford. He has published largely in the area of science and theology, including: *In the Beginning God: Modern Science and the Christian Doctrine of Creation* (1994) and *Earthshaping, Earthkeeping: a Doctrine of Creation* (1999).

Nicholas Wood is a Baptist minister who has served churches within the city and county of Oxford. He is currently Tutorial Fellow in Religion and Culture and Director of the Centre for Christianity and Culture at Regent's Park College. He will shortly be publishing *Faith in a Pluralist Society.*

Acknowledgements

Grateful thanks is offered to those publishers who have allowed previously published material to be reworked and included in this collection.

The chapter 'Movies and Meaning: An Introduction to Reading Film', by Robert Ellis, was first published as an article in *Expository Times*, vol. 112, No 9, 2001, and is reprinted here by kind permission of Sage Publications Ltd (©Sage Publications Ltd 2001).

The chapter 'The Grace of the Valar: *The Lord of the Rings*' by Stratford Caldecott is based on material developed in the author's book *Secret Fire: The Spiritual Vision of J R R Tolkien* (London: DLT, 2003) and an article in the journal *Second Spring*, volume 4, and has been kindly offered for publication here.

The chapter 'Interpreting the Gospel: *The Passion of the Christ*' by Stephen Holmes is based on the article 'Getting Passionate with Mel Gibson' originally published in The Bible Society periodical, *The Bible in TransMission* (Summer 2004), and is included here by kind permission of The Bible Society.

The diagram of the 'Pastoral Cycle' or 'Doing Theology Spiral', on page 63, from Laurie Green, *Let's Do Theology: A Pastoral Cycle Resource Book*, p. 30, is printed by kind permission of the publishers Continuum Books, London (©Continuum Books 2001).

Cover image: *A-1208* by Maurice Estève,1989. Aquarelle sur papier, 56,10 x 49,50 cm. © ADAGP, Paris and DACS, London, 2005.

1
Introduction

On 28th December 1895 August and Louis Lumière showed their film *Arrival of Train at Station.* The audience recoiled with fright at the train steaming towards them. The cinema was born. After a century of technological innovation and mass marketing techniques, the cinema is now a huge global business, whether the products are watched in the new shimmering multi-plexes or via DVD on a flat plasma screen television. Even with the increasing rise of television, the cinema has managed to hold its own, and now experiences something of a revival. Part of the explosion in the UK of television options is the growing number of 'film' channels.

The growth of cinema itself has also spawned a growing academic interest in film as a particular and unique medium, and from the second decade of the twentieth century serious reflection on film began. With the rise of alternative theories of film and the burgeoning of university courses on various aspects of media studies, the impression is certainly that the study of film is on the rise. Much more recently there has been an emerging interest in the relationship between theology and film, or perhaps it may be more accurate to suggest that there has been a growing interest in film among theologians. Films have always drawn both on biblical stories and biblical images, although directors and producers have interpreted them in their own way. The commercial success of *The Passion of the Christ* shows that the biblical story still sells, and the 'secular' appropriation of parts of Genesis chapter 3 in *Pleasantville*, as explored later in the book, suggests that both the knowledge and power of biblical images lives on.

This growing interest in film and theology can be seen at a number of levels. At an academic level a number of books explore a variety of different approaches for entering into this dialogue, and offer a range of models and examples. These include such collections as John May's *New Image of Religious Film*,[1] which arose from an international symposium on religious film, theology and religious culture, Joel Martin's and Conrad Ostwalt's *Screening the Sacred*,[2] Clive March's and Gaye Oritz's

Explorations in Theology and Film: Movies and Meaning,[3] and the book by Robert Johnston, *Reel Spirituality: Theology and Film in Dialogue*.[4] At a much more popular level, the widespread availability of data projectors in churches allows films or clips of films to be shown in a whole variety of church events, including public worship.

This book thus sets out to make a contribution to this flourishing subject, in the hope that it will both encourage and enable continued reflection on this particular aspect of popular culture. It is written with a particular focus on the needs of those working in pastoral situations. With this in mind it does not assume any particular knowledge of film theory or of the debate about the nature of dialogue between theology and film. The book also does not attempt to offer and or even work towards some overarching theory of film criticism, but starts with an open agenda, allowing different voices to be heard. Its aim throughout is to offer resources to those who wish to use a dialogue with film to explore and deepen their faith, and who might help others to do the same.

The first part of the book engages with some of the material on film theory, and offers a number of pieces which explore the more general relationship between theology and film. Robert Ellis' chapter, for example, on 'Movies and Meaning' provides an opening overview of the subject and suggests, among other things, that films can be interpreted or 'read' in theological, mythological and ideological ways. He himself concentrates on the first two kinds of reading. Steve Nolan's chapter, one of the more demanding parts of the book, argues strongly in favour of an ideological approach to understanding film, and also provides the most technical engagement with the realm of film criticism. In some ways his approach differs from others in the book, in that his concern to develop one particular way of reading films – as 'signifying practices' – necessarily offers a critique of other forms of interpretation. He does share common ground with other writers in stressing the importance of story, but emphasizes the need to be alert to the way that a film attempts to draw the viewer into a story which has certain ideological presuppositions. It is only after we have discerned this, he suggests, that we can reflect theologically on what is happening in the film and in the viewers.

We think it to be a healthy feature to offer such a debate within the covers of the book itself. Our hope, in fact, is that this first section may open a small window into a much bigger field, offering a taste of various approaches that readers can follow up for themselves, through references in the notes and through the books mentioned above. The first part continues with a piece by Leonie Caldecott that explores the way one particular genre of film, in this case fantasy, develops ideas and provides resources for spiritual and theological reflection. Other genres could also be explored in the same way, and some of the chapters in the second part offer ideas about the function of other genres within the dialogue between film and theology. The final chapter in this section, by Anthony Clarke, suggests some ways in which the dialogue can be enabled to happen in the setting of a church service or study group.

The second part of the book works out some of the principles surveyed in the first part, in relation to a number of specific films. The eleven different authors have chosen a particular film and sought to engage in dialogue between it and Christian theology. This dialogue is clearly two-directional, allowing a reading of the film to shape theological interests, and then giving space for theology to speak back to the issues raised by the film. We hope that these chapters will model a variety of ways of proceeding with this dialogue, suggesting ways that films can stimulate theological reflection and encouraging readers to make similar journeys with other films which they have watched. The pieces tend to exemplify readings that have been identified in the first section as 'theological' or 'mythological' – understood, mainly, as 'existential' (concerned with typical aspects of the human situation) – often moving from the existential to the theological. However, some of them also show awareness of ideological issues, identifying either a predominant ideology reflected in the making of the film or, more often, an attempt by the film-maker to undermine a popular ideology. In all, the readings accept and reflect the complexity of meanings in a film and also the diversity of intentions. The individual chapters are self-contained and can be read in any order.

The third part of the book is based on a further eleven films but in a form which we hope will be particularly useful for those wishing to use a film as a basis for bible study and reflection in a church context. Each chapter provides the details for the film, a synopsis of the plot that could be used as a foundation to help those involved to explore the film and then a series of questions gathered round a number of themes that aid further reflection. The synopsis is detailed, but also tends to highlight issues that are going to be raised again in the questions. It may be particularly helpful when only clips of a film can be used in a study-group or church service. Again the accounts of individual films within this section are self-contained, but it is recommended that the opening chapters in the first section are read as resources for exploring this dialogue.

The films in the second and third parts have not been chosen because they form a collection which explores common themes, or because they are deliberate representatives of varying genres of film, although some similar themes will emerge and the films are very varied in type. Rather, the diversity of the films emphasizes the point that this book is attempting to bring together in dialogue theology and film in its widest sense. It is our conviction that the theological dialogue is not to be restricted to those films with a biblical basis or a clear religious setting. With the exception, to some degree, of *The Passion of the Christ*, the films discussed in the book are not Christian, but rather secular products from mainstream cinema. Whereas some do have religious characters, use religious images or explore some religious themes, many have no such connection with faith or theology. But they do explore life. And the motivation for this book is that theology should engage with all the various expressions of culture, high and popular, that we come across.

This book, then, encourages a dialogue with that which is 'other' to theology and different from it, in the belief that thereby insight and meaning can be gained. We hope that readers will journey both with us in the book, and without us in their own reflections on film, so that the dialogue may continue.

Notes

[1] John R. May (ed.), *New Image in Religious Film* (Kansas: Sheed & Ward, 1997).

[2] Joel W. Martin and Conrad E. Ostwalt Jr (eds.), *Screening the Sacred: Religion, Myth and Ideology in Popular American Film* (Boulder & Oxford: Westview Press, 1995).

[3] Clive March and Gaye W. Oritz (eds.), *Explorations in Theology and Film: Movies and Meaning* (Oxford: Blackwell, 1997).

[4] Robert K. Johnston, *Reel Spirituality: Theology and Film in Dialogue* (Grand Rapids: Baker Academic, 2000).

Part I
Methods

2
Movies and Meaning:
An Introduction to Reading Films

Robert Ellis

The cinema business is booming. Multi-screen cinemas sprout across our cities, and shelves heaving with videos and DVDs are on display in local video libraries and chain stores. Cinema-going in Britain is enjoying a revival and many homes own a selection of pre-recorded films as well as having their own particular muddle of self-made recordings. DVD is adding another dimension to home entertainment, with the battle over newer formats of DVD recently in the headlines. The British film industry, so much and so often lamented, is producing films which not only win critical acclaim but also gain a handsome box office return. The Hollywood 'dream factory' goes on producing films of variable quality and commercial viability, but every year a few blockbusters appear which seem to grip the popular imagination.

Yet despite the widespread appeal of film, in its various formats, there has until relatively recently been little attempt to reflect theologically on its form and content. This is now changing, and this chapter will outline some of the work done and indicate possibilities for further reflection by its readers. Lest such a project still need justification it ought to be borne in mind that the vast majority of our fellow Britons will this year watch many films. Certainly, more people, even among churchgoers, will watch more films than they will read books! It is fairly commonplace to find theological reflection on various literary forms: poetry, novels, drama. Yet the most accessible and consumed medium is largely ignored.

Departments in universities and colleges are establishing 'Film Studies' as a subject with its own integrity, data and tools. Many arts subjects include the option to study film in one form or another, and it is now not uncommon to find courses in religious studies and its near relations also encouraging such study. Those who teach in this way speak of the way in which the study of film motivates students to participate and empowers them, for students feel that they 'own' films, that they are part

of *their* culture.[1] The appeal of film as a 'pedagogical tool' is also
ascribed to its ready availability, the immediacy of its impact, and the
congeniality to modern audiences of images rather than words.[2]

There is a resistance, perhaps, to taking seriously as data for theological reflection a medium so often dismissed as 'popular' (a loaded, and
imprecise word) and ephemeral. Yet films also raise some basic questions
about religion, faith, and the way we look at the world. These questions
include: 'Who am I?' 'Who are we?' 'What does it mean to be human?'
'Where are we?' 'What's real?' 'What's the relationship between human
experience and transcendence?' 'What's wrong? What's the remedy?'
'Where are we going?'[3] As we shall see, it is precisely in those films
which might at first be dismissed as 'popular' that the most fruitful theological engagement may come.

Films are often 'read' as 'texts'[4] and the variety of approaches to film
parallels literary criticism in general, and biblical criticism in particular.
Indeed, this comparison is interesting. Just as form critics studied the way
in which certain sorts of story conform to certain formal patterns, so also
in film such formal patterns can be discerned and analysed. Reader-
response, and other approaches to texts, have focused on the way in which
the audience is addressed or 'constructed' by the text, and similarly many
film theorists have sought to examine film in such a way. Just as redaction
criticism looked for the 'hand' of the final editor, so some films can be
viewed against the literary texts upon which they are based, or on the previous movie of which they are 'remakes', or in the way a Director
interprets a screenplay. Some writers, notably Robert Jowett and Larry
Kreitzer, have deliberately brought scripture texts and 'film texts' into dialogue in a way which is sometimes creative and fruitful.[5]

Three approaches to the theory of film

Amongst the many approaches to film theory three stand out as the most
generally accessible, each offering theological food for thought.

First there is an approach arising from a branch of French film criticism. *Auteur theory* sees the director as the 'author' of the film and seeks
to trace his or her creative hand through a canon of films. Common
themes, and their development, are followed. Such an approach sees the

director as an especially powerful and creative talent, the master or mistress of the process of film-production. The film is his or her 'text'.

Second, *genre studies* examine the common themes, traits, and iconography[6] of particular genres of films, analysing their appeal and the themes considered most successfully dealt with within the genre. This approach often finds the most creativity at the point where the conventions of a given genre are broken down and transcended.[7]

Third, *star studies* consider the nature and appeal of star performers, and why particular types of star, and particular individual stars, appeal to fans. The history of Hollywood has in certain respects been the history of stars, and an analysis of their changing relationship to audiences, and indeed the changing audience and what it requires in its stars, may be illuminating.

However, each of these approaches, valuable though it is so far as it goes, has certain weaknesses which mean that they can only be pursued with caution. The theological 'reader' needs to be aware of this.

Auteur theory founders on the complexity of the film itself. All sorts of pressures are brought to be bear on directors, and often a film is issued in its final or 'release' form in a version other than the one the director wanted. Especially in older films made under the 'studio system,'[8] the producer of the film has often occupied a position at least as important as the director. In discussion of *Ben-Hur*, for instance, the producer is often lauded more than the director who is spoken of as little more than an artisan.[9] In the cult sci-fi film *Blade Runner* a key line of dialogue was inserted into the final edit against the wishes of the director, and only later was the 'director's cut' issued with the ending he favoured.[10] Such stories are legion, and when one considers the complexity of the process of film production it would seem foolish to ascribe too much power to the director / *auteur*.

A novel is usually the work of one hand. Whereas a novelist normally bears total responsibility for what appears on the pages of his or her book, though in reality an editor, and even a publisher, may have made suggestions or even demands about the final form, in film-making the situation is more complicated. A film is the work of many hands. There are not just the normal contributors to dramatic production, such as writers, actors, directors, various technicians involved in lighting and stage management, but also editors, cameramen, continuity people and producers, and increasingly special effects technicians. Decisions about how a film will be seen are made in the politics of production as a huge number of people vie for their particular input given the constraints of time and money, and often audience focus groups are shown different versions of the film to test commercial responses to storylines and endings. Sometimes the producer overrules everyone, even the director, and is sometimes in turn overruled by those holding the purse strings. Richard Maltby speaks of Hollywood's 'commercial aesthetic' as the criterion which governs the production of films.[11] When one considers the complexity of film-making, whose 'text' is the film? With how many voices does it speak? Will it, can it do more than utter fragments of sense?

That said, it is clearly true to say that some directors really do seem to have the clout, the ego, and the sheer determination to get their way most of the time. A film's credits can be revealing. When Martin Scorsese directs a film, his name will almost certainly appear elsewhere on the credits too, for example, as writer or co-writer, as producer or co-producer. His collaborators will also re-appear in several films indicating partnerships judged to be creatively fruitful. James Cameron, Stanley Kubrick and Steven Spielberg would also have multiple credits.[12] This indicates a far greater total control and suggests to us that sometimes it is proper to speak of a film as a text with an author – though only in a qualified sense. Those who seek theological meaning in a film will be familiar with the way that seeking the 'author's intention' is one possible line of enquiry into the meaning within movies.

However, a realization of the complexity of films and the many hands involved in their creation might lead us to another conclusion regarding their 'message', a concept that will also need careful construal. How does a message emerge from this apparently chaotic process? Often that 'message' will express, accidentally or deliberately, some commonly held or widely assumed sort of truth. The collaborative venture of film-making often yields up a shared and possibly 'unmeant' meaning! Meaning happens. This observation will prepare us for a discussion, below, of the ways meanings emerge from movies, and it will come as no surprise to those who have become familiar with various attempts to 'deconstruct' a text, scriptural or otherwise.

If *auteur* theory has limited application, 'genre studies' have also proved to be limited. As with any system of classification, problems have emerged about what films fit into what genre. The difficulty of fully defining genres has proved debilitating. Of course, *The Magnificent Seven* is a 'western'. To describe it further as an adventure story is merely to unpack something of what 'western' usually means. But what about *Thelma and Louise*? It might be called, and probably has been, any of the following: comedy, adventure, drama, domestic drama, crime. It is frequently referred to as a 'road movie', which is sometimes a 'cross-genre genre'! But few of these labels on their own would prepare an audience adequately for the film they were to see when they go to watch *Thelma and Louise*. Each label gives only a partial insight. A more fruitful way of approaching this film may be to 'read' it 'ideologically' (see below for details). But this might be found no more enlightening by the average audience.

The difficulty of classifying films into types and genres is encountered when one attempts to classify 'religious' films. Some films very obviously deal with 'religious' or theological themes. The most obvious are what I will call the 'Jesus films', but others also have clear religious content. We might think here of *The Exorcist*, and Monty Python's *The Meaning of Life* has a number of sketches which implicitly, or explicitly, challenge received religious values and beliefs. Some films, by contrast, would require a real struggle to extract any theological ore for further smelting. However, in the middle, and largely unexamined, a huge corpus of 'popular'[13] films awaits theological scrutiny and consideration. These films, often with 'meaning' or significance embedded in the complexity of their production, tell stories about how human beings see themselves and their situations, their hopes and their fears. Precisely because they are *popular*, because people pay to see them and to see similar films again and again, it is clear that the 'message' these films communicate resonates with their audiences. In the matter of genre, almost every film is in some sense a 'religious film'.

'Star studies' can lead off in interesting directions. Arnold Schwarzenegger, Bruce Willis, Mel Gibson and Harrison Ford tend to play (as stars have always done) similar sorts of roles, and each present their audiences with different types and images of masculinity with which to identify or reject. The persona of a star comprises both on-screen and off-screen elements. As Richard Dyer has suggested,

> Stars articulate what it is to be a human being in contemporary society; that is, they express the particular notion we hold of the person, of the 'individual' ... they articulate both the promise and the difficulty that the notion of individuality presents for all of us who live by it.[14]

But star studies become speculative and unconvincing when they push their categories of interpretation, often drawn from semiotics and psycho-analytic-derived theories, too far.

The phenomenon of the film star, and its proper and inevitable study, is another ramification of the complexity of film production. Many hands make a film, but, even supposing you had seen them, could you say who directed *Die Hard*, or *The Fugitive*, or *Four Weddings and a Funeral*? Perhaps, but could you say who had produced them, or directed their photography? If you will forgive my presumption, probably not. But if you had seen them you would be more likely to be able to name their *stars*.

A theologian, or indeed an evangelist, may be interested and intrigued to analyse why and how our contemporaries revere and identify with such individuals. What lessons, for instance, might there be in the way that Jesus Christ, himself portrayed as a *Superstar*, is presented to the world in which stars are lionized and imitated? Could star studies prove a fruitful avenue of investigation?

Different ways of 'reading' a movie

Given that film is part of our mass culture, a readily accessible and often enjoyable medium that has a special place in much youth culture, and given also that films raise basic questions about religion, faith, and the way we look at the world, how might we approach films in order to reflect theologically upon them?

Joel W. Martin and Conrad E. Ostwalt Jr organize the essays in their collection *Screening the Sacred*[15] according to a threefold pattern of methodological approaches which they claim to have discerned in the contributors to the book, and more generally in work on religion and film. They suggest that writers on religion and film can be deemed to be theological, mythological or ideological critics, and their work can be examined and tested accordingly. These categories, or modes of 'reading' films, are not prescriptive or definitive, nor are they mutually exclusive. Some films might usefully be read in more than one way, and some in other ways as yet unidentified. Martin and Ostwalt have given useful clues as to how we might access meaning in movies.

1. Theological Criticism
Theological criticism will use such traditional concepts (doctrines) as sin and salvation, grace and hope, as a means of accessing a film's meaning. These concepts provide a 'window to understanding the film's intent'.[16] Sometimes theological criticism will use an allegorical key, and sometimes it will discover Christ figures in films. Examples given here are *Cool Hand Luke, One Flew over the Cuckoo's Nest, Rocky* and *E.T.* While there is sometimes a temptation to find Christ figures too readily, the Christ figures often bestow blessings on those around, transcend their surroundings, and suffer to redeem their communities. A theological approach to film stimulates viewers to think about profound religious themes, and the approach often employs tools used by literary critics focusing on atmosphere, character, plot and tone, features often attributed to the intention of the film's 'author', where appropriate.

2. Mythological Criticism
Mythological criticism focuses on 'universal truth' as opposed to the more particularistic renditions of a given theological tradition. Through human time, and across human cultures, myths have enabled humanity to connect with 'their psychological and religious depths, aspects of their world not normally accessible by their conscious mind.'[17] A mythological reading of a film identifies the way it taps into universal human feelings and reactions, and assumes films have a distinct relationship to archetypes (universal symbols) and communicates them to modern audiences in a meaningful way. In such a way, films enable their audiences to encounter life's deeper questions and meanings. These films often have a hero figure who embarks upon a form of mythic journey in which they confront evil in myriad forms. If they prevail against such foes they undergo a transition to a new dimension of living; if they succumb they help the audience

name the social forces that thwart human fulfilment. Films in mind here include: *Star Wars, Tender Mercies, Field of Dreams, Groundhog Day, Alien*, and many more.

3. Ideological Criticism

Ideological criticism owes much to the work of Louis Althusser who believed that ideology was not a consciously held set of beliefs (like, say, Marxism) but that which connects individuals to socio-economic reality by giving them a way of thinking about the world, themselves, and their role in the world. Thus defined everyone has an ideology, though they may not be aware of it. Many film critics influenced by Althusser see film as a system of representation which portrays and reinforces, or perhaps challenges, given socio-economic relationships and assumptions. *Rocky* is thus seen as a film reinforcing certain racist attitudes in American society, and the use of some religious imagery in the film is all the more alarming; *Blue Velvet*, with imagery drawn from the Garden of Eden explores male gender identity. An ideological reading, then, may discern how the structures of society, culture and institutions function to dis-empower or alienate certain groups.

We might notice an important feature of film and its study here. In general terms, when we watch a play on stage our viewpoint will depend on the director, designer and others who have set up the stage for a scene, and perhaps also our seating position. But in a quite different way, when we watch a film we are *made* to watch it in a particular way. Film is based on illusion,[18] and the camera's position is an element of this. We can be made to watch a particular scene from high or low angles, from over the shoulder of a character, even sometimes 'through their eyes'. The careful construction of each *shot (mise-en-scène)* 'frames' the action in particular ways. All of these techniques affect our view of the people and places we see.

Richard Maltby offers an ideological reading of *Ordinary People* based on the film's *mise-en-scène*, and the way in which one of the characters is repeatedly isolated in camera shot, or framed in doorways or other structures.[19] However, this film, and its proposed reading, also indicates the difficulty and ambiguity of 'reading' a film. The character isolated by Robert Redford's direction is the mother in a family grieving for a dead son, who has been killed in a boating accident. Many reviews of the film cast the mother as villain: she seems the least ready to face her loss, and at the end leaves her husband and surviving son in order to be alone.[20] Critics saw in her a threat to 'family values', but Maltby follows an ideological critique which sees the mother as the victim of patriarchal oppression, and he supports this argument from a careful observation of the way in which the scenes are constructed and framed.

Those whose background is in some of the theological and hermeneutical debates of the last few decades may find something else of interest in *Ordinary People*. Robert Jowett infuriatingly insists on interpreting the film by quoting from and referring to the novel on which it is based.[21] The vast majority of people who see the film will not have read this novel, and his method of interpretation thereby privileges certain viewers with 'inside' information. More significantly, this method refuses to allow the film its own integrity as a 'work of art',[22] its independence. Film critics need to use something more akin to canonical criticism, taking the text of the film as it is.

Martin and Ostwalt can write that

> ... religion, thanks in part to the cinema, is reaching more people than ever. As viewers look toward the screen they are 'seeing' religious themes, theologies, morals, myths, and archetypes represented in a visually compelling medium ...[23]

Their threefold approach to reading film offers a useful way into discovering the meaning which inheres in and is offered by films. There are other methods[24] but theological, mythological and ideological criticisms – together as well as separately – can be convenient and productive tools.

Exploring movies and their meanings
What sorts of theological reflections on film might then be possible? It will be useful for our purposes here to give a list of certain types of issues that may emerge for their audience from films. We are not here classifying films by genre. Rather this is an attempt to indicate how films from a great variety of genres yield and discuss familiar themes, and here I am mainly confining myself to *theological* and *mythological* 'readings' of

films. I leave it to the writer of the next chapter, Steve Nolan, to make the case for a thorough-going *ideological* reading. Thus my listing of 'film types' here is somewhat arbitrary and extremely provisional, merely an aid to discussion and reflection.

1. *'Jesus' films*

When one speaks of 'religious film' many listeners will assume one is speaking of films that relate the story of Jesus of Nazareth. While this has been done many times in many ways, it is difficult to do satisfactorily. Films often appear over-reverential and even 'wooden' in their represen-tation of Jesus himself. John O. Thompson suggests that this is to do with the difficulty of representing the divinity of Jesus Christ in a spatio-tem-poral setting.[25] Yet films which take risks in representing Jesus, like Scorsese's *The Last Temptation of Christ*, are often vilified and even banned. *The Last Temptation* in fact offers a genuine reflection of the humanity of Jesus upon which many of the 'faithful' could usefully reflect. Mel Gibson's *The Passion of the Christ* might be said to suggest the 'otherness' of Christ through the use of an Aramaic script, and maybe even by the barbarity of the suffering depicted; it is a film which has pro-voked controversy for what might be seen as its strong orthodoxy. Rather like Gerd Theissen's book *The Shadow of the Galilean*[26], *Ben-Hur* is a 'Jesus film' in which Jesus never actually appears. It is actually all the more powerful for this, with its vivid representation of the effect Jesus had on people, and the healing power of his death. *Monty Python's Life of Brian* might even be said to come into a similar category.

2. *'Christ' films*

Another, much larger corpus of films might be said to consist of 'Christ films', or films in which a character is 'Christ for' those around him or those watching. The list could be very long, with many rather debatable inclusions, but the figure who 'delivers' others and sacrifices himself is remarkably common. Such 'deliverers' are frequently un-Christ-like in significant ways. The mainstream adventure story often pits, for example, Bruce Willis against some malign threat which has emerged arbitrarily and destructively, threatening to engulf its victims. The *Die Hard* trilogy is a good, and entertaining example. Willis usually wins through despite being pushed to the edge of destruction himself, and against apparently impossible odds. But while Willis' character risks himself, and even behaves selflessly, the 'deliverer' he portrays ultimately beats violence with more 'redemptive' violence.[27] Similarly, the loner who is the hero of the western, *Pale Rider*, is identified by reference to the Book of Revelation and has many 'marks of Christ' about him; but in the end we just get a good old fashioned western shoot-out.

It is in identifying both the points of identity and difference between cinematic 'deliverers' and Christ that fruitful discussion can take place. In contrast to deliverance through violence, Luke Skywalker refuses to fight in the climactic scene of the *Star Wars* trilogy in *Return of the Jedi*. To fight and give in to his anger and hate, the evil emperor tells him, will begin his movement to the dark side. Luke refuses, and is almost himself destroyed before evil destroys itself. But Luke Skywalker makes a problematic Christ-figure. The heroes of *Dead Poets Society* and *The Shawshank Redemption* provide more promising 'Christs', though the congruence is far from complete. *Terminator 2: Judgement Day* is often mentioned in this regard also, since the portrayal of the robotic hero incorporates self-sacrifice, a resurrection of sorts, and the power of the future in the present.[28] The female 'Christ' in *The Fifth Element* is vulnerable and at risk, but represents, as does *Terminator 2*, certain issues in the debate over the 'two natures' of Christ, human and divine.

A promising Christ-figure from recent film is seen in *The Matrix*. The film reminds us again that science fiction is a particularly useful genre for exploring such issues, with its greater imaginative reach. *The Matrix* is also a violent film, but with many biblical allusions, such as the way that Neo Anderson battles against evil and defeats it, which has some parallels to the *Christus Victor* understanding of atonement. In a host of interesting ways traditional Christological concepts such as incarnation and resurrection are explored in such films.

3. 'The Meaning of Life' and 'Who Are We?' films
Many films raise fundamental questions about the meaning of human life. *Forrest Gump*, which arouses such varying reactions even within one viewer let alone a group, uses the motif of a feather borne on the breeze at its beginning and ending to reinforce the central character's question of

whether life is just one thing after another, or whether there is any purpose to it. *Dead Poets Society* raises questions of fundamental meaning, and the TV producer in *The Truman Show* is a little too uncomfortably like certain portrayals of the divine.

Movies which deal with questions about human identity are closely related to those which explore the meaning of life, and include *Blade Runner* with its focus on the role of memory, and *Blood Simple* with its dark and nihilistic vision of a humanity alone and fragmented without hope of redemption or damnation[29]. *Life is Beautiful* and *Schindler's List* show both the evil and the good of which humanity is capable, but offer different visions of how the two interact within the context of Nazi genocide.

4. 'Humanity and sin' films
The cinema shows itself well able to explore the nature of sin, perhaps because it gives its producers an opportunity to be gruesome and appeal to the voyeuristic element in its audience. *Seven* is an unpleasant film, underlit, with colours greyed out, and with almost every outdoor scene set in driving rain in a decaying urban setting. But this rain cannot wash away the sin that gets closer and closer to home. A serial killer works his way through the seven deadly sins, suggesting that the sin of the world finally arrives on our own doorstep, embodied in the person of the leading actor with whom the majority of the audience will feel it may identify. Sin is real; hope of redemption is absent. *The Godfather* and *The Godfather Part II* explore power and corruption and the erosion of ideals (of a sort), as well as the aloneness and alienation of the sinner.

Martin Scorsese's remake of *Cape Fear* gains from being 'read' against the film's original version (despite my criticism above of a similar strategy with regard to *Ordinary People*). The director has had the 'original' very much in mind while shooting his version and continuity with it is provided in a number of ways within Scorsese's film. The modern penchant for ambivalence comes through in the way that, early on at any rate, the 'baddie' is not wholly bad, and the 'goodie' is not wholly good. However, the villain, reciting scripture and speaking in Pentecostal tongues, demonstrates that he who takes vengeance to himself usurps

God's place, and the final images of the film are of rebirth and renewal. It is a remarkable and powerful piece.[30]

Dead Man Walking airs the issues around the death penalty in the story of a nun appointed to be the spiritual advisor and advocate of a murderer on death row. The film manages not to take sides in any facile way, but explores the possibility of forgiveness, and the humanity which lurks beneath our sin, however awful. Sister Helen quotes Jesus as someone who thinks people are worth more than their worst act. Many 'ideological' readings of films identify structural sin: at one level, for example, *Thelma and Louise* is about the way men treat, or mistreat, women. This film also offers some hope, in friendship most of all, and in the ability to transcend a given space and time; yet the question remains as to whether the ending is triumphant, comic or tragic. The screenwriters set out to create a feminist film, though as some thoughtful treatments have pointed out, it is by no means certain that they have been entirely successful.[31]

5. 'What-if?' films, or films about the future

A number of films provide intriguing meditations on the nature of the future and its openness. The romantic comedy *Sliding Doors* shoots two alternative stories which develop for the same characters, hinging on whether the leading lady catches, or misses, an underground train. We are led to reflect on how apparent coincidence can change our lives so completely. Then the two endings converge. Is this a profound suggestion about human freedom and its relation to some sort of providence? The viewer must choose. I offer an extended study of this film in the next section of the book. *The Terminator*, and *Terminator 2: Judgement Day* take their viewers on a mind-blowing loop whereby the future influences the present, and finally a 'visitor' from the future takes action in the present which will mean that he will never exist in the future! *Minority Report* also explores the question of whether the future is fixed or open, and this futuristic crime thriller suggests some ambiguity on the matter.

6. 'Beyondness' films

Many Hollywood films suggest some sort of transcendence or 'beyondness', another world beyond our senses. *Field of Dreams* is amongst them, with its treatment of our relationship with the past; *Ghost* and *Truly*

Madly Deeply both use 'beyondness' as a motif to explore human love and life. Films which go 'beyond' to an afterlife are very revealing. No more does Saint Peter meet the newly deceased at the gates, and any hint of judgement or a personal deity is gone. *What Dreams May Come* and *City of Angels* portray a form of human fulfilment from which such elements have been excised, and all is suffused in a warm glow of human satisfaction and non-value-laden existence. We are back nearer ancient immortality than Christian heaven, with a few guardian angels thrown in for good luck. Is this really what people believe? I suspect it is. What should we say about it?

Such lists can be extended. Other types that immediately spring to mind are 'Good versus Evil' films and 'Apocalypse' films.[32] What this chapter suggests is that there is much in the view that religion is a constant and recurring theme in contemporary popular film, even though organized religion and explicit Christian faith are treated seldom and even then emerge in a frequently poor light.[33] By approaching films with the tools of key Christian concepts, and by being also alert to mythological and ideological considerations, it is possible to see that movies come to us laden with meaning. This meaning not only helps us to understand our contemporary world better, but also furnishes us with accessible ways of airing and discussing key theological issues.

Movies express something of the approved positions of the world in which we live. Whether they are held consciously or unconsciously, these positions have to be identified and understood if true dialogue and effective preaching is to be possible. Paradoxically, while laden with religious images and themes, these films also often implicitly express a view of the world very much at odds with the Christian gospel. Although, and even more *because*, we are entertained by such films, we need to be aware of their implications and able to offer a critique of them. Mythological perspectives on films may provide ripe opportunities for the gospel to fill in universal stories with particularist detail. And we will sometimes stumble across the gospel travelling incognito in some celebrated box office hit. Such a joyful discovery is reason enough to take seriously this powerful and popular medium.

Notes

This chapter is an expanded version of an article first published in *The Expository Times*, Vol. 112, No 9, 2001, and is reprinted here by permission of Sage Publications Ltd (Copyright, Sage Publications Ltd 2001).

[1] Conrad E. Ostwalt, 'Religion and Popular Movies', *Journal of Religion and Film*, 2/3 (1998). This American specialist journal, published on the internet, provides a useful introduction to some of the issues and methods of reflection being employed, some bibliographical leads, and indications of how 'religion and film' is being taught. Web-site: *www.unomaha.edu/~wwwjrf.*

[2] Barbara de Concini, 'Seduction by Visual Image', *Journal of Religion and Film*, 2/3 (1998)

[3] Gordon Mathies, 'Religion and Film: Capturing the Imagination', *Journal of Religion and Film*, 2/3 (1998)

[4] They are often referred to in this way, for instance, in the essays collected in Joanne Hollows and Mark Jancovich (eds.), *Approaches to Popular Film* (Manchester: Manchester University Press, 1995).

[5] See Robert Jewett, *St Paul at the Movies: The Apostle's dialogue with American Culture* (Louisville: Westminster, 1993) and *St Paul Returns to the Movies: Triumph over Shame* (Grand Rapids: Eerdmans, 1999); Larry Kreitzer, *Pauline Images in Fiction and Film: On Reversing the Hermeneutical Flow* (Grand Rapids: Continuum, 1999) and *Gospel Images in Fiction and Film: On Reversing the Hermeneutical Flow* (Sheffield: Continuum, 2002).

[6] A term used to signify the various visual motifs in a given genre (such as costume and props) which provide 'a shorthand system enabling the knowledgeable viewer to glean a great deal of information about the characters and the situation simply from the way the characters are dressed, the kind of clothes they wear, and so on': Richard Maltby, *Hollywood Cinema: An Introduction* (Oxford: Blackwell, 1995), p. 117.

[7] See the chapter on 'Genre' in Maltby, *Hollywood Cinema*, pp. 107-143.

[8] Maltby, *Hollywood Cinema*, pp. 71-93.

[9] William Wyler won an Academy Award for his direction of the film, though the Director of Photography (Andrew Marton) is always given credit for direction of the chariot race, its most celebrated scene.

[10] Maltby, *Hollywood Cinema*, pp. 32, 56n.52.

[11] Maltby, *Hollywood Cinema*, pp. 27-31.

12 In a recent TV documentary about the late Stanley Kubrick we learnt that he had an editing suite in his own home and would invite the editor to his home so that he could supervise the process. We also were given insights into the degree of control he that tried to exercise over writers: *The Last Movie: Stanley Kubrick and 'Eyes Wide Shut'*, produced and directed by Paul Joyce, Lucida Productions for Channel Four Television, 1999.

13 As I have already hinted, this term is capable of a number of meanings, some commercial, others cultural. Too often it is used dismissively in an élitist sense to privilege one taste over another. Here I have used it more neutrally to refer to films which are widely available and widely watched, often made to familiar formats and with familiar stars.

14 Richard Dyer, *Heavenly Bodies* (London: British Film Institute, 1987), p. 8; quoted in Paul MacDonald, 'Star Studies', in Hollows and Jancovich (eds.), *Approaches to Popular Film*, p. 83.

15 Joel W. Martin and Conrad E. Ostwalt Jr (eds.), *Screening the Sacred: Religion, Myth and Ideology in Popular American Film* (Boulder & Oxford: Westview Press, 1995). See esp. Martin's introduction, pp. 1-12, and Ostwalt's concluding essay indicating further lines of exploration, pp. 152-160.

16 Martin and Ostwalt (eds.), *Screening the Sacred*, p. 14; notice how the writers speak of 'the film's intent', not quite casting the director as 'author', but broadening and 'impersonalizing' sources of meaning. They indicate a meaning which is meant to be found.

17 Martin and Ostwalt (eds.), *Screening the Sacred*, p. 66.

18 See, for example, Maltby, *Hollywood Cinema*, chapter 1, and pp. 291ff.

19 Maltby, *Hollywood Cinema*, pp. 221-227.

20 See Maltby, *Hollywood Cinema*, p. 221.

21 Jewett, *St Paul at the Movies*, pp. 90-104.

22 Many critics would be very cautious about using such an expression because of the complexity of film production and the commercial purpose of most, especially Hollywood, films. I think such scruples are too refined. Mozart wrote for money, and a stage production has its own degree of complexity, albeit on a lesser scale.

23 Martin and Ostwalt (eds.), *Screening the Sacred*, p 120.

24 For instance, John R. May, 'Contemporary theories regarding the interpretation of religious film', in John R May (ed.), *New Image in Religious Film* (Kansas: Sheed & Ward, 1997), pp. 17-37.

25 John O. Thompson, 'Jesus as Moving Image: The Question of Movement', in Stanley E. Porter, Michael A Hayes and David Tombs (eds.),

Images of Christ: Ancient and Modern (Sheffield: Sheffield Academic Press, 1997), pp. 290-305.

[26] Gerd Theissen, *The Shadow of the Galilean* (London: SCM Press, 1987).

[27] See Walter Wink, *Engaging the Powers* (Minneapolis: Fortress, 1992), chapter 1.

[28] See chapter 11 below, for a discussion of the issue within *Terminator*.

[29] Larry E. Grimes gives an illuminating reading of *Blood Simple* in 'Shall these bones live? The problem of bodies in Alfred Hitchcock's Psycho and Joel Coen's Blood Simple', in Martin & Ostwalt (eds.), *Screening the Sacred*, pp. 19-29.

[30] See the discussions of Cape Fear in Peter Hasenburg, 'The "Religious" in Film: From King of Kings to The Fisher King', in May (ed.), *New Image of Religious Film*, pp. 41-56, and Reinhold Zwick, 'The Problem of Evil in Contemporary Film', in May (ed.), *New Image of Religious Film*, pp. 72-94.

[31] See the discussion in Margaret R. Miles, *Seeing and Believing: Religion and Values in the Movies* (Boston: Beacon, 1996), pp. 141-148.

[32] In 'Good v. Evil Films' we are largely within the realm of the 'mythological', and the whole *Star Wars* phenomenon is an extended treatment of good versus evil. Many westerns, and their successors in sci-fi, also deal with this great theme. 'Apocalypse Films' deal with the future in a more gloomy way, though despite the borrowing of biblical language and imagery they usually speak about an end of human making rather than of divine ordering. Such films as *Platoon, Waterworld, Armageddon, Dune* and *Apocalypse Now* all tackle this theme.

[33] Organized religion, of a nominal sort, acts as a backdrop to brutal murder and mayhem at the end of *The Godfather*. In *Dead Man Walking* Christianity gets one of its more favourable and sympathetic treatments.

3
Understanding Films:
Reading in the Gaps

Steve Nolan

The problem of mainstream theological film criticism

After somewhat tentative beginnings in the early 1960s, theological writing on film is now as mainstream as theological writing on art or literature. What was once the favoured choice of a handful of secular theologians and progressive Roman Catholic scholars is now widespread, with a trend towards engagement with contemporary culture for the sake of mission as well as theology.

Typical of this kind of engagement is the writing of Robert K. Johnston, in his introduction to the theological task of coming into dialogue with film. Of the five categories of increasingly positive theological response to film he describes (avoidance, caution, dialogue, appropriation and divine encounter), Johnston favours dialogue. He argues that in choosing the films they choose to discuss, theological critics are not imposing outside or alien perspectives, rather 'the movies themselves explicitly deal with religious matters and thus invite a theological response'.[1]

Johnston's observation might be unremarkable were theological critics limiting themselves only to films with more or less obvious theological themes, such as *The Passion of Joan of Arc* (1928), *Becket* (1964), *Babette's Feast* (1987), *Breaking the Waves* (1996) or *The Green Mile* (1999), all of which Johnston describes as films that seem 'uniquely able to mediate the holy, to be the occasion for epiphanies'.[2] However, Johnston believes that 'any filmic story that portrays human experience truthfully has this spiritual capacity'.

Johnston's thesis is that, while certain films are experienced immediately as sacraments of the human or the sacred, others demand an analytical response, and that theological criticism can provide such a response. Theology thus seeks to engage a movie from perspectives that come out of, but move beyond, the movie experience. It seeks a dialogue between filmic elements and convictions and Christian experience and belief.[3]

It is significant that Johnston locates this dialogue in the area of narrative, and argues that 'it is the visual story of a movie with its particular narrative elements that invites communion on its own terms through theological dialogue'.[4]

Johnston's perspective is typical of those that take their cue from John May's idea of film as a 'visual story'. May's professional interest in theology and literature influenced his thinking about theology and film, and explains why he adopted T. S. Eliot's conviction that literature should be judged by Christian faith. May developed a literary approach to film that regarded the theological critic's task to be the discovery of 'the cinematic analogue of the religious or sectarian question'.[5] That is, the critic is interested in a film for its (often superficial) equivalences or parallels to theological themes. This is an approach that has since become mainstream in theological film criticism. For example, the Australian Roman Catholic media critic Peter Malone distinguishes between films that depict what he terms 'the *Jesus-figure*' – more or less straightforward portrayals of the historical Jesus (as in *King of Kings* [1961] and *The Greatest Story Ever Told* [1965]) – and those depicting 'the *Christ-figure*', or characters that somehow resemble Jesus (such as *Cool Hand Luke* [1967]).[6] Similarly, Robert Jewett has aimed to 'dialogue in a prophetic mode' by 'seeking analogies between ancient and modern texts and situations'. To this end he attends to the cultural and historical context of a given biblical passage, setting this alongside a contemporary, popular film with 'thematic and narrative similarities'.[7]

I believe that there is a difficulty with this literary approach: film is *not* literature – and a literary approach is not sympathetic to film. In my view, then, Johnston and May, and most other mainstream theological film critics,[8] have failed to treat film in its own terms, and their myopic preoccupation with film as 'visual story' has missed the specific operation of film, which I will call a 'signifying practice'. By adopting this term from others,[9] I am suggesting that the event of making and watching a film becomes a set of signs pointing us to a range of meanings which will always exceed the signs themselves.

It is a strange anomaly that theology persists in taking a literary approach to films, since the mass of theoretical work developed within film studies has taken another direction, aiming to interpret film in terms of its cultural significance. An unfortunate example of the theological approach is provided by Christopher Deacy, who argues that, because the 'overwhelming evidence' suggests that film is displacing 'some of the roles traditionally associated with religious discourse',[10] there are strong grounds for reading films in terms of contemporary acts of redemption. This is, of course, another example of the search for cinematic analogies to theological questions. From this he advances the circular argument that, because some have emphasized that film can convey religious hopes and values, therefore film is 'at least amenable to a religious reading'.[11] Elsewhere I have written about other problems I find in Deacy's account.[12] He is certainly right to observe that film audiences somehow become part of the film 'text' and so are able to identify with the protagonist, but he fails to engage with the film theory that might explore the nature of this identification, offering as an excuse that the processes by which movies affect spectators are 'intellectually elusive'.[13]

Deacy seems genuinely surprised that film theorists and critics substantially overlook, if not dismiss outright, any interpretation of films in terms of their religious nature and orientation.[14] But the fact is that to earn critical respect theologians must answer the question: what have theology or religious studies brought to the study of film other than subjective opinion? Whereas film theory has been more or less successful in its attempts to analyse and comment culturally on film and cinema, theological film critics have, with few exceptions,[15] pursued May's quest for cinematic analogies and succeeded only in leaving their readers with the question: 'So what?'

By contrast, 'structuralist' film theory has been concerned with the cultural and political impact of film. To read films in terms of the way that spectators construct a meaning for them has highlighted the fact that the meaning of a film is located, not in its production, but in its consumption. Moreover, psychoanalytic film theory has stressed that cinematic representation is consumed in ways that construct the *self-identity* of the spectators. Viewers bring their own meaning to a film, in a way that enables them to create a sense of who they are in the world. I want to suggest that structuralist film theory offers to theology a way to understand film that can enable it to escape from the unproductive pursuit of cinematic analogies for religious questions, and to produce more culturally informed theological reflection on film as it is experienced. We need to be interested in the way that films invite viewers to construct a certain identity for themselves, to ask why they do this and to assess what the results of this process are.

In this chapter, I will highlight some key moments in structuralist film theory. This approach was developed during the 1970s in the British film journal *Screen* and has been described by one of its leading protagonists as the 'encounter of Marxism and psychoanalysis on the terrain of semiotics'.[16] This opaque, labyrinthine, at times 'intellectually elusive' theory is not without its cultured despisers,[17] but it retains the strength of treating film as film: as cinematic *experience*. It offers theology an opportunity to press beyond the 'demand for a surface realism'[18] and the 'subjective taste-ridden criticism'[19] it sponsors. The way forward is to dismantle (or 'deconstruct') the view that film works by representing things as they really are. There is thus an opportunity for theological film criticism to move towards interpretations that are more politically and culturally incisive by reading in the gaps,[20] and thereby to deepen theological dialogue with film and contemporary culture. In this chapter, I will use this theory to develop an interpretive frame through which theology can engage film. The engagement itself I will largely have to leave for another time.

A criticism of realist representation

At one level, *Screen*'s theoretical project can be understood as an extended, if not laborious and at times arcane, attempt to produce a psychoanalytic account of Louis Althusser's theory of ideological *interpellation* applied to cinema. The word 'interpellation' neatly combines both the actions of 'addressing' people and 'interrupting' them amid their daily preoccupations.

1. Louis Althusser: ideology as realistic representation
Althusser himself had been interested in how the ideology of a capitalist system becomes reproduced in the minds of the people it exploits. As a Marxist philosopher, he saw ideology as 'the system of the ideas and *representations* which dominate the mind of a man or a social group',[21] and he argued that what ideology represents is not the *real conditions* of human existence but *imaginary relations* to the real world.[22] For Althusser these imaginary relations are transmitted through 'ideological State apparatuses' (ISAs), through institutions such as church, school, family, law, political system, trade unions, and finally through culture itself. These all 'interpellate' or address individuals as 'subjects' and so make the dominant ideology seem natural and universal. For example, Althusser suggests, when a child is old enough he or she will naturally be sent to school, which as an institution is understood to be 'a neutral environment purged of ideology' a place where teachers are 'respectful of the "conscience" and "freedom" of the children who are entrusted to them'. There, in that safe, supposedly 'neutral' environment, the child will be addressed as a 'pupil' and will assume the position of being a subject within a certain framework of understanding that is just 'given', and within which he or she is naturalized by this ostensibly value-free education.[23]

Building on Althusser's premise, *Screen*'s interest was directed against mainstream Hollywood realism insofar as it made certain representations of reality seem natural and universal and positioned spectators as subjects within that ideologically-constructed reality. During the 1970s the journal explored the concept of a 'signifying practice' (for this term, see above) as a way of uncovering the 'universalizing' and 'naturalizing' strategies[24] by which cinematic realism makes 'what appears on the screen self-evident and natural, a "truth" '.[25]

An initial target was the 'common sense' assumption that 'the camera never lies', an assumption given formulation by André Bazin's notion of 'photographic ontology', or a theory which connected photography with what it really means 'to be'. Bazin argued that 'the essentially objective character of photography' endows the photographic image with a 'quality of credibility absent from all other picturemaking ... . For the first time an image of the world is formed automatically, without the creative intervention of man'.[26] However, Bazin failed to address the paradox that 'photographic ontology' (and cinematic realism) depends on cinematic illusion; the genius of cinema is that it creates the *illusion* of reality.

Bazin's cinematic realism often underwrote what Stephen Heath described as 'the flow of (ideologically complicit) drivel that currently and massively passes as "film-criticism" '.[27] In rejecting this approach, *Screen* drew on the thought of Christian Metz, who studied cinema from the viewpoint of a theory of signs ('cinesemiotics'), and the journal eventually combined this with the psychoanalysis of Jacques Lacan, in order to deconstruct the operations of realist cinema.[28]

2. Christian Metz: connoting 'reality'

Metz directly addressed himself to questions of cinematic reality.[29] Initially interested in the capacity of cinema to connote meaning, Metz drew a distinction between *denotation* as the literal, primary meaning of something – its realist representation – and *connotation* as the implied characteristics suggested by that thing. For example, 'one might say that a word like "mother" *denotes* "a woman who is a parent" but *connotes* qualities such as protection and affection.'[30] For Metz cinema is 'condemned to connotation',[31] and while realist cinema attempts to represent or denote reality as it is, the representation itself constructs or connotes a particular *value-ladened version* of reality. He put this insight into the technical terms of a theory of signs (semiotics) in this way: 'One finds the denotative material (signifier and significate) functioning as the signifier of connotation'.[32]

Metz became interested in the spectator's relation to the signifier, and so in the viewer's relation to a film as a set of signs pointing beyond itself. Against Bazin's theories of cinematic realism, Metz argued that the effect of the cinema 'as a mystical revelation, as "truth" or "reality" '[33] is in fact the product of the factors that are objectively determined by the nature of the medium. Thus the spectator's position in the cinema

> does not derive from a miraculous resemblance between the cinema and
> the natural characteristics of all perception ... it is foreseen and marked
> in advance by the institution (the equipment, the disposition of the audi-
> torium, the mental arrangement that internalizes the two), and also by
> more general characteristics of the psychical apparatus (such as projec-
> tion, the mirror structure, etc).[34]

In other words, the representation of reality, or the cinematic impression of reality, is far from being a natural, to-be-expected phenomenon. It is something 'connoted' by the cinematic signifier, and thus is a construct of the institution of the cinema: 'the impression of reality is also the reality of the impression'.[35]

3. Jean-Louis Baudry: the all-perceiving 'transcendental subject'
For Metz, the spectator in the cinema becomes '*all-perceiving*', 'a great eye and ear without which the perceived would have no one to perceive it …. a pure act of perception … a kind of transcendental subject, anterior to every *there is*'.[36] Metz borrowed the concept of a 'transcendental subject' from Jean-Louis Baudry, who explored the way that the techniques of using the camera shape the working of the film as a signifier. He was thus especially interested in the identification of the spectator with the camera, as one 'eye' identifying with another 'eye'.[37] Baudry took the view that the camera occupies a position between 'objective reality' and the film as a finished product. As such its operations transform reality but in a way that masks the transformation – the camera creates the *impression* of reality.

Baudry made a comparison here with the effect of monocular perspective in *Quattrocento* painting; the system of fixed point perspective which was developed during the Italian Renaissance was a means by which the artist organized the objects visualized. Similarly, the ideology (as discerned by Althusser) which shapes the perspective of a film arranges the position of the spectator or 'subject' within an impression of reality. As Stephen Heath observed, this is a reality that is 'neither absolutely two-dimensional nor absolutely three-dimensional, but something between',[38] a 'narrative space'.

For Baudry, the movement of images and the shifting camera position in cinema undermines 'the unifying … character of the single-perspective image [and implies] a multiplicity of points of view which would neutralize the fixed position of the eye-subject'.[39] However, it is the very mobility of the camera that provides the conditions for the manifestation of the 'transcendental subject', unfettered by the limitation of objective reality for whom the world becomes 'an intentional object'. Baudry argued that, since the spectators of the film constitute its meaning and continuity is necessary for the constitution of meaning, the continuity of the images within the film must be attributed to the activity of the spectator. Being held within the narrative by the camera's movements, the spectator assumes the camera's viewpoint and knowledge as his or her own and in this way becomes the 'transcendental subject', the one who sees all and knows all.

Developing Baudry, Heath noted that there is a connection between the part played by the spectator in creating a continuity of images, and the way that classical Hollywood narrative cinema makes no attempt to hide 'out-of-frame space', or the scene that lies, out of sight for the moment, beyond the frame being shot. Indeed, the Hollywood film deliberately uses out-of-frame space, recapturing it and bringing it into view through the unfolding of the narrative. Here the technique of point-of-view shot, or shot/reverse-shot is crucial in 'the joining of a film's constructions, the *stitching together* of the overlaying metonymies',[40] or what Heath considers to be the operation of *suture*.[41] We shall explore these aspects of the film through considering a fourth theorist, Jean-Pierre Oudart.

4. Jean-Pierre Oudart: the system of 'suture'
The concept of 'suture' was first developed by Lacan's student, Jacques-Alain Miller,[42] and was adopted by Jean-Pierre Oudart who shared the contemporary concern to expose the technologies of ideology. For Lacan, the individual is never fully represented in language, and is consequently compelled to procure a 'fictional' or pseudo-identity of himself or herself.[43] To clarify his point linguistically, Lacan drew a distinction between the content of the statement (*énoncé*) and the act of stating (*énonciation*), that is between the subject *designated* in the statement and the subject *making* the statement.[44] For example, in the paradoxical statement 'I am lying', the subject making the statement is not fully represented by the subject ('I') *of* the statement. In other words, there is a lack in the way that the statement signifies: the subject who is speaking is not fully represented by the linguistic signs he or she is employing, and must consequently 'suture' (or stitch together) a pseudo-identification which is assigned or signified by another person.

For Oudart, the language of the cinema works in the same way as the psychoanalytic process in everyday discourse which is described by the concept of suture. There is a lack opened up by the cinematic *énonciation*, and this is sutured together within an imaginary identification. He had in mind the shot/reverse-shot process.

In a simple shot/reverse-shot process the spectator may question why she is being shown an image of – say – a landscape, and may begin to wonder which character is intended to be the viewer of this scene. Who, within the film, is meant to be looking at the image along with the spectator of the film? Questions are posed about the relevance of the frame to the film, disturbing the pleasure experienced in the initial shot, and threatening to disrupt the ideological positioning of the spectator which the film is achieving. The spectator is left feeling 'aware' that the filmic representation signifies *for* 'an absent field', pointing to someone outside the image. For the spectator, the impression of 'reality' created by the film is thus also being disrupted. Oudart contended that in a cinematic statement constructed around a shot/reverse-shot framework, the lack is abolished in the reverse-shot, when someone (or something) is placed within 'the filmic field', 'the filmic space defined by the same take',[45] the problematic field of representation. The reverse-shot annuls the threat by showing that the initial shot was in fact the point-of-view of a character within the fictional narrative, thereby re-appropriating or suturing the spectator's initial relation to the film.

Arguing that art is a discourse constructed according to codes, themselves the product of ideology, Oudart held that the cinematic discourse predetermines how the subject should read the 'text', while the text itself masks and naturalizes the presence of the figurative codes. Operating beneath perception, the codes create an impression of 'reality' or 'truth', which is threatened when the spectator becomes aware of the frame, but which is overcome by the shot/reverse-shot process. This is 'the system of suture', which 'stitches' or joins the spectator into the texture of the film.

5. Stephen Heath: addressing the implied spectator
Oudart intended a psychoanalytic account of cinematic *interpellation*, which he saw as the 'establishment of an imaginary as real … by the persistence of the ideological effects of the representational system'.[46] However, Heath was critical of what he saw to be 'the muddled status of the concept'[47] of suture and returning to Metz, he drew attention to the

correspondence found between the linguistic sentence and the filmic image.[48]

Arguing that Metz intended the single shot as a statement (*énoncé*), Heath understood the shot as being not just 'there' but 'there-for' someone, addressing an implied spectator, which it does with a kind of 'innocence' which leaves the *énonciation* as open and unspecified. So the spectator is confronted with an image that appears complete, but which is in itself limited by what it addresses, namely the spectator himself or herself. The image enters the signifying chain and its meaning or signification is only completed when appropriated by the subject whom it is entertaining, i.e. the spectator. Arguing that in order to understand cinema as discourse it is necessary 'to understand the relation of that address in the movement of the image, in the movement of and between shots',[49] Heath held that cinema as discourse may be taken to be the constant production of addresses to subjects, happening through an interplay of incompleteness-completion that is characteristic of representation.

Heath regarded suture as 'the effecting of the join of the subject in structures of meaning'.[50] In the chain of discourse set up by the film, the joining or 'suturing' of the subject-spectator to a character in the film shows that there is a lack in a spectator's representation of himself through the signs he accepts as representing or signifying him. Signifiers in the film (characters) make up for the lack of signification in the spectator's self-presentation and – ultimately – sense of identity. Since in a film a spectator is offered multiple positions as a subject, influenced by the ideologies that lie within the making of the film, the effects of ideology can be measured across that multiplicity of positions. For Heath, the ideological mechanism of the film is specified in the operation of the suture, the never-ending process of construction and reconstruction, of absence and presence, of flow and bind, closed in narrative; narrative closure is the moment which 'shifts the spectator as subject in its terms ... [It] is scene and movement, movement and scene, the reconstruction of the subject in the pleasure of that balance'.[51]

A framework for theology to engage with film

In placing some severe question marks against Johnston's and May's literary approach to film, I have suggested that mainstream theological film criticism can even be fundamentally unsympathetic to the nature of film. The structuralist film theory I have outlined was similarly a reaction against literary and moralistic approaches to film. In treating film as 'signifying practice' *Screen* was utilizing a 'hermeneutic of suspicion' aimed at exposing the collusion of Hollywood realist representation with the concerns of ideology. Developing a psycho-semiotic account of cinematic 'address' (*interpellation*), the journal analysed the impression of 'reality' produced by a film; it found this to lie in the effect of what was signified by the characters, suturing spectators of the film into a 'narrative space' and positioning them as unified subjects of ideology. The difficulty with so much mainstream theological film criticism has thus been, not that it attends to 'story', but that in searching for *analogies* to the Christian story it never looks beyond the obvious. My argument is that theological film criticism should comment on the way film affects its viewers, and so how they are made part of a story which has ideological intentions.

I suggest, therefore, that we might take three specific ideas from structuralist film theory to develop an interpretive frame through which theology can engage with film.

First, there is the idea of the spectator's pseudo-identification. In some respects, because of a misunderstanding by Althusser of Lacan, *Screen* downplayed the place of character-actor-star as a focus for spectator identification. In Lacanian terms, the spectator forges the fictional or pseudo-identification with the screen character-actor-star. The salient point is that in making this pseudo-identification the spectator assumes an ego assigned or signified by an other.

Second, there is the idea that the quest for representation sutures the spectator into a narrative space. The spectator's desire to identify with a character-actor-star, mistaken for a representation of the spectator's own self, stitches the spectator into a chain of mistaken representations each (more or less) signifying the unconscious narratives of the spectator's own desire to be represented.[52] Making this pseudo-identification with the screen character-actor-star, the spectator is joined or stitched into the film's narrative space, into the space the film provides for the story to unfold.

This leads to the third idea, that the spectator becomes a participant in a constructed reality that is always already ideological. Lacan described the extent to which individuals are always situated within an unspoken narrative, which is in effect a construction of the individual's subjective 'truth' about the world. Spectators of a film are already participants in a fiction created from their own impressions of reality; thus they readily inhabit the reality constructed for them by Hollywood, a cinematic impression of reality that repositions the spectator within its own narrative.

In what follows I want to apply this interpretive framework. Examining the representations offered for identification by spectators will open the way to understanding the narrative space into which the spectator is sutured, and with it the ideologically constructed reality in which the spectator becomes a participant. The task for theology will then be to engage with the insights of this analysis.

For the sake of this application, in what follows I will make reference to the new sub-genre of post-Cold War 'terrorist hijack' films. These films have new significance post-9/11, but I have three reasons for choosing this genre over another. First, these films feature strong lead characters. Second, they make clear value statements about 'our' American way of life. Third, they feature a predominantly religious (i.e. Muslim) 'other' who serves both to assist audience identification and to encourage participation in the ideology which drives Hollywood realism.

Representing the aspirations of fans

In his definitive study of film stars and their social meaning, Richard Dyer defines stars as 'images in media texts'.[53] For Dyer, stars are representations of people, but unlike characters, they have an existence that endures beyond and is independent of their fictional screen appearances. This independence gives the star a greater reality than his or her screen characters, and serves to disguise the fact that stars are as much constructed personalities as any fictional character. As a consequence, 'the value embodied by a star is … harder to reject as "impossible" or "false", because the star's existence guarantees the existence of the value s/he embodies'.[54] In other words, stars collapse the distinction between their authenticity as a person and the authentication of the narrative characters they play. For Dyer, this operation of stardom is in part due to a noticeable shift in audience perception of stars, a shift from stars as 'embodiments of *ideal* ways of behaving' to stars as 'embodiments of *typical* ways of behaving'.[55]

Specifically, Dyer considers how Will Rogers and Shirley Temple embodied and so reinforced the social values of the American Dream. His point is that the star's image may be used to suppress some of the contradictions that exist in an ideology. Dyer proposes that stars de-politicize the consciousness by individualizing social realism, 'rendering the social personal'. By being 'experienced ... individuated ... and having an existence in the real world', stars displace the political onto the personal, so masking the spectators' awareness of class membership; social differences in the audience are covered up and re-arranged by the impact of the film in personal terms. In this way, films and stars are ideologically significant, both in the general sense of cutting audiences off from politics, and in the narrower sense of reinforcing a given political standpoint: in fact, 'The personal is always political'.[56] Dyer is clear that 'stars are supremely figures of identification ... and this identification is achieved principally through the star's relation to social types'.[57]

One example of this is the character of John McClane (Bruce Willis) in *Die Hard* (John McTiernan, 1988), arguably the film whose global success demonstrated that terrorism could replace Communism as the enemy of choice.[58] McClane is a regular guy with typical character flaws, and like many in the audience, his marriage is rocky. In fact, he and his wife Holly (Bonnie Bedelia) have become estranged, and while he remains a humble NYPD cop, she has left him for a high-powered job in Los Angeles. Unable to accept Holly's success, McClane uses their reunion at the Christmas party to pick up a conversation they had left unfinished at their last meeting six months earlier: he challenges his wife about reverting to her maiden name, Gennero.

Although superficially a simple – if gratuitously violent – action spectacular, *Die Hard* is a subtly complex, multi-layered film. *Die Hard* can be thought of as an old fashioned cowboy flick, whose central theme is the imposition of the law on the Wild West (NYPD cop = east coast lawman; LA = modern day Wild West). But, while McClane may be a flawed enforcer, he is enabled to transcend his defects, overcome the bad guys and recover his girl, because he has internalized his own identification with a Hollywood cowboy. In one scene, terrorist leader, Hans Gruber (Alan Rickman) asks McClane who he is:

Gruber: Just another American who saw too many movies as a child? Another orphan of a bankrupt culture who thinks he's John Wayne? Rambo? Marshall Dillon?
McClane: I was always kinda partial to Roy Rogers actually. I really liked those sequin shirts!

McClane masks his anonymity, by assuming the identity (and name) of a cinematic 'other'.

McClane's choice of Roy Rogers is appropriate since the 'King of the Cowboys' and star of more than 90 feature-length westerns was one of the most beloved figures in show business.[59] By the late 1940s a new production team reinvigorated Rogers' persona 'with color photography, more adult plot lines, and an almost sadistic emphasis on violent action'.[60] To this extent, McClane's 'social type' performs the very identification that the film is offering to the spectators in the cinema. In effect, he plays out on screen the role of the thirtysomething male, who as a child lost himself in identifying with his film-star, role-model hero, and whose actions are now unconsciously directed by that hero as he performs his own heroics. He, in turn, is watched by thirtysomething males, who as children lost themselves in identifications with film star heroes, and who identify now with the reflection of themselves performing the heroics of which they would like to believe themselves capable if, like McClane (who like them is flawed), they are pushed into an extreme situation.

Narrativizing the threat of the other

Post-9/11 it is not difficult to argue that contemporary 'terrorist hi-jack' films function as a myth serving to reinforce a particular manifestation of the fear of the other. Samuel Huntington names this myth as the 'Clash of Civilizations', and according to him the 'Cold War alignments are giving way to civilizational ones rooted in Islam and Orthodoxy'.[61]

The basic plot of the 'terrorist hi-jack' film is undemanding enough. Even with the fall of the Berlin Wall and the collapse of the Soviet Union, western democracy and its capitalist base remains under threat: the

Soviets may now be allies, but a smorgasbord of radical heterogeneity is emerging as the new enemy of the western lifestyle. Naturally, as leader of the 'free' world, the ferocious hostility of these seditious extremists is directed at the USA. Within this context, hi-jack movies track the emergence of one or other terrorist grudge, build the tension of imminent disaster, and successfully resolve the crisis, typically through the actions of one man.

Of all the post-Cold War terrorist action films, Edward Zwick's 1998 film *The Siege* tries to be intelligent and politically adept; it is certainly the most chillingly prescient and interesting for the identifications it offers. According to Jeff Beatty, Military Advisor on *The Siege*, FBI Counter-intelligence Agent Anthony Hubbard (played by Denzel Washington) is

> a pretty accurate portrayal of where our consciousness was about the reality of the threat. I think that law enforcement would react very close to that way in the late 90s. They just weren't there.[62]

Hubbard represents the sophisticated, hi-tech naïveté of an end-of-the-Millennium USA law enforcer. More than this, Hubbard is a man who has seen it all, and still 'believes in the system'.[63] Hubbard's moral focus is established in a mid-picture conversation with the morally complex Elise Kraft (Annette Bening). Suspicious of all true believers, 'present company included', Kraft caricatures Hubbard as 'Catholic School ... President of this ... Captain of that ... Hard work ... Make a difference ... Fair play ... Change the system from within ... Rah, rah, rah!'

'Hub': What about you? What do you believe?
Kraft: Like what?
'Hub': Like right and wrong?
Kraft: It's easy to tell the difference between right and wrong!
'Hub': Is it?
Kraft: Yes! What's hard is choosing the wrong that's more right!

According to Beatty, Hubbard is in a form of denial, and when Islamist extremists hijack a New York bus he thinks in terms of 'old style terrorists who'll want to use the hostages as bargaining counters'.[64] Hubbard represents those Americans in the cinema audience who will travel with the agent from political naïveté to an awareness of the 'Clash of Civilizations'.

The terrorists' ideological identity is as mysterious in *The Siege* as in other films of the sub-genre. Probably Palestinian – in one scene Kraft discusses with Hubbard her sympathy with the Palestinians, who 'seduce you with their suffering' – it transpires that the terrorist cells operating in New York are acting out of a sense of betrayal. Having been trained as a covert network financed by the CIA and handled by Agent Kraft, the followers of Sheik Achmed Bin Talal had fought against Saddam Hussein. Following a change in US policy the Arabs were abandoned by their former US 'friends' and as a result 'they were slaughtered'. Because of her former involvement, and sense of responsibility, Kraft helped to get student visas for those who remained, including her lover Samir Nazhde (Sami Bouajila).

It matters little that the politics of this group of films is uncertain, confused, or even misleading. Films in this sub-genre do not attempt to articulate an accurate portrayal of international relations post-Communism. But they do narrativize the perceived threat of the other (the more potent post-9/11); they turn it into story, and offer it for consumption by US audiences and their political, economic and cultural allies. That they are uncannily prescient has more to do with the fact that, in describing the possible, they focus the fear posed by the other.

Participating in ideological 'reality'
In this post-Cold War context, the 'Green Peril' replaced the 'Red Menace' in the oversimplified lexicography of US media reportage, where '"Islam" denotes a simple thing to which one can refer immediately'.[65] After Communism, Hollywood found Islam a ready-made *bête noire* for at least three reasons. Firstly, the oil crisis of 1973 made an impact on the West's sense of its own security, and altered western perceptions about Muslims. According to Edward Said, the OPEC embargo, which so dramatically affected fuel bills and inflation, melded Arabs and Iranians, Pakistanis and Turks into a single group, defined now by their shared religion as Muslims. The significant point here is that in the public mind

Muslims became associated with western dependence on imported oil, regularly referred to as 'being at the mercy of foreign oil producers'.[66]

Second, the Iranian revolution and hostage crisis of 1978-9 represented an ongoing humiliation to the USA. As Fawaz A. Gerges comments:

> By holding 52 Americans hostage for 444 days, Khomeini's Iran inflicted daily humiliation on the United States, eliciting an intense degree of hostility and a deep and unfamiliar sense of powerlessness. Eventually Iran became a national obsession.[67]

For Said, the trauma of the hostage experience continues to inform American demonology of Islam: 'The preoccupation with Iran continues into the 1990s. With the end of the Cold War [Iran], and along with it "Islam", has come to represent America's major foreign devil'.[68]

Third, the more recent development of actual 'Islamist' terrorism, in particular the terrorist attacks on the World Trade Centre, in February 1993 and September 2001. The effect of these attacks has been to deepen American fears about the security threats associated with Islamists, linking Muslims with domestic terrorism in many American minds. Consequently, Muslim extremists were immediately linked with the April 1995 bombing of a federal building in Oklahoma City, with individual US Arabs becoming targets of harassment.

According to Said, the main purpose of this new wave of large-scale feature films is 'to first demonize and dehumanize Muslims in order, second, to show an intrepid western, usually American, hero killing them off'.[69] The significance of this was not lost on those Arab and Muslim American groups who protested against Twentieth Century Fox's release of *The Siege* in August 1998. They complained precisely because the film deals 'with fanatical Muslim extremists who detonate bombs in New York'.[70] Their protest suggests that, in the case of *The Siege*, the minority ethnic group of American Arabs and Muslims found themselves represented as 'the other' for the majority group.

The obvious corollary is that the main characters offered for identification represent the majority ethnicity. However, it should be noted that Hubbard himself is African American, a clear indication of how far

Hollywood iconography has moved from the heady days when Sidney Poitier became the first – and until 2002 the only – black male actor to win an Academy Award for Best Actor. Hubbard's team includes a Chinese, a Jew (a white American of European origin) and even a Muslim, the Lebanese Frank Haddad (Tony Shalhoub); so Hubbard's colleagues are as ethnically mixed as the American Dream would prescribe. The lack of subtlety in this coded statement about American society's inclusivity serves to narrativize the belief that Americans can successfully distinguish Muslims who love America from Muslims who do not, and will embrace the former while punishing the latter. The fact that in the three days following the 1993 attack on the World Trade Centre 'more than 200 violent attacks against Muslim Americans were recorded'[71] suggests otherwise.

According to Said, a major part of the reason why Americans (and other nationalities) fail successfully to make the distinction is due to the abstraction of 'Islam'. Said notes that, while Robin Wright, Islam expert of the *Los Angeles Times*, acknowledges the 'danger of simplifying a "myriad of Countries" ', the only picture in his five column piece (of January 1991) was of Ayatollah Khomeini:

> He, and Iran, embodied all that was objectionable about Islam, from terrorism and anti-Westernism to being 'the only major monotheistic nation offering a set of rules by which to govern society as well as a set of spiritual beliefs.' That even in Iran there was a major, on-going dispute about what those rules were, and even what 'Islam' was, plus a vociferous debate that contested Khomeini's legacy, were not mentioned. *It was enough to use the word 'Islam' to cover what 'we' were worried about on a world scale.*[72]

As I noted above, the political ambiguity surrounding the terrorist's allegiances in *The Siege* matters little. What matters is that the film narrativizes the perceived threat of the other and so reinforces the ideology of Hollywood realism. By the time that Zwick was making his film 'Islam', 'Muslim' and to some extent 'Palestinian' had become terms to cover what worried 'us'. Holding the values of American culture at its narrative centre, spectators of post-Cold War 'terrorist hijack' films are able to identify with an ordinary guy hero and be 'stitched' into a narrative that is structured around protecting the American way of life against the perceived threat of the Muslim other. Identifying *with* Agent Hubbard, *against* the vaguely drawn other, spectators become participants in the ideology of Hollywood realism.

Understanding the task of theological film criticism

As I have hinted earlier, there are certainly difficulties with structuralist film theory.[73] Nevertheless, reading film as a 'signifying practice' widens the possibilities for theological engagement with film. First, it offers the possibility of exploring the ways in which representation shaped by ideology makes spectators into participants within a 'reality' that is always already ideological. Second, it offers the possibility of analysing particular ideological constructions of the 'reality' represented. Thirdly, it offers the possibility of moving beyond subjective, taste-ridden theological film criticism towards a theological engagement with film as cultural product, as a significant site of cultural debate.

The problem with mainstream theological film criticism is that it attempts to engage with film *without* proper and rigorous analysis of film in its own terms. The interpretive frame I have suggested here offers a way into this kind of analysis: beginning with examining the representations offered for spectators to identify with, leading on to exploring the nature of the narrative space into which spectators are sutured and finally to exposing the ideologically constructed reality in which spectators become participants.

The task of analysis is to understand film as film, film as signifying practice, and to deconstruct film as cultural product; this means reading in the gaps. The task of theological film critics is to shun the search for 'the cinematic analogue of the religious or sectarian question' and respond theologically to what is opened by the analysis.

If, as theological film critics, we want to earn the respect of our 'secular' counterparts, and bring an informed theological contribution to the film critics' table, then we must begin to talk, not to ourselves – about the superficial theological equivalences of realist representation – but to those who identity with and participate in the ideological realities represented inside the film theatre. If we can find the theological courage we might go the extra mile and, out of an understanding of those constructed realities, we might also mount a critique on the constructed 'realities' of our own religious and theological practice.[74] My case is that without this analysis it is impossible properly to understand films, and without this understanding it is impossible properly to reflect theologically about film.

Notes

[1] Robert K. Johnston, *Reel Spirituality: Theology and Film in Dialogue* (Grand Rapids: Baker Academic, 2000), p. 51.

[2] Johnston, *Reel Spirituality*, p. 155.

[3] Johnston, *Reel Spirituality*, p. 152.

[4] Johnston, *Reel Spirituality*, p. 152. Johnston's worked example of dialogue in practice is an extended treatment of the films of the Australian director, Peter Weir.

[5] John R. May and Michael Bird (eds.), *Religion in Film* (Knoxville: University of Tennessee, 1982), p. 26. See also John R. May (ed.), *Images and Likeness: Religious Visions in American Film Classics* (Mahwah: Paulist Press, 1991).

[6] Peter Malone, *Movie Christs and Antichrists* (New York: Crossroad, 1990).

[7] Robert Jewett, *St Paul at the Movies: The Apostle's Dialogue with American Culture* (Louisville: Westminster/John Knox Press, 1993). Larry Kreitzer has taken a similar approach in his series of books finding theological themes in fiction and film. See, for example Larry Kreitzer, *The New Testament in Fiction and Film* (Sheffield: Sheffield Academic Press, 1993).

[8] For a review of the literature see Steve Nolan, 'The books of the films: trends in religious film-analysis', *Literature and Theology*, 12/1 (March 1998), pp. 1-15. For alternative overviews see: John R. May, 'Contemporary theories regarding the interpretation of religious film' in John R. May (ed.), *New Image of Religious Film* (Sheed & Ward, Kansas, 1997), pp. 17-37; Johnston, *Reel Spirituality*, pp. 41-62.

[9] The term, for instance, is used by Julia Kristeva, who argued that meaning exceeds the fixed sense and closed structure of the sign, maintaining that 'signifying practice carried out through *langue* [remains] irreducible to its categories': Julia Kristeva, 'The semiotic activity', *Screen*, 14/1 (Spring 1973), p. 38.

[10] Christopher Deacy, *Screen Christologies* (Cardiff: University of Wales Press, 2001), p. 3.

[11] Deacy, *Screen Christologies*, p. 14.

[12] See my review of his book in *Reviews in Religion and Theology*, 9/5 (2002), pp. 460-65.

[13] Deacy, *Screen Christologies*, p. 91.

[14] Deacy, *Screen Christologies*, pp. 14-16.

[15] For example, Joel W. Martin and Conrad E. Ostwalt Jr (eds.), *Screening the Sacred: Religion, Myth and Ideology in Popular American Film* (Boulder & Oxford: Westview Press, 1995).

[16] Stephen Heath, '*Jaws*, ideology, and film theory', in Bill Nichols (ed.), *Movies and Methods: an Anthology*, Vol. 2, (Berkeley & London: University of California Press, 1985), p. 511.

[17] Notably, Noël Carroll, *Mystifying Movies: Fads & Fallacies in Contemporary Film Theory* (New York: Columbia University Press, 1988); David Bordwell, *Making Meaning: Inference and Rhetoric in the Interpretation of Cinema* (Cambridge, Mass & London: Harvard University Press, 1989); David Bordwell & Noël Carroll (eds.), *Post-Theory: Reconstructing Film Studies* (Madison: University of Wisconsin Press, 1996).

[18] *Screen*, 'Editorial', 13/2 (Summer 1972), p. 2.

[19] *Screen*, 'Editorial', 12/1 (Spring 1971), pp. 4-5.

[20] As the French film journal *Cahiers du cinéma* conceived it, to read in the gaps is to make films 'say what they have to say within what they leave unsaid'. *Cahiers du cinéma*, 'John Ford's *Young Mr Lincoln*', trans. Helen Lackner and Diana Matias, in *Screen*, 13/3 (Autumn 1972), p. 8. *Cahiers*' strategy of 'active reading', attempting to reveal a film's (always displaced) '*structuring absences*', was to be achieved by the doubly structured overdeterminations of Marxism and Freudianism: political ideology and psychoanalysis.

[21] Althusser, 'Ideology and ideological state apparatuses', in Althusser, *Lenin and Philosophy and Other Essays* (London: New Left Books, 1971), p. 149 (emphasis added).

[22] 'What is represented in ideology is therefore not the system of the real relations which govern the existence of individuals, but the imaginary relation of those individuals to the real relation in which they live.' Althusser, 'Ideology and ideological state apparatuses', p. 155.

[23] Althusser, 'Ideology and ideological state apparatuses', p 148.

[24] Terry Eagleton, *Ideology: an Introduction* (London & New York: Verso, 1991), p. 45.

[25] 'Editorial', *Screen*, 13/1 (Spring 1972), p. 3.

[26] André Bazin, 'The ontology of the photographic image', trans. Hugh Gray, in Hugh Gray (ed.), *What is Cinema?* Vol. 1 (Los Angeles & London: University of California Press, 1967), p. 13.

[27] Stephen Heath, 'Introduction: Questions of emphasis', *Screen*, 14/1&2 (Spring/Summer 1973), p. 9.

[28] The hybrid structuralism, forged by British film theory, sought to open the ideological operation of film applying Saussurian insights into film as signifying system, Lacanian psychoanalysis of desire, and Marxist (as proto-structuralist) historical materialism, 'the keystone in the theoretical arch … relating signification and subjectivity to history'. Robert Lapsley & Michael Westlake, *Film Theory: an Introduction* (Manchester: Manchester University Press, 1988), p. 12.

[29] Christian Metz, *Film Language: a Semiotics of the Cinema* trans. Michael Taylor (New York: Oxford University Press, 1974).

[30] *The Oxford Compact English Dictionary* (Oxford: OUP, 2003), p. 226.

[31] Christian Metz, 'The cinema: Language or language system', trans. Michael Taylor, in Metz, *Film Language,* p. 76.

[32] Metz, 'The cinema: Language or language system', p. 80. Metz was indebted to the semiotics of Roland Barthes. See in particular, Roland Barthes, 'Myth today', in Barthes, *Mythologies*, trans. Annette Lavers (London: Vantage Books, 1993), pp. 109-59.

[33] Christian Metz, 'The imaginary signifier', *Screen*, 16/2 (Summer 1975), p. 54.

[34] Metz, 'The imaginary signifier', p. 54.

[35] Christian Metz, 'On the impression of reality in the cinema', trans. Michael Taylor, in Metz, *Film Language*, p. 9.

[36] Metz, 'The imaginary signifier', p. 51.

[37] Jean-Louis Baudry, 'Ideological effects of the basic cinematographic apparatus', in Nichols (ed.), *Movies and Methods,* pp. 531-42.

[38] Rudolf Arnheim, *Film as Art* (London: Faber & Faber, 1958), p. 20, cited in Stephen Heath, *Questions of Cinema* (London & Basingstoke: Macmillan Press, 1981), p. 31.

[39] Baudry, 'Ideological effects', p. 535.

[40] Stephen Heath, 'Narrative space', *Screen*, 17/3 (Autumn 1976), p. 92 (emphasis added).

[41] Stephen Heath, 'Notes on suture', *Screen*, 18/4 (Winter 1977-78), pp. 48-76.

[42] Jean-Pierre Oudart, 'Cinema and suture', *Screen*, 18/4 (Winter 1977-78), pp. 35-47. Thus he explored the close bonds between cinematic identification, cinematic signification and visual perception . The concept was developed by Jacques-Alain Miller for Lacan's Seminar of 1965: see Jacques-Alain Miller, 'Suture (elements of the logic of the signifier)', *Screen*, 18/4 (Winter 1977-78), pp. 24-34.

[43] Jacques Lacan, *The Four Fundamental Concepts of Psychoanalysis*, trans. Alan Sheridan, (Harmondsworth: Penguin, 1979), p. 117.

[44] Jacques Lacan, 'The subversion of the subject and the dialectic of desire in the Freudian unconscious', trans. Alan Sheridan, in Lacan, *Écrits: a Selection* (London: Routledge, 1977), p. 298.

[45] Oudart, 'Cinema and suture', p. 37.

[46] Jean-Pierre Oudart, 'Notes for a theory of representation', trans. Annwyl Williams, in Nick Browne (ed.), *Cahiers du Cinéma: 1969-1972 the Politics of Representation* (London: Routledge, 1990), p. 203.

[47] Heath, 'Notes on suture', p. 62.

[48] 'A close-up of a revolver does not mean "revolver" (a purely virtual lexical unit) but at the very least, and without speaking of the connotation, it signifies "Here is a revolver!"'. Christian Metz, *Film Language*, p. 67.

[49] Heath, 'Notes on suture', p. 63.

[50] Heath, 'Notes on suture', p. 74. For an argument against *suture* see William Rothman, 'Against the system of the suture', *Film Quarterly* (Fall 1975), pp. 45-50.

[51] Heath, 'Narrative space', pp. 99-100.

[52] For Lacan, the signifying chain operates according to the 'laws of the signifier', the discourse of unconscious, displaced desire.

[53] Richard Dyer, *Stars*, 2nd edn. (London: British Film Institute, 1998), p. 10.

[54] Dyer, *Stars*, p. 20.

[55] Dyer, *Stars*, p. 22.

[56] Dyer, *Stars*, p. 28.

[57] Dyer, *Stars*, p. 99.

[58] Steve Bradshaw, *A Warning from Hollywood*, Panorama BBC1 (transmitted 24 March 2002).

[59] Rogers won the *Motion Picture Herald*'s title 'Most Popular Western Star' every year from 1943-54. Patrick Robertson (ed.), *The Guinness Book of*

Movie Facts & Feats, Fourth Edition (Enfield: Guinness Publishing, 1991), p. 71.

[60] See Leonard Maltin on 'Roy Rogers' at www.us.imdb.com

[61] Samuel P Huntington, *The Clash of Civilizations and the Remaking of World Order* (London: Touchstone, 1998), p. 126.

[62] Jeff Beatty, in Bradshaw, *A warning from Hollywood*.

[63] Ken Hollings, 'The Siege', *Sight and Sound*, 9/2 (February 1999), p. 54.

[64] Beatty, in Bradshaw, *A warning from Hollywood*.

[65] Edward W. Said, *Covering Islam: How the Media and the Experts Determine How We See the Rest of the World* (London: Vantage, 1997), p. 41.

[66] Said, *Covering Islam*, pp. 36-7.

[67] Fawaz A Gerges, *America and Political Islam: Clash of Cultures of Clash of Interests* (Cambridge: Cambridge University Press, 1999), pp. 42-3.

[68] Said, *Covering Islam*, p. 7.

[69] Said, *Covering Islam*, pp. xxvi-xxvii.

[70] 'Arab Americans Protest Willis Movie', *StudioBrief*, 27 August 1998, Internet Movie Database, www.us.imdb.com/SB

[71] Gerges, *America and Political Islam*, p. 48.

[72] Said, *Covering Islam*, p. 7 (emphasis added).

[73] I have addressed some of these difficulties explicitly elsewhere. See Steve Nolan, *Faithful Representations: An Application of 1970's Lacanian Film Theory to the Study of Liturgical Subjectivity* (unpublished PhD thesis, The University of Manchester, 2003).

[74] This is the approach I have attempted to develop in a series of theological film reviews in the *Baptist Times* and *Third Way*. See for example my reviews of *Star Wars: Episode One. The Phantom Menace*, in *Baptist Times*, 29 July 1999, p. 8; *Dogma*, in *Third Way*, February 200, p. 27; *American Beauty*, in *Baptist Times*, 13 April 2000, p. 8; *Ali*, in *Baptist Times*, 28 February 2002, p. 5.

4
Transcending the Cave: Fantasy Film as Spiritual and Philosophical Reflection

Léonie Caldecott

When we sit in the dark, contemplating a giant screen, we enter a world presented to us through sophisticated, sometimes almost subliminal cues. Unrestricted by the spatial limitations of theatre or radio, combining the visual with the aural, interweaving writing with music, visual design with dramatic effect, a good film is capable of lifting us out of the here and now to an overwhelming degree. But we also bring to this experience our own concerns, within a whole range of moral, spiritual and philosophical issues. We come as we struggle to make sense of our own lives, as we seek purpose and meaning, as we make choices that contribute greater goodness and love or turn ourselves away from others. The cinematic narrative can transport us through space and time, can give us an overview of a particular life-experience, and can convey atmosphere and cultural referents like no other medium.

Fantasy film, or film with a powerful fantasy element, may take us to a world that seems totally removed from our own. But the distance of this fantasy world creates space that allows it to express things about the culture of the time in which it was created, whilst possibly also giving a critique of that culture. More than that, fantasy film can address the very moral, spiritual and philosophical issues a contemporary audience faces. This we will explore in this chapter.

Reflecting on the culture of technology

Because of the cult status that attaches to *The Matrix*, the Wachowski brothers' trilogy actually tells us a great deal about the cultural moment in which we find ourselves at the beginning of the third millennium. The films are based on a premise with huge philosophical ramifications. What if our very devotion to, and dependence on, high technology ended in a diabolical reversal, whereby the machines that humanity has created to serve its endlessly proliferating material desires eventually turned on their creators, enslaving us as we have enslaved one another? What if mankind pricked its finger once and for all on the enchanted spindle of its own ingenuity, and fell into a sleep from which it would never wake, living a virtual dream-life whilst the robotic sorcerers lived off the basic energy generated from our minds and bodies? What if the machines controlled what is left of the real world? And what if, somehow, against all the odds, a group of human beings managed to struggle out of this fate, out of this computer generated Matrix of lying sensation and false information? What if the citizens of this new Zion began also to reclaim their brothers and sisters from their Platonic shadow-play? And what if one individual, or perhaps a couple, were to sacrifice themselves in order to win back the freedom for at least some of humanity to reclaim their own destiny?

The questions are good ones, and film is in some ways an ideal medium in which to ask them. The cinema bears more than a passing resemblance to the cave in *The Republic*, where we sit watching the flickering images and shadows of the *Matrix* trilogy on the wall. Who will liberate us? What would liberation mean? Our generation increasingly inhabits a virtual reality at one or more removes from the sun and grass outside. We are occupied by computer games, reality TV and internet chat rooms; we have virtual food, virtual politics, virtual economies, virtual relationships; there are jobs that mean nothing in reality, media that feed a kind of addiction to unreality, and endlessly reinvented trivia – anything to distract us from the profound truth of our existence and its purpose. This is nothing less than enslavement to the machine.

In the world of the Matrix represented on screen, the character called Neo gradually discovers that he is the prophesied hero called 'the One'. Being liberated himself, he returns into the Matrix to liberate others. Perhaps the film makers, the enigmatic Wachowski brothers, were trying to do the same, projecting themselves into the artificial reality of the film in order to liberate their audiences. If so, the adventure, whilst containing fascinating elements, does not quite come off. The tightly constructed drama of the first film contrasts with the loose and overblown sequels. All in all, the series is too self-conscious for its own good.

Nevertheless, despite the widely-acknowledged failure of the second and third films, some truth gets through. At the climax, the price of Neo's victory is the surrender of his very being to the enemy, an act of existential subversion whereby the rogue program that threatens to destroy both the Matrix and the world of the machines will be invaded and eliminated in turn. The images themselves speak to us, even when we cannot decode the allegory in all its details. (Who is the Merovingian? Who or what is the Oracle? Is the Architect a *persona* for the machines?) All thinking is in some degree symbolic or metaphorical – even the most seemingly abstract. A medium which deals in powerful, moving and developing images can generate thought at a very deep and almost primal level, sometimes even undercutting the author's conscious intentions.

The conscious, religious referents of *The Matrix* are various – from Zen Buddhism to Gurdieff *via* the Kabbala – but the undeniable intimations of Christianity form a central thread, particularly in the resolution. The sacrifice of one man for the sake of many, the entry into complete darkness (the flesh and blood Neo has been blinded and reduced to a grim desperation by the death of the woman he loves): all this is done in order that the darkness will not overpower the light. Neo is quite literally crucified in a deal with the Matrix whereby a portion of humanity – those in Zion – will be let alone, for a while at least, if he defeats the rogue, self-proliferating programme which is agent Smith. In the last moment of battle, free will becomes the defining trait of a humanity which is reduced to a bare minimum. Neo's assertion, in the face of apparent meaninglessness, 'Because I choose,' tells us a great deal about the condition of the modern imagination at this particular historical moment. 'Welcome to the desert of the real.' We need to pay attention to this state of alienation, to the temptation to find everything empty, if we hope to refresh the springs which will prevent *The Matrix* from becoming a genuine prophecy.

Hints of transcendence
In the end, the *Matrix* films offer no final resolution, no *eucatastrophe,* in the sense intended by J.R.R. Tolkien, simply a truce between Man and Machine. The Tolkienian 'turn' would depend on the existence of a transcendent realm, and not just an internal rearrangement of forces. Only the Oracle seems to hint at some more profound order of reality, outside time

and space, the source of the unpredictable agent of freedom. As the blinded Neo approaches the city of the machines, he rises for a moment above the clouds that cover the planet into a shining realm of light. It is an attempt by the film makers to generate a glimpse of transcendence, for us if not for Neo, yet the glimpse remains no more than a hint, and the story itself leaves us in the dark.

At root, all the stories to do with humanity's immersion in the illusions created by our own technological competence are in some sense ante-deluvian, recalling the position of those portrayed in the Book of Genesis before the great flood: we have laid our hands on knowledge which was not ours by right and which by definition alienates us from communion with God – with the transcendent. To put it another way, we are fallen creatures. If you were to take good (defined as that which *is*) as represented by the number one, and evil (the negation of existence, the 'no' to the Creator) as being nought, the knowledge of good and evil could be interpreted as the binary code at the basis of all computer programmes.

The Matrix is far from being the only film which addresses the alienation of an I.T.-overloaded generation. A number of film makers are taking up the challenge of tackling big issues. Many of them are, at the very least, asking the right questions. They are immersing themselves with increasing honesty in the painful realization that our culture may have taken some wrong turns. These film-makers are genuinely diverse in their outlook, and not necessarily enslaved to what we have come to think of as Hollywood values. M. Night Shyamalan, Brian Synger, Sam Raimi, Hayao Miyazaki and Ang Lee, to name but a few, are proving that the cinema is actually able to put up a powerful showing against the bread-and-Big-Brother-circuses, with which the small screen seeks to subdue and captivate the masses.

One example is the scene at the end of Bryan Synger's *X-Men 2*, where Jean decides to put her telekinetic powers to the ultimate test, sacrificing herself for the sake of the other mutants, who are about to be submerged in the raging waters of a breaching dam. She does this without telling any of her companions what she is up to, and she uses her powers to prevent them from saving her in turn, which would compromise her effort to hold back the raging torrent and enable their plane to take off safely. After they are in the air and the water has claimed Jean for its own, the two men who love her, heretofore rivals, fall into each other's arms and grieve. Another mutant, Nightwalker, quietly intones the twenty-third psalm. It is a scene which could easily have become sentimental, yet it succeeds in conveying at once acute grief and the transcendent dimension in which that grief is assuaged by meaning, by a purpose beyond the here and now. It is what I would call, after Viktor Frankl, a logo-therapeutic moment.

Reflecting on the wonder of nature

One of the most interesting and adaptable directors, Ang Lee, famous for films such as *Sense and Sensibility* and *The Ice Storm*, has also turned his hand to superhero fiction as a genre. *Hulk* too has scenes of cosmic grandeur. What is so interesting about this film, which some critics slated for being too 'slow-moving' at the beginning, is that alongside the special effects and the big green computer-animated monster, there is both a powerful human interest story, and what can only be described as a meditation on the wonder of life, at both microscopic and macrocosmic level. It is certainly a visually beautiful film, bearing out the words of Barbara Niccolosi, the director of Act One, a training programme for Christian writers in Hollywood:

> Great art is found in the combination of mastery of craft, and lyrical or poetic images. A piece 'works' in so far as its imagery speaks 'thousands of words' to the receiver, by combining with their past experience to lead them to new or deeper truths. Unravelling the meaning of art can often be as simple as taking its central images at face value ... A sign of a great work of art is that its central metaphors are so carefully chosen, that the more a viewer plumbs the literal meaning of the metaphor, the more the lyrical meaning is manifest.[1]

In fact Niccolosi was talking specifically about an Ang Lee film, *The Ice Storm*, here. But her assessment of his genius applies every bit as much to *Hulk*. The premise of the film is the same as it was in the comic book: a scientist named Bruce Banner has suffered an alteration to his DNA, so that when he becomes angry he transmogrifies into a huge green hulk which runs amok. In the film, the reasons for the genetic mutation are rendered much more complex than in the comic. Bruce's father, also a geneticist who once worked for the military, experiments on his own DNA, trying to boost his immune system to levels that would make him invulnerable. The whole plot of the film turns on this promethean obsession of the father's. 'I tried to improve on the limits in myself ... to improve on nature, *my* nature. It's the only path to the truth, that gives men the power to go beyond God's boundaries!'

In many ways, *Hulk* is about the passions. It is partly about the lust for power, represented in the military industrial complex by a greedy young entrepreneur who wants to patent the Hulk's invulnerability, and a controlling general who also happens to be the father of Bruce Banner's girlfriend. The military man wants to deal with everything by force. What he fails to appreciate is how brute opposition merely fuels the hazard. Oppose a force of nature (and here the Hulk's colour plays a significant symbolic role) with evil means, and nature herself may turn on you. Science too is put on the stand here. Tinker with the components of life without reference to their moral purpose, and you open Pandora's box. Fail to love your child unconditionally, turn him into a cipher for your own ambition or curiosity, and you create a human time bomb. Ang Lee modelled many of the Hulk's action scenes himself (wearing the sensor suit which would enable the computer generated image to be created), and so the Hulk also represents the potential for rage, fury and frustration in each one of us, as represented by Lee, perhaps particularly in a disjointed post-permissive generation. Yet there is something which can defuse that rage, deflate that exaggerated reaction back into normal proportions – the Hulk's love for Betty.

In *Hulk,* as in *Harry Potter*, a mother has died attempting to save her son from destruction – in this case at the hands of his own father who, having been ordered by his military superior to cease his experiments, destroys his laboratory and tries to destroy the child to whom he passed on his genetic mutation. Later on he will complete this perverse inversion of paternity, by exposing his grown-up son to gamma radiation which will push the mutation to its ultimate conclusion. Directors like Ang Lee are not afraid to tackle big issues and perennial themes: the role of the family in society, and in the development of the individual; the breakdown of the family under the impact of cultural upheaval and the sexual revolution; relations between one generation and the next; the psychodrama associated with masculine and feminine, and the respective influences of mother and father. Such directors are not deterred by the great questions around natural law and the meaning of creation, death and the nature of the soul. And most importantly, again and again, they try to show us the redemptive power of sacrificial love.

Reflecting on sacrificial love

This theme is at the heart of *Crouching Tiger, Hidden Dragon.* Here Ang Lee has gone back to his Chinese roots, basing himself on a plot used in modern Chinese pulp novels, which base themselves on traditional stories and legends. The background is the mysterious company of Wudan warriors, trained physically and spiritually for combat against evil. At the heart of the story is a young girl, Jen, who with the help of her nurse manages to get hold of and learn the content of the Wudan fighting manual. While *Hulk* deals with the crisis of a masculine element gone AWOL, *Crouching Tiger* deals with the feminine equivalent.

The hero Li Mu Bai is attempting to give up his famous sword, the Green Destiny, along with his life as a warrior. The sword is stolen by Jen, and in confronting her Li decides to adopt her as a pupil, in order to prevent her becoming a 'poisoned dragon' like her initial teacher, who is largely motivated by hatred for the men of Wudan, men she considers to hold women in contempt – good for concubines, but not to train as adepts of their mysterious art. As Li Mu Bai fences with Jen – using only a stick against the Green Destiny itself – he teaches: 'No growth without assistance. No action without reaction. No desire without restraint. Now give yourself up and find yourself again.'

Jen has secretly fallen in love with a bandit who attacked her parents' luggage train. However, she is destined for marriage to an eminent man she does not know. The conflict caused by this within the girl, combined with her angry wilfulness in the face of the difficulties besetting her, prevents her being open to Li Mu Bai's teaching. Rather than patiently accept Li's unprecedented offer, or the maternal guidance of his friend Lu Shu Lien, she leads him into mortal danger. At the hands of the true poisoned dragon, the girl's nurse, Li pays with his life for the concern he has shown for her soul. And yet it is his death that produces her conversion. Aghast at the realization of what she has caused, she seeks, too late, to make the antidote for the poison dart which Li has received from Jade Fox. Jen knows that she has helped to cause her nurse's descent into darkness, for she deceived her, along with everyone else: she had withheld information that was in the stolen manual, so that the nurse would never learn to fight as well as herself.

In contrast, Lu Shu Lien represents the true, healthy feminine, the woman who is both maternal and warrior-like at once. The death of Li Mu Bai is a disaster for her, since she was deeply in love with him, and he with her, though this love has never had the opportunity to be fully expressed. Swallowing all trace of resentment, she still acts as a mother to Jen after the tragedy has played itself out, telling her to go and meet her lover at the Wudan mountain and set her life in order. 'Promise me', she tells her, 'whatever path you take in this life, to be true to yourself.' Overcome with remorse, the girl then enacts a very strange form of penance, throwing herself into a deep chasm.

Since Jen is able to fly, we know this cannot be suicide. Nevertheless, most people are puzzled by this ending. It makes sense only in the light of the conversion experience triggered by the sacrificial death of the Master. Earlier in the film, Jen's lover Lo has told her of a story he heard as a child. 'We have a legend', he says. 'Anyone who dares to jump from the mountain, God will grant his wish ... Long ago, a young man's parents were ill. So he jumped. He didn't die, he wasn't even hurt. He floated away, far away, never to return. He knew his wish had come true. If you believe, it will happen. The elders say: A faithful heart makes wishes come true.'

By now, Jen has realized that she does not have a faithful heart. Her motives have been base and self-interested. She has been divided within herself, to a lethal degree. Her lover, on the other hand, has a completely sincere heart, so she asks him to make the wish, knowing that the two of them are one, and that her own heart is not pure enough to make wishes come true. All she has left is her daring. She dares to jump from the mountain. And so she finally does what Li had told her she must do: 'Give yourself up and find yourself again.' Jen leaps into the void, into the unknown. It is a leap of faith, a leap of contrition, a purifying act. Ang

Lee does not tell us what the outcome will be. This remains a mystery, as do all the most personal, interior movements of the human soul. But her image remains with us, recalling that it is not just a matter of waging war against all that we find evil and false outside of ourselves. We must first wage war within our own hearts.

Blessed are the pure in heart, for they shall see God. It may not be the beatific vision, but the cinema is able to give us at least a glimpse of hope for some fulfilment beyond the world we know, when the film maker's heart is in the right place.

Note

[1] Barbara Niccolosi, at http://church of the masses.blogspot.com, 15 March, 2003.

5
Gaining Fresh Insights: Film and Theological Reflection in a Pastoral Setting

Anthony Clarke

Film as significant experience

In pastoral ministry as I knew it, one of the relatively common trials was to hold a conversation in someone else's home with the television on in the background. I would have to judge on each occasion whether I could suggest that the television, which for some is a constant part of life, a background noise that is only ever half watched, might be turned off. Although television is such a dominant contemporary medium, this is clearly a different kind of experience to sitting in a blacked out cinema and watching a film, which, through the screen size and acoustics, confronts us and draws us in. And this is precisely one way of judging the 'success' of a film.

Although our response to any film will always be highly subjective, and the impact of any given film will depend on our own experiences which we bring to the encounter, one aim of a film is to draw us into another world. This may be a whole new world of fantasy or science fiction, such as Middle Earth in *The Lord of the Rings*, it may be another world beyond our experiences, such as that of the Guarani Indians of the eighteenth century in *The Mission*, or it may be the particular life story of another individual in a world that we otherwise recognize such as Helen's life in *Sliding Doors*. Film enables us to dwell for a while in another place, to walk in another's shoes. Film offers us a brief but significant experience of another life.

Throughout the twentieth century, film theory has wrestled with this connection between the world of the film and the world of the viewer. That which is often known as the 'realist' position of 'classic film theory' took its standpoint from the naturalist view that everything is trying to imitate reality.[1] This has its roots in the origins of western philosophy and especially Plato's image of the 'forms' or eternal ideas. Here Plato portrays the experiences of life as a person sitting in a cave and seeing the shadows of objects on the wall in front. What the person can see here and now is not the object itself but a copy of what is real. In the same way the world of our sense perception is a copy of the world of ideal forms. Such an understanding stresses how a film aims to portray reality – we may think of the common phrase, 'the camera never lies' – and so one essential standard by which to judge the success of a film is the extent to which it is able to show the world as it really is, for a film is intended to be a 'window into reality'[2].

Yet there was an opposing view, referred to as the 'formalist' position, which recognized the way that cinema used various cinematic techniques to 'manipulate'[3] reality and so create another world of fiction and fantasy. Although this 'formalist' understanding of cinema was already well known, Antony Easthope suggests that it was finally in the 1970s that the break with the naturalist understanding was decisively made in the area of film studies. At the beginning of the twenty-first century we are all too aware that the camera is normally 'lying' as photographs are airbrushed and digitally altered to suit the occasion. We are likely to feel that the removing of slight imperfections on the face of the model who graces the cover of a glossy magazine is an intentional distortion of reality. But there is a different kind of shaping of the truth in the operations of the cinema, which has always aimed to present us with another reality which comes alongside and confronts our own.

One criticism of current films is now more likely to come from the opposite direction, that they are escapist, that the world they present for us is so removed from the reality that we know that they do not offer a significant experience. While it is certainly true that some 'feel good films' do aim to take us away, for a moment, from 'ordinary life' and immerse us for a while in a different and supposedly 'better' world, very few films might be considered pure escapism. Even if the world that we indwell for a moment stands in contradiction to our own, the significant experience is when an individual viewer brings together this other world alongside her own, so that meaning might be found in this creative tension. It may be seen as escapist to make a film full of images of peace in a time of war, but, on the other hand, to live in this other world for a brief moment may help us to reflect on the reality we know. It is also true, and we will pick this up again later, that the Bible does exactly this. It seems no coincidence that the pages of the prophets combine side by side both words of judgement that arise from the lived reality and pictures of hope for a better future. We need to hear and see another world.

This has always been the case. From the epics of Homer and the plays of Aeschylus through to the novels and plays of modern times, good stories, told well, have always had the ability to take us into another world. This has always involved a partnership between narrator and audience, with the former creating the plot and the characters and the latter adding the imagination needed to make this world live. Cinema follows on this age old tradition of telling stories, again in partnership with the audience, although perhaps requiring less imagination. In the *Odyssey* we travel with Odysseus on his journeys, creating in our minds the awful Cyclops or the enchanting Sirens. In Shakespeare's *Henry* V, the chorus encourage us to 'work, work your thoughts,'[4] so that our minds transform a few actors into vast armies. The chorus continues,

Piece out our imperfections with your thoughts:
Into a thousand parts divide one man,
And make imaginary puissance.

By contrast with this required effort of the imagination, in the film *Master and Commander* we join the ship 'The Surprise' as it travels around Cape Horn, experiencing the violent storms almost to the point of sea-sickness! Not before this modern era has the world of a narrative been so realistically displayed. Yet intrinsically book, play and film are all attempting what Coleridge described as 'the willing suspension of disbelief', which is often wrongly understood as temporary switching off of our rational faculty; rather it is a collaborative partnership between the work of art and the reader or viewer, in which a new world is created.[5]

Film studies is certainly a discipline in this own right, with its own patterns and techniques, a discipline that has attracted a growing and increasingly complex range of theoretical interpretations, as Steve Nolan has argued in a previous chapter. It is not simply literary criticism. Yet I believe that film still holds significant connections with literature and the theatre, as alternative ways in which stories are narrated. From this perspective it is clear that films can be regarded, at one level, as 'texts', albeit highly visualized ones, texts which engage us and which can be 'read' at a variety of levels. Our grasp of cinematic techniques, as well as an understanding of the use of symbol, image and narrative, can help us to 'read' the film. But above all else film brings another world alongside ours and thereby creates a space to reflect on the encounter between these two worlds. Watching a film can and should be entertainment, and this is something to be celebrated, but a 'good' film, like a 'good' book or 'good' play goes beyond this, and becomes a significant experience, that is one in which we encounter what is real. Returning to the beginning of this chapter, this in no way suggests that the film literally reflects the reality of our lives, but in the other world of a film we still encounter what is real for us.

As a significant experience, film may then cause us to stop and reflect. This is a most natural response, and a film that has worked well may send us from the cinema either in animated discussion about those moments that struck us most, or in complete silence. The latter is my particular memory, for example, after seeing *Schindler's List*. Film can and should be the initiative for deeper reflection, which must be something that happens within the church community. This is partly because it is vital that the church engage with the whole range of contemporary culture, which, at a whole variety of levels, is expressed in film. But it is more than a duty to engage with what is beyond the church. Film is a medium which has the power to make another world come to life and so create new and varied experiences, offering in its own right a valuable resource.

The emphasis of 'applied' or 'practical' theology as it has been developed in recent decades has been that experience is a valid, and indeed necessary, point of departure for theological reflection. The literature on applied or practical theology offers a range of methods for this discipline,[6] but the most common tool used is some variation on what is known as the 'pastoral cycle' or 'hermeneutical circle'. Here, as the diagram on page 63 shows,[7] experience is a starting point that leads us on to exploration, reflection and finally a response which then begins the process all over again.

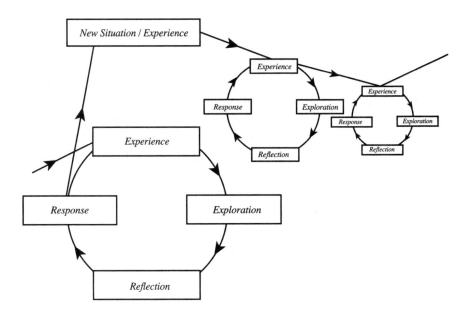

"The Pastoral Cycle" or "Doing Theology Spiral"from *Let's Do Theology: A Pastoral Cycle Resource Book*, by Laurie Green (London: Continuum, 2001).

This hermeneutical circle can act as a guide as we think through our experiences, helping to ensure that the process of reflection is not short-circuited but reaches a valuable conclusion. For the remainder of this chapter I want to consider the whole process of using film as a basis for theological reflection, following the stages of the 'pastoral cycle' in practical theology, whether we engage in such reflection after our own visit to a cinema or as part of a planned use of film in a church context. For many years it has been possible to show a film as part of a home group and use this as a basis for Bible study, but now with the technological advances that make good quality data projectors available at an affordable price it is possible for many churches to use, not only the latest 'Powerpoint' presentations, but also clips of films in church. I remember the slightly open mouths of our cubs and scouts when I showed a short clip of the first Harry Potter film, downloaded from the internet, the Sunday before it was due for general release. There are a number of practical considerations that are important in this respect, particularly ensuring that the projector is powerful enough to show films in daylight and that all legal requirements are met.[8] But there are other matters we must ponder.

Film as an existential exploration
Films are about life! Their setting may sometimes be in an alien world, but they explore themes of right and wrong, good and evil, of love, sacrifice, truth, self-discovery and our journey as individuals and a society. Films explore issues in life that matter and it is in this existential and anthropological arena that film and theology come together. As mentioned in its introduction, this book contains reflections and guides on a whole array of films without attempting to suggest which should or should not be viewed as 'religious' films. Whereas some films clearly set out to portray Christian or religious events, such as the various 'Jesus' films, or explore particular religious themes, it would be theology's loss to confine our reflection to this category alone. The belief in putting together such a book as this is that all films, with very limited exceptions,[9] can be a stimulus for reflection, because the meeting place for the dialogue between theology and film is not the overtly religious but the existential.

The aim of the thousands of sermons that are preached each week and of the Bible study that takes place in a whole variety of small groups is to allow the Christian gospel to speak to life as we live it today in the presence of God. We may begin with the traditionally 'religious' subjects, such as God, salvation and heaven, but these in themselves include significant existential questions about the meaning of life, the possibility of forgiveness, the nature of death. We need the gospel to speak to us about the realities of everyday existence, such as relationships, family life, our political world, and the acceptance of those who are other than we are. And these are the issues explored in films because these are the issues that affect us and matter to us as human beings.

As narratives, films may explore within themselves a range of issues. Some may have a predominant theme that acts as a thread weaving through all the action and dialogue. In *Master and Commander*, for example, the deeper theme that lies behind the dramatic action is that of the nature of leadership, as Captain Jack Aubrey commands his ship in a dangerous pursuit of a French enemy vessel. Other themes and issues may surface, but one may dominate. Other films may raise a number of significant issues at different points during a narrative. *The Mission*, for example, asks searching questions in turn about personal redemption, the nature of the church and the use of violence.

The temptation is often to jump to the end of the process, to move through the hermeneutical circle to the point of reflection too quickly, without spending sufficient time staying with the film and exploring the issues that the film raises. There seem to me to be two aspects to this exploration, which occupies the phase of the circle after the 'experience' of seeing the film. First we need to ponder what the film is 'saying', or allow the film to speak for itself. This is inevitably bound up with the way that we 'read' the film. Steve Nolan, in a previous chapter, appeals to a structuralist account of the nature of film to make this very point; we need to ask, for instance, what kind of reading the film is itself attempting to create in the mind of the viewers, and what ideology this assumes. Either on our own, or talking with others – perhaps on the way back from the cinema – we identify a number of issues which arise from the film and which we want to explore further. For some films, especially with complicated plots, it is only on a second or third viewing that we begin to have a clear picture of the film as a whole. This is not to suggest that there is only one 'reading' of a film, on which we will all agree, and that this corresponds to ideas clearly within the director's mind; what does matter is to listen to the film. This leads to a second aspect of exploration, to explore how the issues the film raises connect with our lives and current experience, the existential questions it asks of us and the challenges it offers. It may well be that what strikes us most in a film is something tangential to the main plot or even the overt message of the film, but which is central to our life at that moment. These two aspects, of course, are not entirely separate, but work together.

But before proceeding with this twin process of allowing the film to speak and exploring further the places where it most seems to connect with our lives, we need to sound various notes of caution.[10]

First, it is the very nature of films that the meaning of a particular film will neither be apparent nor generally agreed upon. Robert Ellis, in a previous chapter, has already highlighted some of the difficulties in seeking the meaning of a film, beginning with the large number of hands involved in its production and ending with the risk involved in offering a film to audiences who will understand it within their own context. We cannot adopt a naive view of popular cultural 'texts', as if they contain one simple clear meaning, but must recognize that there is always a strong 'reader-response' at play. The particular interests and commitments that we bring with us as we view a film will shape the way we respond to, and understand, what we watch. In the introduction to his book *The McDonaldization of the Church*[11] John Drane describes going to see the film *Stigmata* with some friends. Drane comments that he identified several aspects of today's spiritual search reflected in the film: 'questions about suffering, about psychic powers, about the source of religious authority, about whether the church could be trusted as a guardian of the truth, and some other themes besides.' He then began to think how these themes might be used in reflecting on Christian beliefs and practice. One of his companions he notes had a completely opposite reaction, seeing the film as 'a manifestation of sin in the most vulgar form imaginable.' For that person, therefore, there was no sense in discussing it, let alone engaging with it. Other people will not respond to a particular film in the same way as we do. We need to take care that we do not restrict our analysis of people's perceptions to white, middle class Anglo-Saxons, who perceive the world in a cerebral way. We need to allow the film to speak but we must recognize that it will do so in many and varied voices.

Second, we notice that many people seem merely to enjoy a film, engaging with it as a source of excitement or relaxation and taking it at face value, rather than articulating the issues the film explores. This, at least, appears to be their own perception of a good night out. But we need to reflect more profoundly on what actually happens when we and others enter into a different world that a film creates for us. Are we ever 'only' being entertained by a film without its world impinging upon us at some level? Steve Nolan, in his chapter, discusses a number of 'terrorist hijack' films and highlights the way that they reinforce a particular understanding of life, shaping our response to others whom we see as threats. He suggests that these films work at a level below that of explicit reflection, and that we are likely to leave the cinema more than entertained. John Drane, again, notes that many modern films develop our dissatisfaction with the world as we find it, our desire to recover personal fulfilment and a meaningful spirituality, and our belief that there is something 'unreal' about the world in which we live. He identifies these themes in such films as *The Truman Show* (1998), *The Matrix* (1999), and *American Beauty* (1999): these have

> highlighted the contrast between the happy, clean, middle-class values that our culture commends and which we all – at some level – strive for, and the underlying reality of people who wear masks all the time, and who have a real struggle to come to grips with what is real and worthwhile in life. This is an example of the moviemakers reflecting back what we already know to be true: the world we have created for ourselves seems not to be real.[12]

Drane, like Nolan, seems to be suggesting that such films 'work' at a deep level of our hopes and fears, in such a way that we cannot remain unmoved by entering into their world. Joseph Marty, in an essay on the theological interpretation of film, makes a similar point. In a passage which discusses the nature of an 'image', and the danger of reducing the image to the reality it represents (we see something of this in those who live as if their favourite Television soap-opera were real), he recognizes the particular power of film:

> Even if we know that this is just cinema, we cry or rejoice. In the 'projection' of a film, there is a projection and an identification that is immediate. That's the risk of a mediation that does its job so well that it can make us forget the representation.[13]

Films are a major source of entertainment, but we underestimate their narrative power if we restrict them within this boundary.

Third, when using film as an experience to provoke theological reflection, it is important to remember that we will be asked to inhabit temporarily another world that may be very different from our own, but one that may have much closer connections with the world of others. Some films will contain scenes which are uncomfortable and shocking, and may need to be so in order to make their point. Specifically, films may include violence, sex, swearing and blasphemy. A few films considered in this book have an '18' rating, because of the graphic violence they portray, such as *The Passion of the Christ* and *The Killing Fields*, or because of the mixture of the language, violence and the 'adult' theme explored, such as *One Flew Over the Cuckoo's Nest*. If films are going to portray the realities of human life, and if we are to encounter the world around us, as it is captured in film, then these are issues that we will not be able to avoid. Careful decisions will have to be made about which films are appropriate for use in the particular church or Christian group concerned, which will work best and – if only clips are being used – which clips are chosen.

In making these decisions, the first principle must obviously be to respect the rating that has been given to a film, so that films are not shown to those who are too young. This is particularly important when showing clips in a service of public worship. It is, in my view, inappropriate to show even a clip of a film where there will be those present too young to see the whole film, even if you judge the particular excerpt you have chosen to be suitable. There will be occasions when it is appropriate to use all or part of '15' and '18' films but only when all those present are legally able to see the whole film. Second, it will be necessary to keep in mind the sensitivities of the proposed audience. There is certainly a place for offering people an experience beyond that which is safe and comfortable, but in order for the experience to stretch them rather than crush them it is necessary to gauge the right distance. So in using *The Passion of the Christ* with an adult group that I knew only slightly, I was careful to choose a short scene that expressed something of the whole film, without being overwhelmingly violent. Finally, there may be some films, where there is gratuitous violence, voyeuristic sex and unnecessary bad language that we might choose to avoid completely, searching instead for other films that explore the same issues in a different way.

Having sounded these notes of caution we return to the issue of 'exploring' the experience of watching a film. I suggested earlier that such an exploration will have the dual focus of attempting to read the film on its own terms, despite the inherent difficulties this presents, and making the connections between the issues of the film and the issues of our own lives. This can be one of the hardest parts within the cycle, and a church group may need some prompting to move beyond commenting on the particular scenes they have enjoyed. It is a phase that calls for wise and sensitive leadership, which does not impose a meaning previously thought through, but which draws out from the members of the group their own understanding of what they have seen. Such groups are unlikely to be places where more intricate elements of film theory can be assumed or even discussed; it is more likely to be the story of the film which will provide the key. Discussing the narrative can be a useful foundation on which to build other aspects whose significance can then be seen.

Gathering up for example, the plot of *Sliding Doors* – and here a group will remember collectively more then any one individual – immediately raises the issue of how a small, seemingly insignificant event could change the whole of Helen's life. Thinking carefully about the plot of a film can also be a way into exploring its characters, and this can lead to gentle probing about the way we identify with, or respond to, them; this in turn can bring to the surface some of the hidden ideological presuppositions in the film. Working, for example, with a group who have watched a violent film, like *The Siege* (which Steve Nolan considers in an earlier chapter), discussion of the story can lead on to asking about the significance of the fact that the threat posed in the film through its characters is presented as being Arab and Muslim.

A group will need to develop the skill of attentiveness, and attention to detail. Most films will contain scenes, images, and dialogue that contribute something significant to the meaning of the film, even though they may appear only fleetingly. A later chapter on *Pleasantville*, for example, explores the way that Biblical imagery is used at key moments in the film. David, one of the main characters, is offered an apple by a young woman, a scene which is itself also replayed later. A mural painted on a wall is of an apple wrapped in a serpent and the first painting to be seen and appreciated is of the expulsion of Adam and Eve from the garden of Eden. There may be some discussion and disagreement about the significance of these images – and the chapter by Chris Holmwood explores these possibilities – but it is the attentive viewer who notices them and so is able to reflect.

The second part of the process of exploration allows for the specific ways that a film touches our own lives to come to the surface. This has a strong subjective element to it, what is often described when dealing with literature as a 'reader-response'. It is crucial to remember, when leading a

group discussion, that the issue is not what is 'the' true or false understanding of the film, but what are authentic responses from our individual
situations. It means that a wide range of sometimes conflicting responses
are valid, because they emerge from different people's engagement with
the film. One particularly striking example of such a response occurred in
a late night viewing of *Dead Poets Society* at which I was present.
Towards the end of the film, one of the school boys, struggling to cope
with a difficult situation, finds his Father's gun to take his own life. Out of
the direct view of the camera, you hear the gun shot. The silence of the
cinema at this tense moment was broken by an agonizing scream from the
audience, as the action on the screen touched one memory.

In the majority of situations the response generated by a film will not
be so painful, but hopefully will still be real and meaningful. A group
requires the leadership that creates both the space and the permission for
individuals to express and so explore their own individual, and sometimes
quite different reactions. These will depend on people's own stories, and
the way they identify with the characters in the film. A film may raise
issues of relationships, both experiences of failure and hopes for the
future; it may provoke despair or joy; it may leave those watching feeling
encouraged or intensely challenged. These are then the issues on which
we then seek to reflect so that we are able to take forward our own hopes
and struggles. My most recent outing to the cinema was to see *The
Incredibles*, with my six year old son. In between the numerous times the
world was saved we watched the development of a family, albeit one that
was fairly incredible. The children's attention was likely to have been
caught by the actions of the superheros in the family; but the parents
would be likely to notice the way that the routine issues of family life
were displayed, and no doubt the film-makers had this in mind. In this
fantasy film, there were issues of frustration and boredom in an unfulfill-
ing job, parenting at school and at home, and truth-telling in relationships.
These are precisely the kind of issues that we need to reflect on, in the
light of the Gospel.

Theology and film, then, can be involved in a dialogue, and it is in
this creative partnership and tension that new understanding and insight
can be gained. We have discussed the need to live in the world of the film,
to share in this new and other experience. This is combined with an open-

ness that allows the world of the film to speak to our world and to explore the real issues it raises for us. Then we need to allow the gospel to speak to both worlds. If we follow the hermeneutical circle, having lived the experience and explored the issues that a film raises for our lives, we then need to reflect further on these issues, explicitly bringing film and theology together.

Film as Theological Reflection

The aim of bringing theology and film into dialogue is not to find a particular or hidden religious or theological theme within a film, to encounter an image that acts as a symbol or illustration of gospel truth, or even find a positive message in a film we can easily appropriate – valid as these activities may be in other contexts. The aim of dialogue is to bring our own reading of the film side by side with our own reading of Scripture and other religious texts, even and especially when they seem to be utterly diverse, and to see what emerges from the proximity of one to the other.

The dangers of lack of authenticity in dialogue have been been well explored by Gordon Lynch. He surveys the way that those named as 'Generation X' have immersed themselves in various forms of popular culture – in particular TV, film, popular music and video games. He then notes the way that 'alternative worship events draw on the language and resources from beyond that [evangelical] sub-culture whether that be in the form of a story from the *Big Issue* magazine, a contemporary piece of dance music or a visual image from a contemporary film.'[14] Although he recognizes that the use of these contemporary cultural resources is not an attempt to make Christian worship "trendy" or appealing to others, but is 'an attempt to create environments for Christian worship that are culturally authentic for those who have planned the event',[15] Lynch nevertheless believes that there are problems with such an approach. We tend to read a Christian understanding into a secular art-form, and especially into film. He takes *The Matrix* as an example. This is one of the most discussed films in connection with the search for a spiritual message. It draws on some clear Christian images and ideas, one instance of which is Neo Anderson's death and resurrection as central to the emergence of the Chosen One who is able to control the Matrix. However, in interviewing those who had seen the film, Lynch found a variety of responses to it. Some did find clear messianic and gospel overtones. Others, however, saw it as being like *Star Wars* and *Star Trek*, showing signs of New Age or Eastern religious beliefs. The idea of ordinary life being an illusion has clear affinities with Buddhist and Hindu notions of the illusory nature of what we think is reality. It was also possible for some to see this film as being an occult movie. Some of his own students, who were versed in theological reflection, saw no religious significance at all in their first viewing of the film, and found it to be merely an enjoyable piece of science fiction.[16]

Lynch's comments remind us again of the significant 'reader-response' involved in the watching and reflecting on films. To suggest that *The Matrix* is a Christian film, or for that matter a Buddhist or occult film, is to miss the point. Likewise, there is no suggestion that theological reflection is aiming to find the 'right' interpretation of a film, or even presume that such an interpretation exists. Mention has already been made in this and earlier chapters of the 'risk' involved in attempting to convey a particular message through a particular film. The meaning of the film comes in the creative mix of those involved in its filming and final production and in the individual or group who watch it. But I have been arguing that film gives us an experience of another world, raising issues and asking questions. The precise experience and the exact issues and questions will depend on what we bring to the process. It is right and vital, as Christians, that we respond to these experiences that inform and shape us, even if subconsciously and to a limited degree, by thinking things through in the light of the gospel of Christ.

The exact nature of this reflection will depend on the nature of the film. Some films explicitly raise issues on which we will want to reflect from a Christian perspective. So, for example, I have already suggested that *Master and Commander* is in many ways a study of leadership. What are the tactics and relationships and inner qualities of a good, even great, leader? In the formation of those training to become Christian ministers, the writings, teachings and insights of modern secular leadership experts are explored, but always in critical dialogue with the stories in the Gospels which offer us a pattern of leadership in Christ which is both the inspiration and standard of our own human leadership. So also with a film. We may be inspired and challenged by the story from another world, but to this we bring our gospel insights, seeking for both film and biblical account to help us work out our leadership in Christ's way.

Other films may raise awkward questions that challenge our faith. *Schindler's List* may be the best example of such a film discussed in this book, as it brings us face to face with events of the Holocaust. Here we have to face the world in all its darkness and hear the voice that challenges us to find God in this place. A number of films discussed in this present study are based either on a previous book or on true events, or, as in the case of *Schindler's List*, both. This is a particular occasion when it is important to allow the film to speak without deferring always to the book, or becoming embroiled in issues of historicity. With the exception, of course, of those films which are actually documentaries and so purporting to be examining and weighing the historical data, films tell stories, and it is with those stories that we engage. The exact historical details of Oskar Schindler's life do not affect the imperative of hearing the challenge the film presents.

One of the films briefly reviewed in the final section of this volume is *The Mission*. I used a short clip of this film with a small group who were part of an introductory theology course, showing the scene where Mendoza, full of guilt, carries a net full of his heavy armour up the cliffs to the Indian community at the top of the falls. That one clip raised a number of significant issues which the film itself was working with.

- The nature of sin and guilt. Mendoza is a complex character, but we have the general impression that he is ruthless with little sense of conscience. We do not know exactly why he has spent six months in solitude and depression, but we know something about his past, and so the issues and memories that he struggles with.
- The burden of human life. Mendoza carrying the net up the mountain is a moving image, that represents the struggles of human life. But what exactly does the burden Mendoza carry represent, and how are we to interpret it?
- The possibility of salvation. The initial conversation between Mendoza and Father Gabriel in the cell in Ascuncion focuses on possible redemption for Mendoza. Mendoza claims 'There is no life'. Gabriel responds,

'There is a way out, Mendoza.' But the reply is, 'For me there is no redemption.'

• The nature of forgiveness. The conversation then turns to the possibility of Mendoza choosing a penance. Mendoza thinks that there is no penance hard enough, but Gabriel confronts him with the challenge to try. Carrying the net up the mountain is then a working out of this penance. At the end of the scene, when the net is cut Mendoza bursts into tears. It is impossible to tell whether Mendoza is really crying or laughing – it seems deliberately ambiguous – but it is clearly a scene of reconciliation.

Our task is to bring the film and theology into a fruitful dialogue. The image of the burden of the net falling down the mountain into the river is reminiscent of the scene in Bunyan's *Pilgrim's Progress* where Christian's burden falls down at the cross and rolls into the tomb – surely deliberately so. *Pilgrim's Progress* is a classic work of literature and the scene from it that is most frequently depicted is that of Christian's burden. Mendoza carries his weapons and armor, which he used as a slave-trader and with which he killed his brother. They represent his way of life, something of the sin and guilt he feels. This is very similar to *Pilgrim's Progress*. But it is possible that the film goes further. Mendoza's weapons and armor are more than personal belongings – they are the trappings of the state on whose behalf Mendoza worked, and in whose name he attacked the Indians. While there is clearly the sense of personal responsibility for individual actions – the image of *Pilgrim's Progress* – sin and guilt involves more than that. We are caught up in a web of actions involving those around us and wider society. This seems to me to be the meaning of the difficult theme in the Old Testament, that the children will be punished for the sins of their parents.[17] Sin can never be purely individual and self-contained because we are caught up in wider family and society and the film adds to our understanding of the significance and the complexity of the burdens we carry.

The Gospel passage that makes a direct connection with this scene from the film is Matthew 11:28-30, where Jesus offers rest to those who are carrying heavy burdens. The nature of the burden is unspecified and 'rest' is more than a brief respite, but it is an image of salvation. Salvation is graciously offered to those who carry heavy burdens. The image of burdens features again in Matthew's Gospel in 23:1-4. Here Jesus comments on the Pharisees who impose burdens on others without lifting a finger to help. The burden here is the 'unbearable' demands of the law, perhaps what Jesus had in mind earlier. This at first, seems to offer a different image from the film, with its language of penance, drawn from the Catholic tradition. Does Mendoza have to earn his redemption by undergoing a penance that is sufficiently hard? The end is clearly a scene of redemption for Mendoza, who emerges from it a radically changed man. But what is the cause? Is it that, after Gabriel's challenge, he has completed his penance and so deserves redemption? Or is it that the act of cutting the net by the Indian is a most powerful symbol of their forgiveness of him, and so the forgiveness he can know from God?

It seems to me that although the film uses the traditional language of penance, redemption comes from an act of costly grace, as those most injured by Mendoza's sin show him forgiveness. There is another interesting link with *Pilgrim's Progress* here. Christian loses his burden at the cross – Bunyan makes this explicit. There is no cross at this point in *The Mission*. But at the beginning of the film a Catholic priest is attached to a cross by the Guarani, and is sent down the river over the falls to his death. It is out of this incident that Father Gabriel comes to continue to try and work with the Indians. Father Gabriel retrieves the wooden cross this priest wore round his neck and at the end of the film gives it to Mendoza – so the whole film is framed by the cross.

The film may then help us to a deeper understanding of salvation in two ways. First we see that salvation involves reconciliation. This is one of the images that Paul uses, in 2 Corinthians 5:16-21. If this reconciliation is going to be meaningful it must have a vertical dimension, reconciliation with other people, as well as a horizontal dimension, reconciliation with God. Second, it is a journey that is at times hard, as we see in *Pilgrim's Progress*. Jesus offers words of comfort in Matthew 11:28-30, but we must not assume that once we have heard them everything is finished. The story, for example, of Peter in the Gospels, reminds us of the journey he made, that included denial and restoration.

Having drawn a Gospel text and a spiritual classic into dialogue with the film, it may also be helpful to draw on a part of the liturgy of the church. Standing by the communion table, I have often said words that begin:

> Come to this table, not because you must, but because you may;
> not because you are strong, but because you are weak,
> not because you have any claim on heaven's rewards,
> but because you stand in constant need of heaven's mercy and grace.[18]

Although not using the language of burden, this invitation to communion picks up the issues of weakness, sin and the need for grace that are symbolized by the burden. These words express well the Gospel invitation that is experienced in bread and wine. It is also possible to understand the journeys made by Christian and Mendoza in terms of a response to an invitation. Mendoza makes the climb to the top of the mountain because of his encounter with Father Gabriel; it is not described in the language of an invitation to find grace, but as a challenge to do penance, for this is the language that Mendoza understands. The result is not certain, the project may go wrong – Mendoza asks Father Gabriel 'Do *you* dare see it fail?' – but the outcome is an invitation for Mendoza to journey with his burden and to find at the hands of his victims forgiveness and reconciliation with God.

Film and a Lived Response

The 'hermeneutical circle' that we described earlier pushes us on, to live out the consequences of the dialogue in which we have engaged. As Christmas we want to be entertained by the films we see, we enjoy the space to reflect and discuss and express our opinions on what we have seen. But beyond this there is also the challenge to change, to become different in some way because of our dialogue.

As a Christian minister, reflecting on *The Mission* makes me think about my ministry and the way I help others on their journey to find grace. So services of public worship, the repeated rhythm when people corporately find space for God, need to be occasions where those who attend can find God's grace, and this means some recognition of the burdens we carry. In many written services, for example in the Church of England, a prayer of confession is a set part of the service, followed by a prayer of forgiveness or absolution. In some Baptist churches I have attended, there seems little, if any, place for confession, and perhaps the assumption is we have come to praise God as forgiven sinners. This seems to limit the opportunities for those who come to experience God's grace. My desire is always to include opportunity for confession in a service, and also then words of grace and forgiveness, but the challenge is to make this real. And so I have experimented with two ways.

First, I have allowed some distance between a prayer of confession and a promise of forgiveness, so that in some small way the idea of a journey is expressed. Experience tells us that forgiveness and grace normally comes after a process of struggle, and it is possible sometimes to hold onto a sense of our own sin and journey with it before hearing words of forgiveness. During communion, for example, we may have a prayer for forgiveness at the beginning of that part of the service, think about the events of the last supper and Jesus' death, express our thanks to God for the cross, and then finally offer words of forgiveness and grace in the sharing of bread and wine.

Second, I have sometimes used stones as symbols of the burdens we carry, asking people to hold onto their stone while we think together about our lives, and then inviting them physically to come forward and bring their stones to a cross standing in the church. In the very process of getting up, walking and returning to our seats empty-handed we experience God's forgiveness and grace.

Film is a powerful medium that can shock, challenge and disturb. It may be that a dialogue of theology with a film happens gradually, that we assimilate its results over a long period, and that we can reflect on a journey we have made. Equally, one experience of film may make a profound impact. Sometimes both kinds of experience are combined. I recall the visit to the cinema that in some way changed my relationship with films. In 1986 as student in Durham I saw the film *Cry Freedom!*. Captivated by the images of South Africa it had shown, and powerfully drawn in to its pursuit of justice, I left the cinema knowing that life now needed to be different. I did not, however, join the coaches that went down to London to join in the protests against apartheid, and looking back now I feel some measure of regret, and shame, that I did not. The whole journey of thinking through the relation between politics and theology which began then still continues and has practical effects in my life today. Of course, if I had not been at the cinema that evening this journey may have been triggered by another event at another time, but for me it was a film that prompted a lived response. That evening was the first time I had heard the subversive anthem 'God bless Africa'. Whenever I hear it again, it takes me back to that night.

Notes

[1] For a general discussion of classic film theory see Antony Easthope (ed.), *Contemporary Film Theory* (Harlow: Addison Wesley Longman Ltd, 1993), pp. 1-5; John R. May (ed.), *New Image of Religious Film*, (Kansas: Sheed and Ward, 1997), pp. 3-15.

[2] The phrase comes from Siegfried Kracauer writing in the 1940s, quoted in May (ed.), *New Image of Religious Film*, p. 5.

[3] May, *New Image of Religious Film*, p. 5. May suggests that this is how directors such as Alexander Pudovkin and Sergei Eisenstein understood their work.

[4] William Shakespeare, *Henry V*, Act I, Prologue.

[5] I am grateful to Chris Holmwood for this suggestion, taken from his unpublished paper, 'Shakespeare and the Art of Antithesis'.

[6] Two introductions would be Laurie Green, *Let's Do Theology: A Pastoral Cycle Resource Book* (London: Continuum, 2001), and Paul Ballard and John Pritchard, *Practical Theology in Action* (London: SPCK, 1996).

[7] The diagram is taken from Green, *Let's Do Theology*, p. 30.

[8] For copyright information and the use of films within a context of public worship contact: Christian Copyright Licensing Limited, PO Box 1339, Eastbourne, East Sussex, BN21 1AD, 01323 41711, www.ccli.co.uk. They operate a Church Video Licence and can give information on legally using films in a public context.

[9] There are some films on the very extremes of the genre, such as pornography, which, although focussed on significant areas of life, may be unhelpful as experiences for reflection.

[10] I am grateful to some ideas suggested by John Weaver here.

[11] John Drane, *The McDonaldization of the Church* (London: Darton, Longman, & Todd, 2000; reprinted in the U.S. by Smyth & Helwys Publishing, 2001), p.10.

[12] John Drane, *The McDonaldization of the Church*, p.23.

[13] Joseph Marty, 'Toward a Theological reading of Film: Incarnation of the Word of God – Relation, Image and Word', in May (ed.), *New Image of Religious Film*, p. 133.

[14] Gordon Lynch, *After Religion. 'Generation X' and the Search for Meaning*, (London: Darton, Longman & Todd, 2002), pp. 45-6.

[15] Gordon Lynch, *After Religion*, pp. 45-6.

[16] Gordon Lynch, *After Religion*, pp. 58-65.

[17] See Exodus 20:5; Jeremiah 31:29.

[18] Baptist Union of Great Britain, *Patterns and Prayers for Christian Worship* (Oxford: Oxford University Press, 1991), p. 81.

Part II
Reflections

6
Virtual Literalism: *Big Fish*

David Sutcliffe

> *Oh, some people don't believe*
> *That a whale could him receive.*
> *But that does not make my song at all untrue;*
> *There are whales on every side,*
> *With their big mouths open wide—*
> *Just take care, my friend, or one will swallow you.*[1]

Working pastors and evangelists have all been there. We're exploring the significance of the gospel's message in a small group session, and we sense we may be reeling in a human fish for the kingdom, when someone lobs in a big red herring: what about the seven day creation? Must we really believe in Adam and Eve? Others nod and confess that they also find the virgin birth of Jesus Christ hard to swallow, or can't honestly imagine that two of every zoological species from microbe to mammoth entered Noah's big boat. And if some of the Bible isn't really true, then how can we trust it on any questions at all? Oh yes we'd like to believe, but stories like Jonah's big fish let us off the hook, so to speak. Living in the belly of a fish for three days and nights? Well, really!

Established Christians may find themselves in a psychic dichotomy: mentally divided between the competing truths of a sub-cultural Christian ghetto and a public world. Think of Christian teenagers coping with being taught evolutionary theory as a literal reality at school, having been told by their church youth leader that people were created on the sixth day. This lack of mental wholeness proves very disturbing to reflective people, and can no doubt be a contributing factor to the loss of faith. It seems regrettable, therefore, that at British universities some Christian student groups provide spiritual and biblical education for a generation of emerging leaders which works on the model of competition between literal truths, an approach which is historically recent and already outdated.

Stories and truth

In the context of such discussions, Tim Burton's film *Big Fish* could prove a useful stimulant to a conversation concerning the nature of truth and the value of story. This playful production is a tale about the truth of stories in relation to their factual – or fanciful – base. An aging father, Edward Bloom (Albert Finney), is about to die of cancer, so his estranged son, William (Billy Crudup), returns home from Paris with his pregnant French wife Josephine (Marion Cotillard) in an attempt to reconnect with his father while there is still time. The film consists of extravagant stories from Edward's youth intermingled with realistic scenes of his dying days. William doubts the reality of the stories but longs to be able to connect with the real father who seems hidden by his colourful narratives.

So director Tim Burton weaves numerous stories together to form a rich fabric, implicitly and repeatedly asking the viewer, 'What does it mean to say a story is true?' William embodies a modernist outlook of fact-based realism. A story is true only if it actually happened in the real world. His father Ed insists that this sterile view communicates 'all of the facts and none of the flavour', and the film explores what kind of truth is expressed by this old man's non-literal retelling of human experience. Ewan McGregor plays the younger Edward Bloom charming his way through a series of unlikely adventures.

Edward is a colourful character, a well-liked 'social person', full of confidence, romanticism and passion. William by contrast seems earnest, cynical and mundane. Sadly, their disagreement over stories has separated them from each other. William has grown tired of stories. Story-telling is for children, and when the same story has been told 'a thousand times' the experience has grown thin for him. These stories belong to a child's bed time routine rather than the world of serious adult discourse. Brought into the latter world, they become mere 'amusing lies'.

The parallel with those seeking to understand religious faith is apparent. The modernist sceptic is ably represented by William. If the facts of a story are uncertain, then the story must be rejected as being untrue. If there was no man-harbouring outsize fish, then Jonah is simply a children's fable, and its presence in the Bible masquerading as history discredits everything else there. Edward, on the other hand, stands for a post-modern outlook. Truth for him is a personal construction reflecting

much more than mere facts, a view well illustrated in the opening eponymous Big Fish story. Does he really believe he caught an uncatchable fish
on the day of his son's birth by offering it a wedding ring? Or is this a
delightful fiction to illuminate the challenge and power of lifelong love?

William's total rejection of his father mirrors a modernist person's
total rejection of religious truth. A breakdown of communication has
occurred. Connection based on attempts to force science and religion into
telling the same literal truth will prove generally unfeasible. If William
simply focuses on the literal absurdity of his father's stories, the two will
remain estranged.

All this is masterfully portrayed in the opening scene in which the
Big Fish tale of William's birth is told in four different settings. William
has heard this all before, and when his father stole centre-stage with a repetition of this particular tale at William's wedding, the groom finally
snapped and rejected him, subsequently communicating only through his
mother Sandra, excellently played by Jessica Lange.

Ironically enough, this film is framed by the narration of the sceptical
son telling his father's story. Looking back he has decided it is impossible
to separate the man from the myth, the story from the reality, so he has
decided to tell the story of the father by telling his stories. And so the
opening Big Fish birth story is completed by William himself.

The classic Hollywood theme of father-son relationships is explored
in a fresh format, and the emotive power of the closing death-bed scenes
is all the greater for eschewing mawkish declarations of lately-realized
love in favour of the making of one last story to enable the old man to die
well. William's ability to share in the creative task of story-telling on this
final occasion embodies his acceptance of his larger-than-life father,
whom he had once seen as a mere fake. It also symbolizes a hope that
'science and religion are intellectual cousins under the skin'.[2]

Virtual literalism
Some may feel that the film points us in the direction of seeing the whole
of the Bible as mere fiction. This would suggest that the stories of the
film, and indeed those of the Bible, are true only in the sense that traditional fables are true. The fanciful content is naturally to be dismissed, but
we may accept the moral lesson of the story as its truth.

Marcus Borg, in a recent book discussing a modern reader's approach to the Bible, distinguishes between natural literalism and conscious literalism.[3] *Natural literalism* belongs to the pre-scientific age, when, in the absence of modern cosmology and evolutionary biology, people, unsurprisingly, accepted biblical accounts – for example those of creation – as being realistic descriptions of physical events. By contrast, *conscious literalism* is a modern attitude found in people who, though perfectly aware of the widely-accepted discoveries of modern science, deliberately insist that a literal reading of biblical creation stories should be an article of faith.

Offering a way of hearing biblical stories positively today, Borg uses the term *postcritical naïveté* to describe a reception of a story as true, that is as a narrative carrying life-enhancing meaning, even though we know its facts may not be literally accurate:

> This way of hearing stories is widespread in premodern cultures. In Arabia, traditional storytellers begin their stories with 'This was and this was not ...' A North American storyteller begins telling the tribe's story of creation: 'Now I don't know if it happened this way or not, but I know this story is true ...'[4]

In mulling over the themes of the film I devised another term for this attitude: *virtual literalism*. To enjoy fully a virtual reality experience we must not be focusing on the fact that the sensory information received is a mere contrivance, but we must allow ourselves to enter fully into the computer-generated narrative world. Virtual literalism should be carefully distinguished from the psychic dichotomy alluded to above, in which one simply lives in two separate world views according to whether one is operating in a religious or a secular sphere. A good story received with virtual literalism integrates life by charging emotions, thoughts, relationships and actions with a positive energy, though we may be aware that non-literal aspects of the story are immediately apparent, or might be revealed by reflective analysis.

Burton's film provides numerous stories through which the nature of virtual literalism may be explored, as we shall see. One of *Big Fish*'s most charming tales is that of Edward's courtship of his future wife Sandra.

After an elaborate diversion in the circus world, itself drawing from a range of fairytale motifs, including werewolves and giants, Edward has discovered the name of his lovely bride-to-be: Sandra Templeton. With unabashed romanticism, Edward woos Sandra, and his imaginative approaches culminate in the planting of a vast field of daffodils (her favourite flower) outside her bedroom window.

One feels that the field of daffodils story is an obvious exaggeration of reality. But which reality? Physical reality may well have proved susceptible to the story-teller's hyperbole, but what we might refer to as emotional reality has been accurately expressed – more accurately than if it were constrained by literal reality. The motif of the overnight field of daffodils faithfully reflects Edward's love for Sandra. As the story unfolds we learn that this love has remained alive throughout his lifetime. Against the expectation of his realist son, we learn that Edward was apparently always faithful to Sandra, even when invited to share love with the eccentric but alluring Jennifer Hill (Helena Bonham Carter). Or at least, that is Jennifer's story, and this is the only one we have!

The affection between Edward and Sandra is most beautifully explored in one central scene when the old man is taking a bath with his pyjamas still on – 'I was drying out' – and is joined in the water by the fully-dressed Sandra. As she leans lovingly against his chest and he strokes her chin in a characteristic gesture of fondness, there is a sense of deep joy. This man has lived out his stories. His patently-exaggerated nuptial tales have expressed, nurtured and inspired a deeply enduring love. Edward's essentially good nature is shaped by his stories. They give him courage, love, confidence and determination. So is the daffodil story true? Not if we are counting plants; but 'it's oh, so true', if we are talking about lasting passion colouring emotional life and inspiring loving choices. This is much richer than simply drawing the moral that one should remain faithful to one's partner. This is virtual literalism in action!

In another repeated story, Edward Bloom believes he has seen the circumstances of his own death in a witch's glass eye. This information, accepted at face value – we might say, accepted as virtually true – enables him to face other mortal dangers with confidence. Edward trusts his life to the story's power by facing peril on the grounds of its virtual truth. Besieged by a film-maker's classic man-eating tree, the woodland spell is broken as he remembers aloud – 'This isn't how I die!' So Edward has faith in the power of his own story. A story that is virtually literally true can save our lives.

Now one can imagine Edward being backed into a corner by some investigator and asked: was the giant Karl really twelve feet tall? Well, no, as we see at Edward's funeral. He is certainly a big guy, but not twelve feet big; that is, however, hardly the point. Did the poet Norther Winslow really spend twelve years writing a three-line poem? Well, perhaps he wrote a few more words than that, but again that is not the point. Were the twins Jing and Ping really joined from the waist downward? Well no, we see them later each with their own pair of legs (again, at the funeral), but to picture them as Siamese twins adds colour.

The point is that a good story has transformational power when held trustfully within the human heart and respectfully by human culture; this is a power that transcends any literal reading. The death-defying story is true, not because Edward will one day drown in a real river, but because courage is a true attribute of the human heart. But for it to be not only true but also *effective*, Edward transcends his doubts about its literal detail and allows it to colour his thoughts, his self-understanding and his actions. For him, it is virtually literally true.

Feeling, telling and living the story

As people routinely use technical equipment without a conscious reflection on its workings, so we might use story without a frequent conscious assent to narrative and psychological technicalities. Of course, one can stop and laboriously dissect what we mean when we say that Jonah was in the big fish for three days, and of course educated Christians should be able to conduct such a dissection, but in daily religious experience only the spiritual equivalent of a techno-nerd would do this very often at all.

So Edward Bloom leads us to flee from a cold, routine, religious reductionism and calls us to feel, tell and live the story. We are able to receive the story as virtually literally true, just as a biologist declaring undying love to her lover need not detain him with analyses of blood pressure, pupil dilation, hormonal aspects of sexual arousal, and the evolutionary imperative to mate, but simply feels, tells and lives the story of love.

This virtual literalism is nicely illustrated by the film maker's techniques. Burton chose to make minimal use of computer generated images when telling his hero's impossible tales because he wanted the viewer to perceive them as being as literally true as possible. So the field of daffodils was literally planted by a team of gardeners over a weekend. In one scene, Edward's car is left stranded at the top of a tree after a fantastical storm. Burton insists on putting a real car in a real tree for his filming, feeling that people could sense if it were a computer-generated illusion. He wants people to feel that the story, for all its beyond-reality events, is in another sense realistic. He wants us to receive the story with virtual literalism.

To assist its virtually literal reception, story may draw from the collective associations of historical motifs but without necessarily portraying a literally historically accurate picture. Some have criticized *Big Fish* for its depiction of Edward at war.[5] Which war? Korean? Then why do the entertainers speak a Chinese language? Did he jump from the right sort of plane? Historical anomalies may serve to remind us that we are not intended to be taking the story literally. But historical motifs enable us to feel the associations of an era or an incident and this helps create the right emotional landscape for receiving the story virtually literally.

The historical and geographical vagueness of the Jonah tale is of course well-known. But Trevor Dennis writes of the power of Nineveh to create the right emotional conditions for the reception of the story:

> The significance of Nineveh in the book of Jonah is crystal clear. Though almost certainly the city had long gone by the time the work was written, it still represented for the Jew all that was evil, all that was brutal, ruthless and destructive ... Nineveh occupied much the same place in the minds of Jews after the exile as is filled in the minds of contemporary Jews by Hitler's Berlin.[6]

Virtual literalism as gracious creativity

Stories have areas of competence. To learn positively from a narrative we must consider its trajectory. Jonah's tale moves as an exploration of relations between a reluctant Jewish prophet, a gracious God and various Gentiles. It is not one from which we may legitimately learn of piscine physiology, nor the size of Nineveh, as these matters are tangential to the story's path.

Similarly, *Big Fish* is a poor guide on American racism, depicting as it does a 1950s Alabama quite content with a black doctor treating well-to-do white families. And the film is hardly a well-rounded lead on how to be a good partner. How did Sandra manage when her popular husband was so often away on business? How did she cope with a man for whom the family home was seen as confining? He is self-confident to the point of arrogance, and, like a carefree clergyman with a nationwide parish, shared the goodness of his nature with all and sundry, leaving his wife to manage the household, and wait dutifully and adoringly by the white picket fence.

In one scene, Jennifer Hill is visited by Edward's sceptical son William. Jennifer is a single woman who, as a child, had fallen for Edward and, after a failed marriage, had found that Edward was able to spend some time alone with her. When William visits, she is clearly still very fond of him – she's the only one to call him 'Eddie' – and is disturbed to learn of his imminent death.

This mysterious other woman in Edward's life explains to William that for Edward there are only two kinds of women – 'your mother and everyone else'. Jennifer turns out to have been the witch Edward knew as a child – logically impossible as William, inevitably, points out – but disturbingly perhaps true in Edward's mind. Women are either perfect wives or witches.

But William is not confident in his father's story of marital fidelity, and so he asks Jennifer straight out, 'Were you having an affair?' After commenting on his directness, she replies: 'You have one image of your father. It would be wrong for me to go and change it. Especially this late in the game.' Subsequently she tells a story of how Edward resisted her attempt at seduction, declaring that there was only one woman for him. Jennifer is using story to re-create Edward in the mind of his son, William. What actually happened between Edward and Jennifer we will never know: we only have her story. But we may recall Jennifer's early dismissal of her piano student who wanted to know if he had to give back to his mum the money for the lesson. Jennifer's reply? 'I won't tell her if you won't.' While a small detail in the film, it stands as an agreement to create a particular understanding in the mind of another person.

But perhaps stories are all we have to find meaning in the mind-numbingly vast soup of events in our universe. Factual reality is complex beyond our comprehension. How many events impinge upon us in a typical day? How many emotions pass through our minds? How many reasons do we have for every action we take? We necessarily use reality in a highly selectively manner to create and communicate truth in a story. Most people do this every day as they give an account of their day to a member of their household, creating a narrative by drawing from very many experiences indeed those few events which communicate the particular emotional or relational truths they wish to highlight.

Perhaps Jennifer's story of Edward's faithfulness accurately reflects a particular event. But there would have been very many other events in their relationship. She chooses to tell William a story which reflects the truth that his father loved his mother in a unique manner. She graciously creates a good story to reinforce an image of his father as a faithful hero.

Jonah's tale graciously creates a new understanding for a Jewish audience of both God and Gentiles. The narrative emphasizes God's loving care for the people of the non-Jewish world, and shows the Gentiles as both pious seamen and people capable of responding to a call to change for the better. It is the only prophetic book which depicts an oracle spoken in a foreign city,[7] and Nineveh's positive response creates a sense of the limitless concern and power of God.

For centuries, the book of Jonah has been a set reading at Yom Kippur, the annual solemn fast in the Jewish year. Received by the community as being virtually literally true, it recreates divinity in the listeners' minds, nurturing a sense of God as one who is eager to forgive. The story helps to shape the people to seek reconciliation not only within the Jewish world, but also beyond.[8] Recalling Dennis' remarks on Nineveh as being as evocative of enemy brutality as is Berlin today, the story has the potential to inspire gracious actions even towards recently hated enemies.

Towards the end of *Big Fish*, by Edward's death bed, Dr Bennett offers to tell the 'real story' of William's birth in contrast to his father's celebrated Big Fish version. Edward was away on business in Wichita. 'It was a perfect delivery and your father was sorry not to be there. It wasn't the custom then for men to be in the delivery room, so I can't see it would have made much difference had he been there. So that's the real story of how you were born.' The doctor says he might choose Edward's fancy version involving a fish and a wedding ring. William clings doggedly to his preference for the 'real' version. But his father's extravagant birth story celebrates the mystery of life and the power and challenge of love, and points to the child as being of special significance, as do those of biblical heroes from Moses through Samson to Jesus.

But, back in the hospital, Edward wakes up, and wants his son William to tell him not a birth story, but a death story. His father begins it, but then William creates the truth of how his father will die. In this story, William helps Edward escape from the hospital, wheels him to his old red charger, and drives him to the river, avoiding the slow church traffic (ponder the symbolism here!).

William narrates: 'As we get close to the river we see that everybody is already there – and I mean everyone. It's unbelievable.' Edward responds: 'The story of my life.' His son concludes the story: 'And the strange thing is, there's not a sad face to be found. Everybody is so glad to see you and send you off right.' William carries his father past the well-wishing crowd of characters from Edward's life-story, into the river, where, after gesturing to Sandra, 'my girl in the river', he is released into the water and becomes the big fish he always was. All this time, Edward is physically in the hospital, dying in a bed surrounded by hospital paraphernalia. And so William has graciously created a good story to help his father die. In doing this, William becomes a storyteller himself and enables his father's spirit to live on.

Virtual literalism, a stream of stories and ultimate reality

Biochemist J. B. S. Haldane once remarked that even the Archbishop of Canterbury was 65% water.[9] One might as well say this book is 100% paper and ink. Stories challenge banal reductionism with a sense of ultimate hope.

In William's story, as he dies, Edward becomes the big fish. Twice in the film he has seen this fish as a beautiful woman swimming in the river. The big fish is elusive, feminine, uncatchable and yet is also the embodiment of Edward's stories and of his soul. She even once surprises the realist William by disturbing him as he cleans out the pool. William's narration remarks that Edward will live on in his stories. The big fish is the story of stories: Edward, who seems not to exist independently of his stories lives as the stories live. This is a kind of resurrection, a hint at an ultimate reality.

Another image of ultimate reality looms darkly in the film: the strange town of Spectre, originally cut off from the outside world and superficially a paradise of calm. It is a place drawn partly with biblical imagery, including the sight of a naked woman in a beautiful setting threatened by a serpent, and a welcoming figure checking the names of visitors against a written record – an angel with the book of life? And yet there is something unmistakeably creepy about this place. Sickly smiles and stagnant relationships, along with a sense of being trapped, stimulate a revulsion in the viewer. Edward will not succumb to its spell and declares in the middle of a dance: 'I have to leave. Tonight ... This town is more than any man can ask for. And if I were to end up here I'd consider myself lucky. But the truth is I'm not ready to end up anywhere.' Edward later returns to the town to rescue it from the outside world. But, though he polishes this sterile image of heaven, he leaves it behind, never to come back. Instead the film offers a dynamic and narrative form of immortality: the Big Fish, the man's essence, his stories, go on. Perhaps none of us will be ready to 'end up' anywhere.

The Hebrew scriptures show God as speaking the world into existence. The Christian scriptures describe their Saviour as being the Word – or the story – made flesh. Stories are all we have. If the story lives, we live. The Archbishop's body may be by now primarily atmospheric moisture, but something certainly still marches on – whether his soul or his sermons!

Matthew's Gospel depicts Jesus as reacting to a demand from scribes and Pharisees for a sign, in spite of the sundry miracles that have already been performed. They seem to require a personal physical-reality proof of Jesus' claims. In reply, Matthew's Jesus refers them to stories past and future: the sign of the prophet Jonah:

> For just as Jonah was three days and three nights in the belly of the sea monster, so for three days and three nights the Son of Man will be in the heart of the earth.[10]

Some literalist critics have criticized this text on the grounds that Jesus was not in fact in the tomb for the third night, or have been tempted to use it to try to recalibrate our understanding of the passion narrative's timing[11]. This seems an absurdly over-literal reading of Matthew's Jesus' symbolic remarks.

What we have here is a stream of stories, all inspiring us to live out the truth that in the face of death (fish's belly, tomb, threats to the reader's well-being) and sin (Jonah's reluctance and Nineveh's wickedness, humanity's violent rejection of Jesus, lack of authenticity in the reader's soul) life can still triumph (repentance, resurrection and reconciliation). Various interlinked stories might be discerned, including these seven:

• A beautifully-crafted tale of a prophet and a big fish
• The styling of Jesus' encounter with some Jewish authorities, in the source called 'Q' (lost)
• Matthew's re-styling of the same encounter
• Luke's re-styling of the same encounter
• The great story of the resurrection of Jesus Christ
• The story of Matthew's original audience (reconstructed)
• Our own life story as we read Matthew's account

To suppose that the main point of these stories is to carry a large amount of literal freight is to miss the point. Karl the giant was not twelve feet tall. Jonah did not literally compose a comic psalm of praise inside a big fish which was swimming under the earth for 72 hours.[12] But by receiving the stories virtually literally, as part of our community and part of our soul, we refuse to draw the conclusion that sin and death will prevail.

All of these stories point us in the direction of grace, life, hope and love. They find an echo in our souls and communities which inspires us to hope that indeed, life will go on. They woo us to believe that if there is an ultimate reality, if there is everlasting life, then the best way to prepare for it will be to allow our souls to be inspired by resurrection stories of life, love and grace. The old Apostle reckoned that love lasts forever (1 Corinthians 13:13). Our story-filled souls have a glimmering hope that he was on to something.

Let me give the last word to a character created by master storyteller C. S. Lewis. Puddleglum, when in a spot of bother from the White Witch, says this:

> Suppose we *have* only dreamed, or made up, all those things – trees and grass and sun and moon and stars and Aslan himself. Suppose we have. Then all I can say is that, in that case, the made-up things seem a good deal more important than the real ones. Suppose this black pit of a kingdom of yours *is* the only world. Well, it strikes me as a pretty poor one. And that's a funny thing when you come to think of it. We're just babies making up a game, if you're right. But four babies playing a game can make a play-world that licks your real world hollow … I'm on Aslan's side even if there isn't any Aslan to lead it. I'm going to live as like a Narnian as I can even if there isn't any Narnia.[13]

Notes

[1] Traditional, found at www.cyberhymnal.org, accessed 2/12/2004.

[2] John Polkinghorne, *Quarks, Chaos and Christianity*, (London: Triangle, 1994).

[3] Marcus J Borg, *Reading the Bible Again for the First Time: Taking the Bible Seriously, but not Literally* (New York: Harper San Francisco, 2002), p. 8

[4] Borg, *Reading the Bible Again for the First Time*, p. 50.

[5] See the Director's Commentary on the *Big Fish* DVD, in which Tim Burton anecdotally refers to such criticism.

[6] Trevor Dennis, *Lo and Behold: The Power of Old Testament Storytelling* (London: SPCK, 1991), p. 138.

[7] James Limburg, *Jonah* (London: SCM Press, 1993), p. 22.

[8] Rosemary Nixon, *The Message of Jonah* (Leicester: IVP, 2003), p. 39.

[9] Steven Rose, *The Chemistry of Life* (London: Penguin, 1999), p. 22.

[10] Matthew 12:40, New Revised Standard Version.

[11] Donald A. Hagner, *Matthew 1 – 13*. Word Biblical Commentary (Dallas: Word Publications, 1993), p. 354.

[12] Dennis, *Lo and Behold*, p. 144.

[13] C. S. Lewis, *The Silver Chair* (Harmondsworth: Penguin, 1977), p. 156–7.

7
When Text Becomes Voice:
You've Got Mail
Paul Fiddes

The 'Romantic Comedy' is a genre which is often despised by film critics. Given the dismissive title 'Romcom', it is denigrated as superficial entertainment, hopelessly escapist and surrendering all realism to the demands of a happy ending. The example of William Shakespeare, who spent a considerably part of his dramatic career writing romantic comedies might, however, alert us to the fact that this kind of play can explore relationships between the self and the 'other' in the most profound way, and that the mistakes, deceptions, misunderstandings and disguises that litter its scenes can be the means of raising the most disturbing questions about the relation between appearance and reality. In our present age, often dubbed 'postmodern', it is the romantic comedy that can make us aware of issues of the identity of the self in a complicated world of myriad signs. The 'Romcom' is indeed a suitable dialogue partner for Christian theology which arises from the 'Divine Comedy', no less so than films of tragedy, violence and crime – and perhaps more so. In this article I want to focus these considerations mainly on one Hollywood movie, *You've Got Mail* (1998).

The written text and the spoken word
This film, directed by Norah Ephron and produced by Laura Schuler Donner, portrays two residents of New York who own bookshops of very different characters. Kathleen Kelly (Meg Ryan) owns 'The Shop Around the Corner', a small neighbourhood children's bookshop whose staff love books and know a great deal about them, and whose owner reads to the children who come into the shop for a regular story-hour. Joe Fox (Tom Hanks) is joint-owner of the family business, a giant chain of book super-stores which offer huge stocks, heavily discounted prices and expresso coffee bars. When the film opens Kathleen and Joe do not know each other under their real names, but have in fact been conducting an anony-

mous email correspondence under the identities of 'NY 152' (Joe) and 'Shopgirl' (Kathleen). Through the internet they believe they have come to know each other at a deep level and to understand each other; they share their inner feelings in a way they cannot do with the partners with whom they are living, and they have a growing affection for each other. Each day they look forward to going on line with their computers, and hearing the powerful words 'You've got mail'. The film opens with each of them rather guiltily reaching for their laptops when their partners have left their apartments.

Before long the crisis comes for Kathleen: Fox Books opens a new superstore close by her shop on the West Side of Manhattan, and her business – with all that it stands for in human relationships – is threatened. Her shop was left to her by her mother when she died, and it has had a beloved place in the community for more than 40 years. With all that she cares for about to be destroyed, she confides in the one friend that she has come to trust, her internet correspondent. But when she meets Joe Fox in the flesh, not realizing that she has already met him on the internet, she takes an instant dislike to someone she regards as interested in books only as a commercial product 'like cans of olive-oil'. He finds her to be moralistic, hopelessly sentimental and unbusiness-like. As they talk at a party and in coffee shops, and as she takes the fight to survive to the media, they seem to bring out the worst in each other. With their words during the day they hurt and wound each other, while at night they resort to the internet to pour out their regret to each other for the way they are behaving. Ironically, he gives her the strength to believe in herself and to resist the threat, while she puts him in touch with a more sensitive side of himself that he tends to suppress.

This story of communication on two levels stands as a paradigm for the relation between such concepts as 'text', 'voice' and 'presence' which have been at the heart of recent discussion about the nature of language and human community. Thinkers such as Jacques Derrida point out that the whole world around us can be envisaged as a system of signs – or signifiers – which we 'read' in order to make sense of our place in the world and through which we relate to others. 'Text' does not have to be written down on paper, or appear on the screens of computers and mobile phones, but consists of all material forms which point beyond themselves to something or someone else.[1] We only have to think of the notion of 'body language' to see the truth of this: we communicate not just through words but through gestures, physical reactions and the way we dress. The old idea that nature itself was a kind of book that could be read has been revived in our time, but shorn of the kind of moralism that we find in a speech of the Duke in Shakespeare's play *As You Like It.* Exiled to live in the forest he reflects that he can learn more from nature than from the court whence he has been banished:

> … this our life, exempt from public haunt,
> Finds tongues in trees, books in the running brooks,
> Sermons in stones, and good in everything.[2]

Now, the revolution of thought which has happened in the period that is sometimes called 'postmodern', and which can be seen reflected in a great deal of popular culture, is that there is 'nothing outside the text'. We cannot escape from being involved in textuality. In older ideas about language and signs, it was assumed that there were subjects with consciousness – especially human beings, and very especially God – who existed behind or beyond the signs and who imposed their presence on others by merely *using* signs. The signs in the world, and words in particular, were simply tools that could be employed to control the world. The individual mind could likewise use words to dominate and impose its will on others. We now see, however, that the relation between the individual self and signs is more complicated than this. Language is there ahead of all individuals who live in the world, and helps to shape them and the way that they live in community. We are born into a world whose signs are already there before us. Moreover, the meaning of a sign comes from its connection to other signs – indeed, its *difference* from other signs.[3] A leaf, we might say, gives out its particular message to those who see it because it is *not* a flower-petal or a snow-flake. Each sign contains the trace of another, of what is *not* present. Difference and 'otherness' must be respected, whether in words or in people, and cannot be simply swamped in a desire to force our presence on others and to be the master of all we survey. What this observation might mean for the presence of God I want to leave for a moment, promising to return to it.

Written texts, such as books, letters and emails can help to open us up to a sense of difference and otherness. The words within a book take their meaning from the whole network of words in which they are placed. This meaning, moreover, is not completely fixed and completed. In the first place, since words refer to each other, or contain traces of each other, there is an endless process of interaction between them (theorists say: 'the signifier becomes the signified') and so new meaning is always being created, is always surplus or excessive to strict requirements.[4] In the second place written texts can always have new meanings in different contexts – in the various times and places in which they are read – and they draw the readers in to make their own contribution to what is going on between the covers. Written texts are a kind of open space in which to play. Perhaps this is the attraction of the email in our age; in the sphere of cyberspace the participants are often released from the restrictions and inhibitions that face-to-face encounter can bring, can take on new identities and try out new experiences. The danger is that this world of the text can become self-enclosed, a self-referencing web in which the users are trapped, unable to make connections between the text on the screen and the 'text' of their everyday lives. What is important to establish is not an exact correspondence between one system of signs and another, as if one can be a mirror-image of another, but the integration of the two (or however many there are) – what theorists tend to call 'inter-textuality'. Otherwise the written or electronic text becomes a mere fantasy of what we desire.

On the other hand, there is a temptation to think that in using our voices to communicate directly with others, in a bodily meeting, we are avoiding the ambiguous and complicated medium of signs. We think that we are achieving a direct presence of our being to others, that the voice somehow makes an immediate link between our consciousness and the one who is listening to us.[5] The parody here is of the English-speaking person in a foreign country who shouts louder to make the other understand what the speaker wants. In placing reliance upon the voice to impose – even inflict – our presence on others we miss all the signs that the other is giving out, and fail to give attention to the other as he or she (or it) is. The voice becomes a vehicle of domination and oppression. Used properly in true conversation, where talk flows to and fro between sympathetic participants, the voice can of course be an instrument of liberation – but often the opposite happens.

Voice, self and domination

With this brief review of contemporary theory about 'text', 'presence' and 'voice' we return to *You've Got Mail*, and we find a cinematic world in which written text is placed alongside the spoken word. Joe and Kathleen open their minds and hearts to each other through the email text, while they try to impose their wills on each other in the struggle of their voiced conversation. One kind of communication seems to open possibilities up, while the other closes relationship down, each partner not recognizing the other for what he or she really is. At the same time, of course, the film itself is a distinct text, a network of visual and auditory signs, which comes into encounter with the text of our own lives. If it is good art, there will be a healthy and life-giving inter-textuality. If it is poor art, it will remain a mere fantasy of desire.

The writers – Norah and Delia Ephron – have deliberately drawn attention to these various worlds of text, and the way that they interact. One way is by making the two main characters into bookshop owners, so that we are continually presented with the theme of the way that books – written texts – make an impact on our lives, and especially on the lives of children. As she recalls watching her mother deal with customers in the shop, Kathleen reflects that 'it wasn't that she was just selling books; she was helping people become whatever it was that they were going to turn out to be. Because when you read a book as a child it becomes part of your identity ... .'

By contrast, in the play ('Parfumerie') on which the film is based, written in 1937 by the Hungarian writer Miklos Laszlo (1903-1973), the characters corresponding to Joe and Kathleen are assistants in a shop selling perfumes and soaps. The earlier Hollywood film, *The Shop Around the Corner* – directed by Ernst Lubitsch in 1940 – which was the first screen adaptation of Laszlo's play, portrays the leading characters as fellow-assistants in a leather goods store. The 1949 film *In the Good Old Summertime*, a musical re-make of the 1940 film starring Judy Garland, has the two characters as assistants in a music store. The Ephrons intensify the theme of textuality by changing the venue to two bookshops, each with a different philosophy about the place of books in society. Further, in all the previous versions of the story (including a Broadway musical, *She Loves Me*), the two characters correspond with each other anonymously through letters and the post. Re-casting the letters as email not only updates the story, but makes more clear the contrast between the two forms of communication, since we see Joe and Kathleen responding to each other instantly through written text, typing their messages online in 'real time', giving scope for us to see their relationship in the very process of development. The juxtaposition of the two worlds of written text and everyday life is also made by the way the scenes have been shot: pictures of Joe and Kathleen typing at their computers are interleaved with shots of the two walking to work through the 'village' of west-side New York, nearly meeting each other, with the voice-overs of the messages continuing over the top.

The relation of voice, text and presence is highlighted by a theme that links several scenes. After a disastrous meeting, and conflict, between Joe and Kathleen at a party, Joe confesses in an email that he sometimes becomes 'the worst version of himself' when in the presence of someone who provokes him: 'instead of just smiling and moving on you *zing* them. Hello, it's Mr. Nasty ...' Kathleen replies that she has the opposite problem. What happens to her when she is provoked is that she becomes tongue-tied and her mind goes blank; then she spends all night tossing and turning, trying to figure out what she should say: 'What should I say, for instance, to the bottom-dweller who recently belittled my existence? Nothing. Nothing.' Joe, whose behaviour is actually being referred to, replies: 'Wouldn't it be wonderful if I could pass all my zingers to you, and then I would never behave badly, and you could behave badly all the time, and we'd both be happy.' But he continues, 'On the other hand I must warn you that when you finally have the pleasure of saying the thing you mean to say at the moment you mean to say it, remorse inevitably follows.' Both recognize that there is a gap between the true self and the words which are voiced, either because the words cannot be found, or because words that one seems to have found do not finally communicate what lies beneath the surface of the self.

Attempts to use words in order to control others, through a dominating voice, will always fail to touch what is really there in human relations.

The world of signs is far more complicated and requires more attention to the other. Kathleen discovers this in a scene in a coffee shop with Joe (to which I will return), when she finally hits on the words that she is seeking to hurt him: 'If I really knew you I know what I would find there: instead of a brain a cash register, instead of a heart a bottom line.' She exults that she had had a breakthrough: 'For the first time in my life, when confronted by a horrible, insensitive person, I know exactly what I wanted to say and I said it.' He comments with rueful admiration that 'I think you have a gift for it. That was a perfect blend of poetry and meanness.' Towards the end of the conversation she scores another hit with the words 'You are nothing but a suit', to which he can only say 'That's my cue' and bid her goodnight. Yet, as her internet friend has predicted, she afterwards deeply regrets what she has said. In a later scene she contradicts her earlier sentiment, saying 'I don't mean to say things like that.'

The spirit and the letter

Theological reflection on this film begins by placing alongside 'text' and 'voice' the New Testament pairing of 'letter' and 'spirit', but not as simple equivalents. The Apostle Paul observes in 2 Corinthians 3:6 that 'the letter kills, but the Spirit gives life', so offering at once both a way of interpreting written texts and a summary of the way of salvation through Christ. In both dimensions this Pauline saying has had a long-lasting effect on the thought of the Christian church. As a key to interpretation, it has urged the reader to look beyond the literal surface of a text – in this case the Mosaic law in the Old Testament – and to seek the inner, spiritual meaning, thereby encouraging a free range of allegorical and typological reading of the scriptures by such scholars as Origen and Augustine. With regard to salvation, it has promised freedom from the condemnation that comes from failing to keep the letter of the law, and has opened up the possibility of new life in accord with the spirit of the risen Jesus, which is to be identified in some way with the Holy Spirit of God. In this sense the text was often appealed to by such Reformers as Luther and Calvin.

In our day, however, suspicion has fallen upon what used to be seen as a liberating maxim. The postmodern mood prefers to say: 'the Spirit kills and the letter makes alive'. As Geoffrey Hartman has put it, 'The roles of letter and spirit are reversed: the letter of the text lives on and undoes idealizations that seek to get rid of the letter.'[6] By 'the letter that makes alive' such critics are referring to what we have already seen to be the expansive space of the written text, in which meanings proliferate, and by which new possibilities are continually opened up for the reader. By 'the spirit that kills' is meant a superior principle which supposedly stands outside the texts and signs of the world (a 'transcendental signified'),[7] an ideology that offers a total explanation of life and to which people appeal when they want to oppress the weak. For many people, God would fall into this category, or would be seen as a support for various systems of thought, or human hierarchies of power, which are used to dominate others. The 'Spirit' that is outside the text is envisaged as timeless, a presence that makes itself felt because it is supposedly not touched by time, change and human suffering.

Properly employed, however, the insight of the Apostle Paul is indeed a liberating one. Whether in written texts, or in the voiced word, we are to look for the breathing of the Spirit of God that confronts all legalism and oppressive ideologies and opens up an awareness of the other. 'The letter kills', when a legalistic principle which merely protects the self is applied within any network of signs, whether a religious text or the life of a community which uses age-old images and symbols. God, we may say, is not an ideology which constricts life, because God has committed God's own self to the text of the world. God is not only outside our sign systems, but *inside* them at the same time, so it is true to say that 'there is nothing (simply) outside the text.' There is a long Christian tradition that nature is a kind of book, a second book alongside scripture, because God has created it through the divine word: 'In the beginning was the Word, and the word was with God, and the word was God ... All things came into being through him' (John 1:1-3). Theologians in our age have reflected further on what it means for God to be committed to the world of signs, to the myriad things and persons that point beyond themselves to God as Creator; many have concluded that this engagement is so intimate that God has willingly taken time, change and suffering into the divine life.

In *You've Got Mail* we can see the force of an ideology that fails to register the difference of others from ourselves. Joe has fallen into the habit of quoting lines from the film *The Godfather* as a kind of guide to life (another piece of inter-texuality), a practice that the writers of the film say they picked up from observing male friends in conversation. One favourite phrase is: 'It's not personal, it's business', which he uses to justify his tactics in crushing yet another small bookshop. This has become 'the letter that kills', whether it is contained in an email to Kathleen or in the spoken word. Near to the end, in a scene where Joe visits Kathleen in her flat when she is ill with 'flu, taking her flowers with the expressed hope that 'I might be your friend' despite putting her out of business, she rounds on his use of the phrase 'It wasn't personal':

> What is that supposed to mean? I'm so sick of that. All that means is that it wasn't personal to you. It was personal to me. It was personal to a lot of people. And what's so wrong with being personal anyway?

To this he can only reply, quietly, 'Nothing'. In the interaction between them one can see through the expression on his face that she is making him re-think his personal law, to seek for the spirit in the letter.

Disguise, deception and exploring relationships

By this stage in the film, however, something has changed in the way that Joe is viewing his encounters with Kathleen outside cyberspace. He has come to know her true identity, while for the moment she remains ignorant of his. Somewhat earlier they had arranged to meet in a coffee shop, she carrying a book and a flower to mark her out. Nervous of meeting the one whom he believes he is falling in love with, he sends a friend to look through the window. His friend remarks – to his great joy – on how beautiful the girl is who is waiting for him, adding, however, that 'if you don't like Kathleen Kelly, you 'aint going to like this girl'. He looks for himself, and discovers who 'Shopgirl' is.

From this point the plot takes the typical form of the Shakespearean romantic comedy, such as *Twelfth Night, As You Like It* and *The Merchant of Venice*. That is, one of the pair of destined lovers is disguised when in the company of the other, and has an advantage of knowledge over the other in all conversations. Viola is disguised as a page-boy in talking about love with the Duke Orsino; Rosalind is disguised as a young man playing at being 'Rosalind', and so leads Orlando a fine dance in the forest; and Portia, who has disguised herself as a young male lawyer, can talk with her new husband Bassanio (during and after wearing the disguise) about the commitments of marriage. It is a convention of Shakespearean comedy that the heroine, putting on male clothing, at once becomes unrecognizable to her lover. The disguise that Joe wears is one suitable for the environment of cyberspace: it is the disguise of the assumed internet identity. From the moment of discovery in the coffee shop he is in disguise both in the email exchange and in physical encounter in a way that she is not.

At first this discovery and disguise leads only to more hurt for both of them. Joe sits down at the table in the coffee shop with Kathleen, very much against her will, and pretends to wait with her for the mysterious stranger who never – of course – turns up. They are both angry with each other, though only Joe's hostility is sharpened by the extreme confusion he feels. It is now that she scores the triumph, so much regretted in retrospect, of telling him exactly how worthless not only his business but his whole life is. For the first time he is genuinely wounded, and she for her part is both disappointed and puzzled at being 'stood up' by the person upon whom she has come to rely. After a silence, the next internet message from him, headed 'Where I was' and carefully constructed, is full of irony, and yet also a growing sense of love:

> I cannot tell you what happened last night, but I beg you from the bottom of my heart to forgive me for ... . *not being there* [deleted] ... . *what happened.* I feel terrible that you found yourself in a situation that caused you additional pain. But I'm absolutely sure that whatever you said last night was provoked, even deserved ... . You were expecting to see someone you trusted and met the enemy instead. The fault is mine. Some day I'll explain everything. Meanwhile, I'm still here. Talk to me.

The point of such disguise and deception in Shakespearean comedy is not only to cause entertaining confusions. It is to allow the one who wears the disguise to explore feelings of love in a way that would not otherwise be possible. The disguise gives rise to ambiguities, half-truths and ironies with which to probe the nature of the developing relationship. So hiding the truth brings the truth to light, as comedy turns the world upside down in order to settle it the right way up. There is already something broken in life before the comedy opens; what is real lies deep beneath the world of appearances, and bringing further disorder into the situation can help to find it. There is no escape from the often confusing world of multiple signs to be read, and 'thickening' the textuality by making the signs even more complicated can be a way of discovering what is true about relationships. From another angle, the comedy reminds us that we all play roles in our relationships with others. We present a set of signs to others that corresponds, yet does not full equate, with whom we truly are. The role-playing that goes on in a comedy gives an opportunity to test out the genuiness of various identities. Those watching a play or a film may identify with the characters and so share in the playing of the roles.

Thus, love and understanding can actually develop through the tangles of the situation in a comedy, which has been produced by a trick or a set of mistakes. In Shakespeare's *Twelfth Night*, for instance, Viola, wearing her disguise as a page-boy, can speak of her love to the Duke with a depth and subtlety that communicates with him at an intuitive level, and prepares him for the moment when she is revealed as his 'fancy's queen':

VIOLA: … .My Father had a daughter lov'd a man
         As it might be, perhaps were I a woman,
         I should your lordship.
ORSINO: … .But died thy sister of her love, my boy?
VIOLA: I am all the daughters of my father's house,
         And all the brothers too: and yet I know not.[8]

Towards the end of the film, as Kathleen and Joe are enjoying each other's company, there is a similar playing with the theme of 'if only …' If only they had not been 'Fox Books' and 'The Shop Around the Corner', and had just met as they were, then, Joe declares,

'I would have asked for your number, and I wouldn't have been able to wait twenty four hours before calling you up and saying, "How about coffee, say, or drinks, or dinner, or a movie … . for as long as we both shall live" '

In this kind of indirect declaration of love, there is room for an interplay of emotions between the characters so that we believe in the union between them when it finally comes. There is encouragement to find the spirit within the letter. Before the final disclosure to Kathleen, Joe makes his final plea to Kathleen in such a mode of ambiguity: 'Let me ask you something. How can you forgive this guy for standing you up, and not forgive me for this tiny little thing of putting you out of business? Oh how I wish you would.'

Such conversation is not the assertion of a person's presence through an oppressive voice, but is talk that is fully aware of the other. A Christian theologian will understand this kind of speech as an entering into a liberating conversation that is already going on within God's own self. The voices that weave together in the to-and-fro of human speech need not be imposing themselves on each other; they can be responding in a sensitive way, aware of the difference of the other and his or her particular contribution to the whole. When this happens they are sharing in the life and the love of God, which can only be described as like a relationship between a father and a son (or a mother and a daughter), opened up to new depths of relationship and to new experiences in the future by a Spirit of hope. The 'persons' in God, three movements of self-giving love, are utterly different from each other, emptying themselves out for the sake of each other, yet at the same time one in creative purpose. We catch the echoes of their 'conversation', movements of love which are like a father speaking to a son and the son responding with a glad 'yes' (Amen); so too 'through Christ we say Amen to the Father' (2 Cor. 1:20). Such a vision of participation in the triune God is not, of course, actually portrayed in the film we are considering. There is nothing overtly 'religious' about this film. But it exposes patterns of text, voice and presence in human life where a Christian thinker can see the presence of God.

The end and the final End

We may regret the fact that the character who is given privileged knowledge of the situation, and so wears the disguise is not – as in Shakespeare – the woman, but the man. We might have preferred Kathleen to have had the strength and initiative of Shakespeare's heroines. But perhaps it is apt that Joe takes the role of the loving deceiver since it puts him into the position of receiving several rebukes from Kathleen which he takes to heart and which prepare him – and us – for the moment when they will meet truly face to face, with all the veils removed. Kathleen has by now embarked on a new career of writing children's books, and both she and Joe have split up with their respective partners. The scene is set for the denouement.

At the end of the film Kathleen sets off for the small neighbourhood park where her mysterious friend, NY 152, has proposed they should meet. She will recognize him because he will be taking his dog, Brinkley, for a walk, whose antics have featured in many of the emails. Before he comes into sight she hears him calling out the name of the dog, and so at this moment the written text becomes a spoken voice. When they meet, to share the kiss that ends the film, she whispers: 'I wanted it to be you. I wanted it to be you so badly'. Text has become voice, but a voice that is no longer oppressive, in the context of the relationship that we have seen develop and the desire we have felt growing.

All endings in human art offer us an echo and an image of the final End. For some it will simply anticipate the ending of life in death, but for Christian believers it will be the promise of God's new creation, of the consummation of all things when all relationships will be re-made in the image of God. As the Apostle Paul puts it in his great poem on love, 'Now we see as in a mirror, dimly, but then we will see face to face. Now I know only in part; then I will know fully, even as I have been fully known' (1 Cor. 13:12). We might update his first sentence like this: 'Now we see as in a computer screen, dimly, but then face to face'. Text has to become voice. The signs of the world, whether in written texts or in the textuality of everyday life, need to be filled with the sound of human conversation, and finally with the Word of God that brought about creation in the first place and that still sustains it. Then all the confusions of our relationships will be clarified and deepened in a new community living in a new city. From time to time we catch a glimpse of this final disclosure, at moments of intense human encounter such as this film portrays at its ending. For Christians, text also becomes voice each time the Eucharist is celebrated, and the written words of Christ in the Gospels 'This is my body, this is my blood' are spoken by the one who presides at the table, creating a meeting-place where disciples encounter their Lord 'face to face'⁹ and can see each other more clearly as well.

But some doubts remain. Is this a 'fantasy' ending to the film, in which Joe gets his reward far too easily? Does it merely offer an escape from life, a happy-ever-after world which fails to connect with the world in which we are living? We never feel this about Shakespeare's comedies, as some dark strain remains in the final harmony, some note of discord or incompleteness: one of the characters remains unreconciled, or we are made aware of the passing of time and the threat of death pressing in, or there is something about the relation between the lovers that makes us suspect that troubled times lie ahead in the midst of the happiness.

In the 'if only' conversation between Joe and Kathleen, before the final disclosure, as they imagine a future together that might have been, Joe says: 'the only thing we would fight about would be which video to rent on a Saturday night'. Kathleen retorts 'Well, who fights about that?' and Joe answers, 'Some people, but not us'. This dialogue, charming and light-weight as it is, inevitably makes us ask whether there might be more serious matters for these two highly-opinionated people to differ about. After all, the film does not endorse the ideology of corporate business, to which Joe seems to remain committed, and to which Kathleen remains opposed. Significantly, as Kathleen glances across the Park and discovers who her internet friend really is, a whole gamut of emotions passes across her face. As portrayed by Meg Ryan with great skill and imagination, looks of bafflement and vexation alternate with those of surprise and joy. We do not doubt the love between them, and we believe Kathleen when she says 'I wanted it to be you', but we also wonder whether there will be storms on the horizon of this Spring day in New York.

The incompleteness of endings in life, spoilt as they are by human failings, is a blurred image of the final End which will be perfect and yet still incomplete, characterized by change 'from one degree of glory to another' (2 Cor. 3:18). This is an End which brings both closure and openness.¹⁰ The Christian hope for the end of all things is a new beginning in which there will be room for the development of persons, in which there will be journeys to make, adventures to be had and purposes to be fulfilled. In short, the divine voice which says 'Come, for all is now ready' will not remove the need for signs on the way. God's commitment to text will never end. The symbol of the resurrection of the body makes clear that the world to come, in which we shall see face to face and know as we are known, will be a world of signs to be read and stories to be lived.

Notes

[1] Jacques Derrida, 'Afterword', trans. Samuel Weber, in Derrida, *Limited Inc.* (Evanston: Northwestern University Press, 1988), p. 148.

[2] Shakespeare, *As You Like It*, Act II, Scene 1, 15-18.

[3] See Jacques Derrida, 'Différance', in *Derrida, Speech and Phenomena and Other Essays on Husserl's Theory of Signs*, trans. David Allison (Evanston: Northwestern University Press, 1973).

[4] Jacques Derrida, 'Semiology and Grammatology' in Derrida, *Positions*, trans. Alan Bass (Chicago: The University of Chicago Press, 1981), p. 26; Derrida, *Of Grammatology*, trans. Gayatri Soivak (Baltimore: The Johns Hopkins University Press, 1976), p. 62.

[5] See Derrida, *Grammatology*, pp. 12, 20.

[6] Geoffrey H. Hartman, *Easy Pieces* (New York: Columbia University Press, 1985), p. 194.

[7] Derrida, 'Semiology and Grammatology', pp. 30-1.

[8] Shakespeare, *Twelfth Night*, Act II, Scene 4,107-122.

[9] Cf. the eucharistic hymn by the Baptist hymn writer, Horatius Bonar, 'Here, O my Lord, I see thee face to face;/ Here would I touch and handle things unseen.'

[10] For this idea, see Paul S. Fiddes, *The Promised End. Eschatology in Theology and Literature* (Oxford: Blackwell, 2000), pp. 26-8, 154-7.

8
Bucking the System:
One Flew Over the Cuckoo's Nest

Nicholas Wood

Vinery, mintery, cutery, corn,
Apple seed and apple thorn;
Wire, briar, limber lock,
Three geese in a flock:
One flew east,
One flew west,
And one flew over the cuckoo's nest.

A line from a lesser-known American nursery rhyme provided the title for Ken Kesey's best-selling novel,[1] subsequently produced as a stage play with Kirk Douglas in the lead role, before the Czech director Milos Forman brought its themes of rebellion and redemption to a wider audience through his award-winning film in 1975. In the film the sympathetic anti-hero R. P. McMurphy is portrayed by Jack Nicholson.

The cuckoo's disturbing presence
Randle P. McMurphy is a free-spirited convict who feigns insanity in order to escape the penitentiary. He finds himself instead in the state mental hospital and its regimented routine, under the iron grip of Nurse Mildred Ratched – an Oscar-winning performance by Louise Fletcher in her first film role. Forman and his production team assemble a fine ensemble cast including Danny de Vito in an early role, and with Christopher Lloyd among several others making their film debuts. Forman, an established director who was already noted for his adaptation of the French *cinéma vérité* approach, said of the film that it must 'first be very real, then entertaining and then a comedy'.[2]

The movie was actually filmed in the Oregon State Hospital/Asylum in Salem, and the film's realistic portrayal of early sixties mental health 'care' owes much to the atmosphere created by this authentic setting. The real medical superintendent, Dr Dean R. Brooks, actually portrays the consultant at the film hospital, Dr. Spivey. Many other members of the hospital community, patients, support staff and medics, worked both in front and behind the cameras; indeed Brooks, who was known for his innovative approach to mental health care, succeeded in having 89 members of the hospital on the film payroll!

Events are set in 1963, with a telling allusion to the Berlin Wall. McMurphy finds the inflexible regime of the hospital utterly dispiriting, but is determined to resist and is constantly finding ways to subvert it and undermine the authority of Nurse Ratched. Much of the film centres on the battle of wills between McMurphy and Ratched, in which gradually the patient is able to win over the other inmates. When the Baseball World Series is on TV, McMurphy attempts to have the routine changed in order that the ward can watch the ball game. When this is refused he tries to lift a huge marble washstand in the bathroom in order to break the window and escape to a bar downtown where they can see the match, but the stand is too heavy and he fails. Nevertheless, refusing to admit defeat, he rounds on the onlookers: 'But I tried, didn't I? God-damn it; at least I did that!'

Into a closed, regulated and sedated community the disruptive McMurphy brings an anarchic sense of freedom and the possibility of joy and hope. He begins a card school, gambling for cigarettes. In recreation periods he creates a basketball team, including the huge but apparently deaf and dumb Native American 'Chief' Bromden (played by Creek Indian Will Sampson, also in his film debut). On one occasion McMurphy hijacks the hospital bus and takes the patients from his ward down the river to the coast for a fishing trip on a boat. In a neat reversal of roles, he persuades the harbour master that the men are all doctors from the institution. But in fact this risky escapade does bring a new sense of identity to the patients whom McMurphy calls, not unaffectionately, the 'nuts'. He tells Martini (de Vito), 'You're not an idiot. Huh! You're not a goddam loony now, boy. You're a fisherman!'

The authorities recognize McMurphy's potential for disruption, but it is Nurse Ratched who surprisingly requests that he is left on the ward since, as she puts it in rather sinister fashion, 'I think we might be able to help him'. In fact she is determined to break him and win the battle for control. It gradually dawns on McMurphy that he has exchanged a time-limited stretch in the penitentiary for an apparently unlimited period in the hospital. Ironically a number of patients turn out to be there on a voluntary basis and choose not to leave, whilst McMurphy, who has engineered his own presence on the ward, is now a captive. He protests to the young innocent Billy (Brad Dourif): 'What are ya doin' here for Christ's sake? What's funny about that? Jesus, I mean, you guys do nothin' but complain about how you can't stand it in this place here and then you haven't got the guts just to walk out!' He observes, acutely, 'You're no crazier than the average asshole out walking on the streets!' These are, as Nurse Ratched somewhat understatedly comments, 'very challenging observations', and it is clear that his challenge will not go unmet.

Gradually McMurphy's powerful critique of the system begins to win over the others who start to express their own views. The underlying tensions and evident frustrations inevitably boil over into a fight during one of the regular group therapy sessions, in which the 'Chief' comes to McMurphy's assistance and they find themselves together under restraint, awaiting electric shock treatment. In sharing a packet of 'Juicy Fruit' gum the chief responds with a quiet 'Thank you', and it is revealed to McMurphy's delight (and the audience's surprised amusement) that he can hear and talk all along! For his own purposes it has suited him to deceive the authorities. 'You fooled 'em chief!', McMurphy declares, 'You fooled 'em. You fooled 'em all.' At last McMurphy has identified a kindred spirit who can buck the system and with whom he can plan an escape to freedom in Canada.

One night at Christmastime, in an attempt to create some festivity, and even perhaps some 'normality', McMurphy smuggles alcohol and women into the ward and they have a party. He steals the keys from the now unconscious night orderly and prepares to take his leave from the others. Inevitably the episode ends in chaos as the ward is effectively destroyed. McMurphy ultimately refuses the opportunity to leave, and stays in order to help the naïve Billy fulfil his ambition to lose his virginity with Candy, one of the women friends McMurphy has sneaked into the asylum. Eventually they all fall into a drunken stupor.

Next morning Nurse Ratched returns and wreaks her revenge. Dusting off her now soiled white nurse's cap, the symbol of her power and authority, she reasserts her control and drives the apron-stringed Billy, only briefly in possession of his manhood, to suicide by threatening to reveal his sordid doings to his mother. McMurphy goes berserk and grabs the nurse by the throat, attempting to strangle her in retaliation. McMurphy is restrained and taken upstairs whence, despite rumours of his escape, he eventually returns 'meek as a lamb'. He has undergone a frontal lobotomy, an extreme brain surgical procedure widely used at the time for difficult cases of disruptive patients.

Chief Bromden realizes what has been done and knows that their plan for escape to Canada cannot now be achieved. In a moving climax the chief hugs his friend and then smothers him with a pillow, knowing that for McMurphy such a continued 'existence' would have been a travesty. Then, achieving what his friend had earlier failed to do, exerting a super-human effort Bromden wrenches the marble washstand from its place and smashes it through the window. Empowered by McMurphy's inspiration the Chief flees and makes his way to freedom, into a landscape at once open and threatening. Unlike the novel, where by this stage many inmates have already chosen to leave, the other patients apparently remain incarcerated, and it is unclear whether or not they will take the opportunity for freedom and the new life which McMurphy's inspiring example has made possible. It may be that it is only one who flies the 'cuckoo's nest'.

To comfort the disturbed – or to disturb the comfortable?

As its many awards suggest,[3] the film made an enormous impact at the time of its release. I can still recall the sense of shock in the cinema audience as it becomes apparent just what has been done to McMurphy in order to control the chaos his free spirit has brought to the institution. Equally, as Chief Bromden wrests the washstand from its place and hurls it through the window, the whole audience roared in approval with a heartfelt 'Yes!' The music rises to a crescendo as the chief staggers across the ward with his great burden, but then fades to nothingness as the credits roll. Such was its impact that the audience also left the cinema in almost total silence. Clearly the movie, like the novel, resonated with issues of the time: the Cold War, Vietnam, Watergate and the Nixon presidency. But it also touched deep themes which appeal across both time and culture, for example, the relative positions of insider and outsider, and the importance of questions of power and control. It also raises significant theological themes: freedom, sacrifice, incarnation, appearance and reality, identity and community.

Fittingly it was a film producer, Richard Rowland, who coined the phrase 'the lunatics have taken over the asylum', as a response to the formation of a new Hollywood production company, United Artists, by Charlie Chaplin, Mary Pickford, Douglas Fairbanks and D. W. Griffith in 1919. *One Flew Over the Cuckoo's Nest* was a United Artists' production, and begs the whole question as to who is sane and who is mad, whose grasp of reality is more secure, who is in charge of the system, who is running the asylum. Whilst explicit in the scene in which McMurphy passes off patients as doctors to the harbour master, the idea runs implicitly throughout the film.

In terms of the typology outlined by Robert Ellis in the earlier chapter 'Movies and Meaning', *One Flew Over the Cuckoo's Nest* is generally seen as a 'Christ-film', and from the summary I have given it is evident as to why this is an appropriate category for the movie. To all appearances the inmates of the institution are locked away from reality and are held securely not only by its locked doors and barred windows, but by a regime which dehumanizes by its rigidity and control. But since many of the patients are there on a voluntary basis it emerges that on another level they are also held by their own inability or unwillingness to engage with the wide-open spaces of the world beyond the asylum. They are not willing or able to challenge the institution, to buck the system. McMurphy's irruption onto the scene not only breaks them out of the physical limitations of their environment but also begins to enable the inmates of the institution to question their mental as well as their physical imprisonment.

In theological terms we might say that McMurphy's incarceration in the asylum might be viewed as a type of incarnation as he brings new life and energy to what for many inmates has become a form of living death. Like a cuckoo's egg hatching in the wrong nest, he represents a different reality; indeed he embodies it through his very words, his attitudes and his provocative actions. The prologue to the Fourth Gospel expresses these truths in relation to the life of Jesus and points out the paradox that he was not received in the place he should have been most welcome. 'He was in the world … yet the world did not know him' (John 1:10).

This might be compared with the Synoptic Gospels' portrayal of the ministry of Jesus as the in-breaking of the Kingdom of God, full of vitality and joy, into a world held captive by evil and death, sickness and sin. Just as in the Gospel accounts signs of healing and new life and a sense of joy always accompany the ministry of Jesus, so too the presence of the irrepressible McMurphy in *One Flew Over the Cuckoo's Nest* is associated with healing, fun and laughter. Just as Jesus resists the narrow rules of the religious leaders of his time and challenges his hearers to live a life of freedom in the Kingdom of God, so McMurphy resists the inflexible rules of the institution and challenges the inmates to take their freedom and live life to the full. In the hospital therapy pool he shares with them a form of 'baptism', and in the boating trip there are obvious resonances with the many Gospel stories related to fishing and fishermen. As Jesus calls the fishermen Peter and Andrew and tells them they will now have a new role, 'Follow me and I will make you fish for people',[4] so McMurphy gives a new identity to the asylum patients in the course of a fishing trip. Now they are fishermen become 'doctors': the patients have become healers.

Inevitably, also like Jesus, McMurphy pays the price of freedom: he suffers his own form of crucifixion;[5] he is tortured and apparently destroyed by the system. Just as Christian tradition has interpreted the death of Christ through the typology of the 'Suffering Servant' described in the prophecy of Isaiah, 'Like a lamb that is led to the slaughter, and like a sheep that before its shearers is silent, so he opened not his mouth',[6] McMurphy is returned to the ward 'meek as a lamb'. Although it is the Chief who finally brings his existence to a close, it is the hospital regime that has already taken his life force. For both Jesus of Nazareth and Randle P. McMurphy theirs is a costly rebellion. The system always wins – or does it?

The parallel is not quite exhausted, for both Christian gospel and *One Flew Over the Cuckoo's Nest* offer the possibility of 'resurrection', of hope beyond the reality of death. The spirit of freedom lives on in the lives of those whom these two 'Christ' figures have touched. The disciples of Jesus suddenly discover that the strangely different yet still recognizable figure of the risen Christ has not after all been destroyed by death: they discover his presence on the road, at the meal-table, in all the old familiar places. The spirit of Jesus lives on in the community he has brought into being and when they meet they know his risen presence. As the history of the church amply demonstrates, the new freedom which Jesus brought can quickly revert to old habits of heart and mind, but the hope and the possibility of something different is real, even if tenuous and fragile.

Similarly, as Chief Bromden hurls the marble washstand through the window and lopes towards the wide-open spaces of the beckoning horizon, the audience cheers not simply for him but also because we recognize that in him the spirit of McMurphy is not after all defeated. Forman and the screenplay writers underline this through an interesting line of dialogue found in the film but not in the novel. As Bromden smothers his friend to put an end to his suffering, he says, 'Let's go'. The connotation could not be clearer; the *two* of them will after all make real their planned escape to Canada. Despite our worst fears, the system has not finally won and the hope of joy and freedom remains a real, if precarious, possibility. McMurphy lives on through his friend and the film leaves open the possibility that others of those whom McMurphy has touched will follow Bromden into this new reality. The ambiguous ending of the film captures something of the Gospel accounts of resurrection, full of possibility, yet open to a future that has yet to be clearly determined.

This also means that McMurphy's death, like that of Jesus in Christian tradition, is one of self-sacrifice and vicarious suffering. He was (in a sense) voluntarily in the asylum in the first place, and when he had a chance to leave, he again chooses to remain to be with his friends and especially to help Billy, perhaps the most vulnerable member of the community. The Lukan tradition especially emphasizes Jesus' concern for the marginalized, but as we have already noted, Jesus' association with the poor, the outcast and the sinner is a common thread through the Gospel material. Although in the film Billy dies as well as McMurphy, and it is unclear if others as well as the Chief take the opportunity for freedom and new life, nevertheless McMurphy's life and death have been a source of inspiration to the others, the system is broken, and the Chief, at least, embraces the wide-open future which McMurphy's sacrifice has made possible.

Disturbing – or just disturbed?

There remains for some Christians, however, a serious problem over this use of typology in representing Randle P. McMurphy as a 'Christ-figure'. In Britain the film is an 18-certificate movie. There are scenes of violence, sexual references, and considerable strong language. McMurphy is a womanizer, a drunkard, and a blasphemer. Can we seriously suggest that such a man can stand as a figure for Christ? Is this not simply a portrayal of a profoundly dysfunctional human being, less a radical disturber of the peace than a troubled man, one who is just plain disturbed? Actually, I want to suggest that if anything this makes the parallel even stronger, for this is remarkably similar to the way Jesus was represented by his opponents, according to the Gospel tradition. He was a disturbing presence who was thought at least on one occasion even by his family to be mad, or by others as so disturbed as to be demon-possessed. 'When [Jesus'] family heard about it, they set out to take charge of him, because people were saying, "He's gone mad". Some teachers of the law who had come from Jerusalem were saying, "He has Beelzebul in him!" ' (Mark 3:21-22).

Jesus too had a reputation as a womanizer and a drunkard, the friend of prostitutes and sinners, perhaps viewed as a man who, in the modern idiom, 'worked hard and played hard' – and his critics were none too sure about the 'work' element! So, on one occasion when he was dining with Levi the tax collector, Pharisaic scribes complained to the disciples, 'Why does he eat with tax-collectors and sinners?' (Mark 2:16).

This aspect of the Jesus tradition, though a misrepresentation by his enemies, is perhaps a helpful corrective to the sentimental portraits of Jesus so beloved of our Victorian forebears who bequeathed to subsequent generations the notion of 'Gentle Jesus, meek and mild'. Of course, we need to beware the tendency of every generation simply to remake Christ in our own image. The point I want to make is that if Randle P. McMurphy seems to us an unlikely and even scandalous ideal as some sort of saviour figure, that was precisely how Jesus appeared to many of his contemporaries. And Jesus himself is reportedly aware of his reputation where, in comparison with the austere and ascetic figure of John the Baptist, he knows that he appears to be a considerable contrast: 'The Son of Man came eating and drinking, and you say, "Look at him! He eats too much and drinks too much wine, and he is a friend of tax collectors and sinners." ' (Luke 7:43).

I am not suggesting that Jesus and McMurphy actually behave in identical ways, but that there are strong parallels in the way that each in his own context is *perceived*. Because of our Victorian inheritance public sensibilities are easily shocked when stereotypical and innocuous images of Christ are challenged, as the playwright Dennis Potter discovered when his play *Son of Man* was presented on BBC TV in 1969. But it is important to recognize that it is the strong characters, the charismatic personalities, and those people who are challenging, who are the ones who get noticed and who often fall foul of those with a vested interest in maintaining the status quo.

As has often been remarked, if alienated and marginal people in any society are to be included rather than excluded, if those whom we label 'disturbed' are to be comforted, then this is likely to be a profoundly uncomfortable experience for those already at ease in the world as it is: the comfortable will be disturbed, the complacent will be challenged in the process of overturning the present order. But we all know that without such radical challenge the combined power of inertia on the one hand, and of vested interest on the other, will ensure that there will be little likelihood of comfort for those who do not really 'belong'.

The dialogue between the film and the Gospel story reminds us that when communities are confronted by the strange intrusion of the 'cuckoo', the first response is to try and make the intruder conform. If that fails then the next reaction is likely to be rejection; indeed it is not uncommon to characterize those who are different, who do not share the commonly held view, as 'mad'. If such figures persist in challenging the norms of society, that rejection may well take violent form. For both Jesus and McMurphy conformity was enforced. Yet such 'Christ-figures' may well be saying something both profound and true to such societies, about the nature of community and about important issues of identity and inclusion. They certainly remind us of the cost of nonconformity in many cultures throughout history and to the present day.

But they also offer the possibility of change, even if won at the cost of personal sacrifice. Both Jesus and McMurphy, in being willing to stand out from the crowd and to stand up to the 'powers that be', pay the price

for bucking the system. Yet through the strength of their respective characters they demonstrate the possibilities of engaging new areas of human
experience; indeed they not only see but help to develop the hidden potential in others. Such people make real the possibility of living not simply
outside but rather beyond the 'system', overcoming all that hinders and
frustrates human flourishing, in order to live a life of genuine freedom, of
fulfilment, joy and hope. They remind us that challenging and noncon-
formist figures should not always be dismissed as 'mad' or 'disturbed',
but can serve to disturb the complacency and comfort of the majority.

Perhaps a film such as *One Flew Over the Cuckoo's Nest* can help us
look with fresh eyes at the Gospel story and allow the person of Jesus to
break free from the domesticating constraints of 2,000 years of Christian
tradition in order to be once again not just the comforter of the outcast,
nor even the challenger of the complacent, but rather the radical and disturbing presence which clearly he was.

Notes

[1] Ken Kesey, *'One Flew Over the Cuckoo's Nest'*, (Methuen, 1962,
republished London: Picador/Pan Macmillan, 1973).

[2] In the background information given in the DVD edition of the film,
Warner Home Video (UK) 1998.

[3] Nominated for nine academy awards, the film won five Oscars: Best
Picture, Best Director, Best Adapted Screenplay, Best Actor (Jack Nicholson),
and Best Actress (Louise Fletcher) in addition to six Golden Globes and six
Baftas (with the addition of Best Debut/Supporting Actor, Brad Dourif).

[4] Mark 1:17.

[5] In the novel the parallel is even clearer with a cruciform 'gurney', the
table to which an inmate is strapped for 'treatment'. McMurphy even asks the
question as to whether he too is to be given a crown of thorns.

[6] Isaiah 53:7.

9
Taking the Waves by 'Surprise':
Master and Commander

Sally Bedborough

The film *Master and Commander* is set in the year 1805. The month is April and as the action begins we are told that: *Napoleon is master of Europe. Only the British fleet stands before him. Oceans are now battle-fields.*

The scene is set: forget the national titles and focus on the distilled drama of a battle on the high seas. The ship that commands our attention is called the *Surprise*, its master is Captain Jack Aubrey who sails to 'the far side of the world' in pursuit of the enemy ship, the *Acheron*. Bearing in mind that in Greek mythology the *Acheron* is one of the five Underworld rivers and is also known as the River of Woe, a classic tale of good versus evil becomes visible: the hero goes into the far country to destroy the enemy. This film invites us to compare the *Acheron* to an enemy that is not physical or tangible, but an illusive, often invisible, force of evil in our world.

A Leader above all Leaders

Captain Jack Aubrey, 'Lucky Jack' to his men, is an inspiring leader. The crew would follow him anywhere; they trust him completely. In one of the opening scenes, there is discussion at the captain's table of a mythical leader, one Nelson: 'not a great seaman' we are told, 'but a great leader', and, 'with Nelson you felt your heart glow.' In the opening battle with the *Acheron*, the captain has ordered his troops to go 'straight at 'em'. In the discussion at the captain's table, a seed of comparison is planted between these two leaders as the first mate shares his memories of this great leader with his fellow officers. He recalls, 'He used to say, "never mind manoeu-vres, just go straight at 'em" '. But as time goes on, Aubrey is elevated even beyond this mythical leader. After a truly marvellous display of nav-igation, Jack dodges the *Acheron* and brings the *Surprise* up on the privateer's tail. One of the officers declares 'That's real seamanship!'

leading us to conclude that in Jack Aubrey we have not only a great leader, but also a great seaman.

It is evident that Jack Aubrey has come to be an admired and trusted captain. How has this come about? Besides his proven skill as a navigator, he identifies with the fabric of his ship. After the first encounter with the enemy in battle, the *Acheron* has proved herself to be a superior warship, with mysterious properties that make her impervious to the firepower of the *Surprise*. Stephen, the ship's doctor and the captain's friend, asks innocently: 'But the *Surprise* is an aged man o' war … . am I not correct?' The captain immediately springs to the defence of his ship and compares the ship with himself. 'Would you call me old?' he asks Stephen. Then he proceeds to point out the ship's characteristics of strength, beauty and speed. Later, our attention is drawn to a piece of wood on the ship's deck that bears the initials J.A. and the date: 1785. One officer points this out to a young midshipman and says: 'He's known this ship - man and boy. There's enough of his blood in the woodwork of this ship to almost be a relation.'

Ingredients of Greatness

Despite the fact that Aubrey is the authoritarian and macho leader required by a Hollywood blockbuster, the real nature of leadership is explored with some degree of insight and humanity. Captain Aubrey's leadership style is dogmatic, there is no doubt, but given the maleness of the situation, historically and culturally, we can attempt to peel off this veneer and to dig deeper. Jack Aubrey is not a two-dimensional fighter; besides the strong sense of identification with his ship, we see revealed some other significant and nurturing qualities.

First, there is tenderness. We stumble on this quality of the captain when Blakeley, just a slip of a lad, takes a hit in the first battle and has to have his arm amputated. The captain visits him in sick bay, and although Lucky Jack is reticent, he embodies a wordless tenderness and compassion. Here is a leader who draws close, who shows empathy and who breathes inspiration and hope into his people. In the case of young Blakeley, the captain gives him one of his own possessions: a book about Nelson. We recall that Nelson has the same injury. What else could inspire and open up future possibilities in such a way?

Second, the captain has vulnerability. This emerges in the aftermath of choosing the lesser of two evils, when a valued seaman, Warley, is sacrificed for the safety and survival of the ship and its whole crew. This is a Christ-like sacrifice because the young seaman concerned has provided the key to understanding the impervious nature of the *Acheron*'s bows. Present at the Boston docks when the French privateer was built, he is able to describe the boat's construction to a colleague, who in turn builds a model of it. So, here is a man who understands the machinations of the enemy, who provides insider information and specialist knowledge that eventually leads to the disabling of the enemy vessel. Within a storm, Warley falls from the topmost rigging of the ship. The mast is broken but acts as an anchor because it remains attached to the ship via the rigging, delaying progress and threatening the destruction of the ship. Warley is trying to reach the mast to use it as a lifeline but the captain and other crew have the agonizing task of cutting free the restraining ropes and rigging, casting Warley adrift on the high seas.

The next scene finds Aubrey grappling with his decision. The captain is sorrowful and reflective; his mastery is shot through with pain. Here is a captain whose responsibility to his crew has cost him dearly. His pain makes him vulnerable and yet it heralds a new possibility. The ship's doctor, Stephen, identifies Aubrey's struggle with his own experience of losing patients. The doctor acknowledges that lives lost in surgery or from subsequent infections, are always more difficult to bear than losses sustained in the battle itself. He comforts the captain by crystallizing the truth: 'the enemy killed him, not me'.

Third, then, the captain embodies the nature of partnership. In this partnership there is honesty and openness, but this is not a partnership of equals. I would cast Stephen as the Psalmist, providing the honest voice of questioning, disagreement and anger. But he also embodies a privileged relationship with the captain. They play wonderful music together on the cello and the violin and this harmony emphasizes difference but also declares their bond. The doctor is a naturalist and is keen to explore the Galapagos Islands, which they pass in their pursuit of the *Acheron*. When circumstances change, and time is of the essence to shorten the distance between the enemy and the *Surprise*, the promise offered to Stephen is revoked. The captain defends himself by claiming he has the bigger picture in mind, and it is only Steven who has the luxury of looking at life through a microscope.

Despite 'Lucky Jack's' leadership, all does not remain well in the ship, and Aubrey tackles this with a further quality – honesty. A period of doldrums brings intense heat and an absence of any breeze, and discloses an enemy within. These stifling conditions result in a stale and motionless state for the ship. It is in this stagnancy that the bitterness and resentment of the crew festers and comes to a head. It is here that the fears and inner chaos of the men are externalized and focussed onto the weaker character of Hollom. This marginalized figure becomes the scapegoat. Hollom is an ineffectual and indecisive officer resented and disrespected by the crew. He cannot decide whether to raise the alarm in the opening scene, he is sent up the mast to assist Warley, but Hollom becomes rigid with fear. When Warley falls to his death it is Hollom who is blamed. An old seaman who is full of bible quotes and misquotes propels the momentum of resentment towards Hollom. Eventually, Hollom is tortured by guilt and by the menacing attitudes of the men. He becomes the scapegoat, is named 'Jonah' and in the impasse of the doldrums, when no life-giving wind is present, human turmoil is intensified.

René Girard explores the mechanism of scapegoating, using the phrase in an everyday sense, and not in the religious sense of Leviticus 16. He draws attention to how internal violence and hatred within individuals is often directed and focussed onto one single individual. This individual is then victimized. This process has the dual 'benefits' both of uniting the group and dealing with personal chaos by externalizing it.[1] Do we recognize this process in ourselves? As we close ranks nationally, socially and religiously to preserve our territory or our purity? As we shift our discomfort about our own inadequacies onto the shoulders of modern day scapegoats? As the blame culture thrives and gains momentum? The theme of scapegoating highlights the chaos of our own natures and our tendency to avoid our own struggles by transferring them to others.

The captain recognizes that Hollom is a typical victim: marginalized and vulnerable. He advises Hollom to 'find strength within yourself and you will earn their respect.' Hollom never does find this strength, or perhaps in a tragic way strength is only found as he decides to take his own life. He jumps ship clutching a canon ball to compound his weight as he journeys into the chaos.

The captain's words and actions at Hollom's funeral reinforce the message that he is on the side of the victim and not the oppressor. Captain Aubrey names their lack of solidarity with Hollom and leads the crew in asking forgiveness. One member of the crew hands the bible, opened at the book of Jonah, to the captain. But Aubrey refuses to use scripture in this way and instead says these words: 'The simple truth is that not all of us become the men we once hoped we might be.'

The one who wishes to be the greatest
In the midst of adventure, patriotic service and amazing storms, this study of leadership is played out.[2] The significant and nurturing qualities of the captain cannot, however, mask the sometimes questionable nature of his leadership.

1. The greatest or the least ... ?
A theme that is introduced very early in the film concerns the tendency of authority to corrupt its leaders. This is a question that is revisited in light of Captain Aubrey's on-going actions and decisions. Where does the commitment to one's duty end and the demon of personal pride bite in? The 'psalmist' voice of Stephen declares that Aubrey's passion to seek and destroy the larger ship of the enemy smacks of pride. It appears that Aubrey has already exceeded his naval orders and we are drawn to ponder his motivation. Is he a true autocrat? What do we make of Aubrey's integrity when he revokes a promise to his friend? Does the captain's advice to Hollom to be 'neither a friend nor a tyrant' suggest something of an automaton? And yet, other officers surround Aubrey and within this group he has a more open and trusting relationship with Stephen.

Aubrey also holds to the opinion that 'men must be governed'. When challenged on this by Stephen, the captain justifies his words by alluding to the hierarchy in nature. Stephen counters, 'there is no disdain in nature.' Does Aubrey hold the crew in disdain? Are they pawns in his proud game? This scene holds the distinct possibility that Aubrey is working to his own agenda for success and that the crew are minor players in this epic. But Aubrey also makes a plea for order and duty. He states that 'it is only hard work and discipline that keep this little wooden world afloat.' Breaking the rules of obeisance in this context could endanger the buoyancy of the entire ship and its crew. Rather than hierarchy spelling disdain, this is perhaps more like an overstated view of the natural functioning of roles within a group.

2. A Gospel view of human leadership

Human leadership as modelled by Jesus is above all things unpredictable. His ministry is tailored to the specific needs of each one of his followers, reflecting God's nature that accomplishes the same thing through a variety of methods. Howard Friend urges leaders to recover a 'sacred centre' that is formed from the inner longings and yearnings of our hearts. Rooted in the sacred centre, it becomes possible to live and minister authentically and to ride the waves of chaos and uncertainty. He writes:

> Effective leaders foster a tolerance for uncertainty, even chaos. This appropriate tolerance is hard to define, but clarity, firmness, and consistency must be woven with a willingness to be uncertain and incomplete.[3]

Human leadership demands an ability to be flexible and 'open-textured' to the environment. The only formula is: there is no formula! Each group is made up of a unique blend of personalities and gifts, of strengths and weaknesses. What works in one context is anathema to another.

Leadership is a way of living, so Walter C. Wright suggests. As we live constantly in relationships, and as God offers us leadership within relationship, Wright goes further and suggests that our human leadership is relational. His definition of leadership is: ' ... a relationship in which one person seeks to influence the thoughts, behaviours, beliefs or values of another person.'[4] But this is not to say that leadership is about domination or manipulation. Wright maintains that this relationship is based on trust, and trust is gained through mutual understanding and faith between the parties in the relationship.

Jesus had complete understanding of the human heart and as we seek to reflect Christ's leadership, we must make this understanding our priority also. Although our understanding will only ever be partial, our dependence on God and our valuing of the 'sacred centre' of the other is key to creating unity, harnessing strengths and gifts, and nurturing the frail and needy. Ultimately, our understanding of, and belief and trust in, each other frees us to become the people we have potential to be; we are enabled to move towards the unique design for which God intends us.

3. Aubrey's example

Aubrey is first and foremost a flexible leader. He has a range of ploys in his arsenal of attack and defence. His tactics include: drawing close to the enemy; retreating in the fog; rigging up a decoy; giving chase; running; and sailing around the enemy to come up on its tail. Perhaps most importantly, although the mission to seek and destroy the enemy takes precedence over a promise made, ultimately Aubrey can be flexible enough to shelve the main focus of his mission and to give priority to the life of his friend and colleague, Stephen.

It is Stephen who challenges the captain's decision to press on against their formidable enemy. The doctor is aware that the crew will follow 'Lucky Jack' anywhere, confident of victory. The question raised is one of integrity: is this a just command, or manipulation of the willing and trusting crew? If we consider the character of the doctor who is averse to fighting, here there is clear evidence that the captain's influence has an impact on Stephen's beliefs and values. Although the doctor is certainly not part of the warring troops, he does engage in the final battle. Perhaps to repay the debt he owes to the captain for his life, or because he has been influenced by the single-mindedness of this trusted captain. Through travelling in a growing atmosphere of trust, the doctor finally joins the mission of the entire crew.

Aubrey's understanding of his men is realistic; his eyes are open to their best qualities but he is also fully aware of their shadow-sides. He understands their superstitions because he has lived the life; he advises the doctor that 'not everything is in your book, Stephen.' This understanding culminates in Aubrey's empowering of others, a theme that is threaded through the film, with the resulting growth and development of the officers and crew.

Flexibility, relational leadership based on understanding and trust, and an ability to empower others are all examples of leadership to which we might aspire. Additionally, the quality of humour lights up this leader's character and surely is an indispensable ingredient of life, let alone leadership!

The One who brought order from the chaos
Although the film offers us this study in human leadership, set in the context of an heroic chase and victory, there are occasions when the film itself encourages us to ponder a bigger picture, especially for those who have ears to hear. This is particularly true in the Jonah motif, which we have already touched upon. Do the fortunes of 'Lucky Jack' and the *Surprise* rest only on human intuition, judgement and skill, coupled with some degree of unknowable 'fortune', or, as for Jonah, is there a God also involved in these same events? Two other incidents point us in this direction.

The first arises out of Steven's enthusiasm for natural history. Remember the date in which the film is set is 1805. Although Darwin has yet to write his famous treatise on evolution, *The Origin of Species by Natural Selection,* there is still a good deal of conversation and debate going on about natural science and the observable changes within a species. Stephen also enthuses the young one-armed midshipman, Blakeley, as together they study pictures of camouflaged creatures. This is a scene that grows in significance as towards the end of the film Aubrey learns this very lesson from the natural order and camouflages his ship in readiness for the final battle. Blakeley asks the doctor, 'Does God make them change or do they also change themselves?' The doctor replies, 'Does God makes them change? Yes, certainly! But do they also change themselves? Now that is the question isn't it?'

Certainly Stephen is articulating an attempt to hold together some understanding of God with his burgeoning understanding of nature. But we are also invited to contemplate the role of God in the wider world and the partnership into which God invites us, along with the corresponding possibility of transformation. We may recall the captain's words at Hollom's funeral, that 'not all of us become the men we once hoped we might be' and acknowledge that it is through relationship with God and in partnership with him that transformation flourishes.

The second comes towards the end of the film, after the battle with the *Acheron*, when we look in on a simple funeral service for the English men who have died. After leading the ship's crew in the Lord's Prayer, Aubrey reads out the names of those who have died. Their bodies, stitched into their hammocks are then lowered into the sea as Aubrey leads a prayer: 'We therefore commit their bodies to the deep, to be turned into corruption, looking for the resurrection of the body when the sea shall give up her dead in the life of the world to come, through our Lord Jesus Christ.'

This scene comes towards the end of the film, when there is a temporary pocket of peace and attainment. The focus of the film has been on the gripping chase through the oceans. Aubrey's strength has been in his ability to negotiate the hostile forces of the seas while remaining focussed on his mission to capture the enemy. Throughout the film the ship encounters a medley of weather conditions: storms of ice, wind, rain and fog which bring chaos into the frame, a chaos against which they constantly battle, and which will only be defeated when the depths of the sea give up their dead. It is an Old Testament theme that chaos exists in opposition to God's rule, and that God has ultimate authority over it. Chaos cannot be avoided; it is a base line ingredient of life. The Book of Genesis depicts creation itself as being brought forth by God from chaos – not from nothing, as we traditionally read it. The Good News translation captures this: 'The earth was formless and desolate. The raging ocean that covered everything was engulfed in total darkness, and the Spirit of God was moving over the water' (Gen. 1:2). And as Psalm 24 tells us, it is God who 'founded the earth upon the seas and made it firm ...' But even so, chaos still bubbles up through the spaces around God's ordering.

Our tendency in these individualistic times is to compare our range of contexts with the varied weather conditions of storm or peace. Valid as that is, this film encourages us to see these storms in a wider context. A backdrop of spiritual conditions is boiling away chaotically, but the master and commander skilfully guides his ship through them. Walter Brueggemann calls for a shift of focus from individual sin and guilt to a broader concept of universal chaos:

A serious theological recognition of chaos in biblical faith opens the
Bible beyond the conventional, simplistic preoccupation with sin and
guilt that so pervades our society. Such a recognition suggests that the
large theological issue to be considered in our culture is not some small
moralistic question, but the largest issue of the ordering of life in the
world that can already be seen to be at risk.[5]

This film helps us to affirm that our journey is undertaken with all
humankind on a sea that is perpetually stormy. Our hope is in the God
who steers us through the very real storms and chaos of life. Although we
can be realistic about the disorder of our world, we can also have hope
and assurance in our pilot and captain. One day the sea will give up its
dead and chaos will finally be conquered. Meanwhile, bringing order
from chaos is not about perpetual peace or certainty, but in the resources
to weather the storms.

Although we do not find the image of a sea captain used of God in
scripture[6], we do have a picture of the captain-like behaviour of Jesus as
he and his disciples are marooned on the Sea of Galilee in a fierce earth-
quake-like storm. This quality of the Almighty finds expression in
Christ's saving act as he stills the storm and successfully navigates to the
shore, finding another pocket of peace. *Master and Commander*, then,
encourages us to reflect not only on the nature of human leadership, but
also on the possibilities of divine leadership. That which is the best in the
human leadership of Jack Aubrey gives us a glimpse of the nature of God
revealed in both the old covenant and the new through Jesus Christ.

We might compare God's love of creation with this captain's love of,
and identification with, his ship. What better picture can we have of God's
involvement with creation, involvement even to the point of identification? Isaiah ponders God's passionate love in these words: 'Can a mother
forget the baby at her breast and have no compassion on the child she has
borne? Though she may forget, I will not forget you! See, I have engraved
you on the palms of my hands; your walls are ever before me' (Isa.
49:15,16). Here, the initials of humankind are etched into the part of God
that holds and creates; here, God promises to continue enfolding and
forming humanity. Can we see God's initials also etched on the fabric of
the world and of all creation? Just as we see the artist's signature on her

handiwork; just as we see the captain's initials carved into the fabric of his ship?

This captain reminds us of the God who offers hope in the midst of our most painful experiences. Aubrey hands Blakeley the book about Nelson, the leader who bears the same wounds as the young midshipman. We might imagine God handing us the book of testimony to God's own self, the record of the experiences of Jesus who has suffered every wound known to human beings and who lives to inspire and nourish our vision.

The captain and Warley – the seaman who fell from the mast and died in the chaos of the ocean – hint, at that point in the film, at facets of the divine nature. Salvation pivots on the self-giving and pain of both God and God's son, Jesus. Even as the captain has ultimate responsibility in sending Warley up the mast and is fully involved in cutting him free in order to free the whole crew, so God bears the agonizing involvement in Christ's death on the cross. Just as Warley's life is lost so that the ship can move forward, so Christ died that we might be no longer tethered in the seas of chaos. We are no longer anchored in the storm and battered by it, but free to negotiate its channels, its crests and its troughs with God at the helm.

Coming Close

We are familiar with ideas of God having a 'bird's eye view' and a broader perspective on our world. And yet even with our limited perspective, we can offer something to God because of our partnership. We are unequal partners, but we are invited to come close to God in trust and reliance: 'In this dependence, we make an amazing discovery: that God who does not need dependence freely desires to be dependent on us for the completeness of fellowship, for the joy of the dance.'[7] There is, perhaps, an example of this mutuality in the way that the doctor's study of 'surprising' nature gives rise to the captain's final plan of disguise. Perhaps in this partnership we see an illustration of how God might 'get a purchase on the human scene in a way not otherwise possible.'[8]

To press this partnership even further, could it be that even as Stephen comforts the captain of the *Surprise*, our comforting of God is a possibility? Who are we to offer anything – let alone comfort or support – to the God above all gods? It is God who comforts *us* because God understands our human struggles. And yet is this not a new context of mutuality? God's pain and loss in the death of God's son opens the way for us to come close and to identify with *God's* pain. God's loss has been a human loss, God has spoken in our language and we have heard and understood because God has used the currency with which we are familiar. We are bound together in our common struggle against the enemy.

While not every line or action of this film can be assimilated into our theological reflection, its themes provide hooks on which we can hang our thoughts. The theme of human leadership includes the ingredients of tenderness, vulnerability and partnership, along with honest integrity. These ingredients in turn breed trust and mutuality, and create unity. In the light of the story of Jesus in the Gospels, we can see that the leadership of Captain Aubrey, while not divulging much of a servant heart, does embody flexibility, along with elements of understanding of the 'sacred centre' of human beings. We may doubt the captain's motives at points in the film, but he draws out the best in his crew and enables and empowers them to grow into the people they always hoped to be. *Master and Commander* offers an image of leadership that is focussed on a common enemy and is flexible enough to cope with uncertainty and tumult.

These reflections lead us to ponder the nature of God's leadership. We have a God who is fully involved with creation and identified with it, who offers us partnership that is based on harmony, including difference and dissonance. This film invites us to consider how our partnership with God brings about transformation, and how we might negotiate the chaos of our world until the time that chaos is finally stilled. This story hints at the distinction between the unseen spiritual forces of evil in our world and the general chaos of our lives. The result is a comment on the stormy journeys we undertake, even as it holds out the promise of transformation that is possible when we align our course with that of God.

Notes

[1] René Girard, *Violence and the Sacred*, trans. Patrick Gregory (London: Athlone Press, 1995), pp. 96-106. Cf. Michael Kirwan, *Discovering Girard* (London: Darton, Longman & Todd, 2004), p. 49.

[2] In this section of the chapter, the conversation of Jesus with his disciples about the nature of rule and greatness in Mark 10:35-45 is constantly in the background.

[3] Howard E. Friend Jr, *Recovering the Sacred Center: Church Renewal from the Inside Out* (Valley Forge: Judson Press, 1998), p. 113.

[4] Walter C. Wright Jr, *Relational Leadership: A Biblical Model for Leadership Service* (Carlisle: Paternoster Press, 2000), p. 2.

[5] Walter Brueggemann, *Reverberations of Faith: A Theological Handbook of Old Testament Themes* (Louisville: Westminster/John Knox Press, 2002), p. 29.

[6] Derek J. Tidball, *Builders & Fools: Leadership the Bible Way* (Leicester: IVP, 1999), p.104.

[7] Paul Fiddes, *Participating in God: A Pastoral Doctrine of the Trinity* (London: Darton, Longman & Todd, 2000), p. 108.

[8] H.H. Farmer, *The World and God* (London: Nisbet, 1993), p. 24; cf. p. 70. Quoted in Kirwan, *Discovering Girard,* p. 71.

10
Pondering Providence: *Sliding Doors*
Robert Ellis

Ideas about the future

A number of popular films have explored ideas about the future, and in particular the question of whether the future is fixed or open to us. *Terminator 2*, discussed elsewhere in this volume, is one such film, where Arnold Schwarzenegger's character comes from the future into the present to change the course of events; this gives a new twist on an old time-travel theme. The *Back to the Future* trilogy worked at these ideas too, but warned its characters not to attempt to deflect the course of events in their past. These two films both raise the question of whether the future can alter the past. But other films ask whether the future itself is alterable. For instance, more recently *Minority Report* offered the subtle suggestion that the future is not completely fixed. Whereas certain outcomes are perhaps more likely than others there is still the possibility that the 'less likely' future – the subject of the 'minority report' – may be actualized depending upon choices made in the developing present. *Sliding Doors* makes a contribution to this filmic discussion that is remarkable both for its profundity and its lightness of touch. It raises issues about the future that may be subject to 'theological criticism'[1] and are very appropriately discussed within the framework of Christian ideas of fate or providence.

Is the future fixed? Are you now in circumstances over which you have had meaningful influence, or are you the 'pawn' of fate or providence? For example, and more specifically, is your current job one that 'had your name on it' – with dates, of course – in an *inevitable* way? Was the 'chance meeting' with the love of your life just that, or was it ordained in some Grand Plan? Might you really, in fact, have been doing other work, or even been married to another person, if *you* had so chosen? Or are the basic contours of your life in some way set, but in such a way as to give you the opportunity to exercise a certain amount of free choice over the details within them?

Sliding Doors explores such questions as it tells the story of Helen, a young woman PR executive, and her amours and friends. The sliding doors of the title feature at the beginning and end of the film and indicate crucial points at which the story comes to what we might call 'crisis' points – points at which decisive events change the course of what will follow. The doors slide shut on an underground train at the beginning of the film, and on an elevator at the end of the film, and they close off certain sequences of events or possible actions. The sliding doors remind us of the way in which our actions are to some extent always irreversible and mutually exclusive: the doors close on some possible outcome in the same way that our choices appear to curtail possible futures. But, as we see from Helen's story, the sliding doors not only cut her off from certain outcomes they also open up new possibilities. New things are possible precisely because other things are excluded, in the same way that our choices seem to close off but also open up new routes into the future. Such closings and openings are real at every moment, when we actualize 'x' rather than 'y' at any given moment. If we choose to leave our house at 7.45 we may get to work on time, while if we dawdle we will be late and the possibility of being punctual gives way to the possibility of being sacked. This is what Helen found in *Sliding Doors* as the opening credits begin to roll. In fact, a very great deal happens before the credits have finished so the viewer needs to watch closely!

But while some of the events in these opening minutes of the film are within Helen's own powers of influence in a clear way, others are less so. Interestingly, both of the events that occur at the sliding doors appear to be 'coincidences', indeed the first of these decisive events is not one where any of the main protagonists seems to exercise direct volition. Events happen around them, and to them. Sometimes we seem to be in control of our fate; at other times we seem to be victims of circumstances beyond our control. Do our lives happen to us, or do we in some sense direct them, or at least partially direct them? Or does some higher purpose, or perhaps impersonal fate, shape our lives in whole or in part?

Providence
The idea of 'providence' is often thought to refer to the notion that God's care for us provides for our needs and shelters us from harm. Historically

a distinction has often been made between a 'general', or indirect, and 'special', or more direct, providence. The former has sometimes been taken to mean that God creates and sustains the world in being with beneficent structures and provisions such as the passing of the seasons and the provision of food and shelter. On the other hand, special or particular providence is believed to focus God's care much more specifically on to individuals and particular circumstances. By special providence God may be believed to influence or determine *micro* events in human lives rather than simply the *macro* conditions within which those lives are lived. So a deistic view of the world would seem to have little place for this kind of special providence, God having retreated from creation, like the watchmaker who winds up the watch and then leaves it to run. By contrast, positions as far apart as a theological determinism and process thought find room in one way or another for special providence, for some sense that God does not retreat from the world, but either wholly determines or at the very least exercises some influence upon, particular and minute events.

Etymologically, 'providence' is derived from *pro video*, seeing ahead. But theologically it also comes to mean that which we then do to prepare for what is to come. Amongst the advertisements jostling for my attention in the newspaper recently was one for Friends Provident, the provider of pensions, life insurance and savings plans. Their motto is 'Life's better with friends', and they want to befriend you and help you to save, to plan ahead and to provide for those rainy days or retirement. Here we see clearly how the word 'providence' means fore-seeing, looking ahead, and our 'friends' at Friends Provident want to help us to look ahead, plan, provide, be ready for the unexpected. They want us, with them, to be *provident*. When Christians use this word 'providence' in relation to God something similar is in mind: we want to talk about God's looking to our future, and God's on-going caring for us, a care that is sure and reliable. The idea of providence relates to God's looking ahead and putting in hand that which needs to be done in order to provide for us. This insight is a common one in many parts of scripture, notably in the Psalms. Psalm 27, which we may use as one of our biblical reference points in such a discussion, speaks eloquently about God's protection.

Yet this stress on God's foreseeing the future seems often to be understood as God's *determining* the future. We may reflect on the way that some members of our churches routinely speak about God's 'overruling'. But it seems to me that this cannot be the case in any rigid sense. The Old Testament prophets, even as they preach that God is the Lord of history, also invite, cajole, plead, for the people to respond, to make the future that God wills for them, not that their sin wastes. We continue this ourselves when we invite others to make their own response to God, because God allows them space. The future, even in God's provident care is *not* fixed and set. Rather it offers human persons a choice. We may go further than this, beyond the scope of the film and this reflection, and suggest that the whole of creation is able to choose and respond to God.[2] In the broadest possible terms this choice is between life and death,[3] or at least, between clusters of possibilities which may, to a greater or lesser extent, actualize God's purpose, or deflect ourselves and creation from it. Is it possible to make a choice that God does not also will? Surely scripture suggests that it is,[4] and that the future is not fixed or wholly determined, and is partly within our influence, although perhaps not wholly. And as well as the apparently random and coincidental factors which clearly affect Helen's life in this film, we may also want to affirm that God is also, in some mysterious way, exerting some kind of influence upon events in and through the observable causes.

The story
Sliding Doors is a rather unusual example of the movie genre known as a romantic comedy, and it explores the themes I have discussed by using a simple but effective dramatic device. It does not simply tell the story of Helen's life. It actually tells us *two* parallel stories of Helen's life, two different and mutually exclusive sequences of events which unfold from one point. As the credits begin at the start of the film, Helen (Gwyneth Paltrow) has arrived late for work on Monday. An indiscretion on the previous Friday and her late arrival now result in her sacking. She wanders disconsolately back to the underground station to return home to the flat she shares with her lover, a writer and 'kept man'. A tiny detail distinguishes her trip to the train. In the rush to the underground platform a child delays her for a moment on the stairs, and so she misses the train;

the sliding doors close leaving her frustrated on the platform. But then the film goes into rewind. We see her retracing her steps just as we might if we pressed the rewind button on our video or DVD player, and the film does a second take. This time, as she nears the platform for the second time the child is pulled out of the way by its mother; she gets there in time to stop the sliding doors closing, and she boards the train. A moment, a tiny detail outside of her control, but it makes all the difference in the world.

In the film we then enter two parallel story-lines from that moment. We might say by implication, that there could be a myriad other such moments in the film where similar divergences might take place, where a choice might be made differently, or when some external factor or circumstance intervenes. But we are left with just these two parallel courses, indicating a major turning point and the shift in relationships it precipitates. In one parallel story-line, she catches the train, catches her boyfriend at home in bed with another woman, and breaks up with him. On that journey home she has chatted with a fellow-passenger, James (John Hannah), and ends up in a relationship with him that heals her hurt and changes her life in all sorts of positive ways. In the other, having missed the train, she falls victim to a series of misfortunes and arrives home much later, and after the other woman has gone. She then continues in a story-line sequence in which she is being cheated on and gains no support to help her address her professional crisis. Her boyfriend Gerry (John Lynch) seems to want to end his affair with Lydia (Jeanne Tripplehorn) but fails to muster the willpower. Suspicion of his infidelity grows and finally Helen catches the couple together.

In both story-lines, Helen learns that she is pregnant. By this time, in the first story-line, she is having a rough time with James following a misunderstanding, while in the second story-line the news coincides with her certainty of Gerry's cheating. Both plots now move towards their climax. In story-line one she is reconciled with James in a scene that looks like the happy ending most of the audience will have wanted, but is then involved in a serious road accident. In story-line two, she runs from Gerry in disgust, slips and tumbles down stairs. Both story-lines now show us ambulances, sirens blaring, en route to hospital. We then sit by two hospital beds, both occupied by Helen. James holds her close and testifies undying love, but Helen's life slips away – so much for the happy ending of the happy story-line. In the parallel plot Gerry also declares repentance and love, but a recovering Helen will not hear it and sends him away.

Story-line one is now over, and only story-line two remains. Discharged from hospital Helen waits for the elevator. Inside it we find James who has been visiting his elderly mother. The sliding doors open, Helen steps in alongside him. James makes a weak joke, a reference to a classic Monty Python script. Helen replies with the quip from the show – but we know that she only knows this answer because of dialogue in the 'wrong' storyline, the first one! The characters exchange quirky smiles and the sliding doors close and the credits roll once more. Will there be a happy ending after all?

It is fortunate for the viewer that Helen has a new hair-do in the first of these parallel plots, so we can see which story-line is which as they unfold. But strangely, while the plot lines run in parallel they also intersect at certain points. The pregnancy is the most significant example, but at other moments Helen ends up in the same bar, or walking beside the same river, in both plot lines at the 'same time'. Crises that call for decision in the parallel plots seem to match up in a similar way. It is as if, whatever tiny detail changed the course of her life, there is a similar 'shaping process' at work in it in both parallel versions.

Most interestingly, at the end there is the very major 'intersection' I have described in the hospital. The viewer is faced with a challenging question: has the plot line which seemed the 'happiest' really turned out to be so, or is the long term happiness found in the other, apparently more unhappy plot line? And as the two parallel lines converge in an unlikely way we ask: is there some purpose shaping this life? Beyond the details that differ – sometimes very important details – is there also a common shape to these parallel lives? Was Helen bound to end up with James, for instance, albeit in different ways and at different moments? Were they 'meant' for one another?

While there are other critical moments on the way in both parallel lines, inevitably our minds go back to that initial scene on the underground. Do we believe that such moments, which can radically change our lives, like catching or missing a train, are *chance*? Or do we believe that God somehow moves, even makes, the mother pull the child out of the way – or not – in order to direct the course of Helen's life, and indeed the lives of those around her, for their fate is also altered by hers? Or is there some kind of hint in the way in which these very different stories yet resemble one another, a hint that somehow there is a purpose shaping our lives beyond the details?

Helen's life was radically different because of that moment on the underground. Obviously Helen's life is a story, but *our* lives can also change completely at such apparently tiny and inconsequential moments, just as they can through choices over which we agonize and appear to have more of a measure of control. Is there, as Hamlet muses, a 'divinity which shapes our ends, rough-hew them how we will'?[5]

Fate, providence, freedom

Half-way through *Sliding Doors*, James tells Helen to step out bravely in a new venture, saying 'Go on, try it, all things work for the best'. Perhaps this is an allusion to Romans 8:28: 'We know that all things work together for good' (NRSV). On James' lips these words do not appear, in the context of the film, to be a bold affirmation of Christian faith. Rather, they sound more like a kind of optimistic trust in fate – a rather different, secularized notion of providence. The official movie website speaks of the story-line in terms of Helen's 'destiny';[6] whereas other online reviews commonly speak of the story as an exploration of 'fate'.[7] James seems to be suggesting that somehow the hidden hand of fate will benevolently protect Helen. It appears to be the happier side of an attitude that sometimes speaks of the bullet with a soldier's name on!

The movie, in any case, does not seem to be speaking of the Christian notion of providence when it tells Helen's stories. If it is consciously exploring any theme, and I believe it is, this is something connected but different. It is difficult, of course, to analyse coherently 'some kind of belief in fate.' Such beliefs will vary from person to person, and perhaps culture to culture. But by analogy with Paul's speech on the Areopagus[8] we might suggest that Christian interpreters could associate this idea of a (benevolent) fate with the Christian idea of providence.

God's providence, like James' view of fate, is usually thought to be a protective force – and that is certainly one of Psalm 27's major themes. The psalmist speaks of God 'hiding' him, and of being saved from his enemies. But the psalm is more complex than that. Some say that it is two psalms, and it is certainly a psalm with a clear change of mood from one part to the next.[9] In the first, the psalmist affirms and celebrates God's protection, and speaks of longing to be able to spend a lifetime reflecting upon the ways of God. But in the second the tone changes; now the psalmist urgently seeks reassurance, pleads for God to hear him and save him, and seeks the protection that earlier was celebrated.

It does not take very long for us to realize with the psalmist, either from personal experience or observation, that faith in God is a poor insurance policy, if by that we mean 'protection from misfortune or calamity'. The wicked seem to prosper now, just as in the time of scripture, while the relatively good suffer. Who could contemplate the concentration camps of the twentieth century, or the ethnic cleansing of the last few decades, or countless personal disasters inflicted by fellow human beings or forces of nature, and say simply that 'faith in God protects us'?

In *Sliding Doors*, both parallel plots begin with misfortune, albeit partly self-induced. And both go through more misfortune, and finally come to a real life and death calamity. These events seem to happen partly because of human choices and partly because of what seems to be an impersonal coincidence. Yet still the viewer might muse on the 'shaping' of these parallel lives which seem, in the two *Sliding Doors* stories, to have certain common features. Our perspective, as people living our own story-lines, makes it difficult to discern this shaping. It was Kierkegaard who remarked that life has to be lived forwards but can only be understood backwards.[10] Sometimes what seems like protection to us in immediate experience turns out to be an illusion. And what seems like disaster turns out to be the possibility and ground of new hope and new beginnings.

How might we make sense of this 'shape' given to our lives, shape that may be given beyond our genuinely free individual choices and beyond the ebb and flow of what Churchill called 'events'? To say that God *has* purposes for our lives is not to say that God *imposes* purposes on us, but it might suggest that God, whom we affirm knows best for us and works with us, might keep on offering us the opportunity to actualize that purpose. Process theologians speak of God offering an 'initial aim' to all actual entities, including human persons, at every moment.[11] That aim, an outcome or cluster of related or equally desirable outcomes perhaps, represents the best which God wisely foresees (*pro video*) for us. It is not necessary to adopt wholesale the technical language of the process theologians to see how this kind of imagery can be a helpful way of imagining the way God deals with us, still presenting his purpose with clarity and winsomeness but not foisting it upon us. We may choose to actualize some other outcome. Perhaps sometimes the choice we would have made is taken out of our hands by circumstance, like the child who delayed Helen on the stairs. But even when we do turn our back on God's purpose, or are otherwise deflected from it, God carries on working with us from where we are and wherever we end up, still presenting us with opportunities to realign ourselves with his gracious will.

Something like this interpretation of divine providence may offer a Christian understanding of the kind of possibilities that are exemplified in the story-lines of *Sliding Doors*, where the films suggest that some impersonal fate may be at work. This would mean that both versions of Helen's life were equally legitimate and possible, but also suggest that the features common to the two story-lines might be common because they represent in some way God's continuing prompting and leading of Helen towards God's will for her. Of course, even this is not guaranteed. They may also reflect Helen's habitual 'wrong' choices, or they may simply be coincidences that fool us into seeing patterns where there are none; we should not even rule out the possibility that God seeks to lead Helen into adversity for some reason hidden from our understanding. But that said, these common features do also intimate that whatever our wrong choices, and however circumstances conspire against us, God goes on working with us and for us according to God's gracious will. This may account for the common shape to the two stories.

What seems at first sight to be the happier story-line becomes, again at first sight, the sadder one. Does this suggest that sometimes we are too close to our own circumstances to make such judgements, that with Kierkegaard we not only need to look backwards but to see things in the long perspective? The problem with such a position is that, looking back on our lives, the turn of events sometimes seems to take on a greater and greater sense of inevitability, as if things had to happen just as they did. *Sliding Doors*, and much in scripture, seem to challenge that perspective.

Instead it may be truer to say that if one story-line seemed happier and the other less so, we should recall that God, human freedom and creaturely interaction have more to say on every story-line. We may mess up even the most promising of situations! More hopefully, God is not absent even from the most unpromising of circumstances; even the film's second story-line can be redeemed by God's gracious purpose.

All of this means that while the stories have a common shape, perhaps indicating the persistence and power of God's prompting, there is also real freedom here in this creation. For would we want to suggest that God intended that Helen should be run over and then die, or that she should tumble down the stairs and lose her unborn child? It would be a hard pastor who would be comfortable with such divine intentions, and instead I would want to argue that in various ways we also see in the two parallel stories of this film that God does not will every event, nor does God intervene to prevent every calamity. God goes on working with us in calamity, promising to be with us in the valley of the shadow of death (Psa. 23:4), rather than promising miraculous delivery from it.

We need then to say something else quite explicitly about providence. The future is not completely fixed. With the evangelists and the prophets I want to say that we are called upon to work with God in making it. While Helen is in a sense the victim, the passive sufferer of an initial circumstance, it is also the case that she then made, or failed to make, a number of positive choices which also affected what happened to her. We too are victims of circumstances beyond our control, which may nor may not be shaped by God, but we also have certain things which we can decide. Our lives, like Helen's, can follow different and equally possible, and maybe valid, courses. The shaping remains in them both, whatever way we choose. In part, to affirm the providence of God is to affirm that we can never put ourselves outside God's persistent concern and care.

In Psalm 27 the psalmist both knew that God *was* his light and his salvation, and yet he also urgently pleaded with God *to be* just that. Amidst the ups and the downs, the forces that we cannot and can control, the things we do and things that happen to us, the future that is fairly settled and the future that is open, the psalmist knows that he is not alone. Somehow and in some way, even as he suffers misfortunes which may or may not turn out to be secret boons, God is with him and is his protection.

This protection is, I am sure, real, but is not a guarantee that only nice things will happen to us, or even that everything that happens to us is *meant* to happen to us.

God is ready always to hear and join our laments, to 'advise', to help us pick up the threads, to show us again that new things are possible despite everything. This conviction about the providential God arises from the witness of scripture and in particular from the death and resurrection of Jesus. The God who created order from chaos at the beginning, and who pulled resurrection from death in the life of Jesus, is always looking to make order from chaos and bring hope from despair. God's attention to detail amounts to numbering the hairs on our heads; in the details of our lives God continually adjusts and readjusts the divine purposes as God seeks to guide us into the divine will and towards good endings. God does indeed exercise a 'special providence', though it is not one that overrides our own freedom or the freedom of the world; in amongst the ups and downs, and ins and outs, there is a force which works for the good, for our good, even in the most unpromising of circumstances. *We* call this providence, and one way of reading *Sliding Doors* is to argue that amid the freedom, the chance and the tragedy, there is some suggestion that such a loving divine force is at work. Before such mystery the appropriate theological response is awe, trust and hope, as we give ourselves day by day to God's infinite and benevolent resources amid the choices, coincidences and calamities of our lives.

Notes

[1] I discuss the notion of the 'theological' reading of films in chapter 2 above. Also see Joel W. Martin and Conrad E. Ostwalt Jr, *Screening the Sacred: Religion, Myth and Ideology in Popular American Film* (Boulder & Oxford: Westview Press, 1995).

[2] Free will is often ascribed to the human part of creation, but a very strong case might be made for seeing the whole of creation as being self-determining: whether free will is too anthropomorphic a way of describing this self-determination might be borne in mind, but it is perhaps appropriate to speak of this creaturely self-determination at least by analogy with human free will. See Keith Ward, *Divine Action* (London: Collins, 1990), esp. pp. 74-102, 119-133; John B. Cobb Jr & David Ray Griffin, *Process Theology: An Introductory*

Exposition (Philadelphia: Westminster, 1976), esp. pp. 63-79. See also my 'Covenant and Creation' in *Bound for Glory: God, Church and World in Covenant*, (Oxford: Whitley, 2002), pp. 20-33.

3 Deuteronomy 30:19: 'I call heaven and earth to witness against you today that I have set before you life and death, blessings and curses. Choose life so that you and your descendants may live'.

4 For example consider Exodus 32: 11-14, 1 Samuel 15: 35, Isaiah 1:2, Jeremiah 3:7, Jonah 4:2. For a fuller discussion of this theme see Clark Pinnock, *Most Moved Mover* (Carlisle: Paternoster, 2001) and John Sanders, *God Who Risks: A Theology of Providence*, (Downers Grove Illinois: IVP, 1998) and my own *Answering God: Towards a Theology of Intercession* (Milton Keynes: Paternoster, 2005).

5 William Shakespeare, *Hamlet*, Act V, Scene 2, 10-11.

6 http://www.columbus.com.lb/columbus/lib/sliding_doors.htm, accessed 22/12/2004.

7 For example http://www.fuzzydog.com/zzslidingdoors.htm, accessed 22/12/2004.

8 Acts 17: 16ff.

9 Artur Weiser believes the psalm to have been formed by combining two originally independent songs. See Weiser, *The Psalms: A Commentary* (London: SCM, 1962), pp. 245ff. John Eaton dismisses such ideas in his *Psalms* (SCM: London, 1967), pp. 85ff.

10 This aphorism is ubiquitous, originating in a journal entry for 1843: see Alistair Hannay (ed.), *Soren Kierkegaard: Paper & Journals: A Selection* (Harmondsworth: Penguin, 1996). It is widely quoted, e.g. in John Cottingham, *Philosophy and the Good Life* (Cambridge: Cambridge University Press, 1998), p. 50n86. It also begins W.H. Auden's introductory selection of Kierkegaard's writings entitled *The Living Thoughts of Kierkegaard* (New York: New York Review of Books, 1999).

11 See John B. Cobb Jr, *A Christian Natural Theology* (Philadelphia: Westminster, 1965), pp. 151ff.

11
Fatherhood, Fate and Faith:
The Terminator Series

Simon Carver

Taking pop-culture seriously

Not long ago, in the church of which I am the minister, I planned a series of sermons that drew on films for illustrations.[1] Some films in our series looked at the harsh realities of life,[2] and others used sport and gentle fantasy to explore important issues,[3] but one film stood out as different, and, while unashamedly violent, offered some interesting thoughts about human and divine relationships.[4] In one way, *Terminator 2* was the easiest film on which to draw for illustrations, in that where some other films had vague allusions, this film, like much science fiction, did seem to make some pretty obvious points about fatherhood, fate and faith.

The *Terminator* series of films,[5] unlike other such series does not degenerate into a lowest common denominator or an 'in-it-for-the-money' franchise (another honourable exception is *The Godfather* series); nor is it usual for series films to be produced as far apart as those in the *Terminator* series. The first came out in 1984, the second in 1991 and the third in 2003. It seems from the ending of the third film that a fourth is inevitable, although age and political ambition may prevent Arnold Schwarzenegger from fulfilling this particular destiny. There were some rather cruel jibes by film critics when the third film came out that the subheading – 'the rise of the machines' – was referring to a Stannah stairlift.

As a boy I grew up reading *Superman* comics. It seemed quite remarkable how many comparisons could be made between the story of Superman and that of Jesus. An example is the connection between Superman's stay in his fortress of solitude before, as it were, he 'came out' as Superman and the time that Jesus spent in the wilderness. Superman heard the voice of his father speak to him, just as Jesus heard his Father's voice during his baptism. Superman's creators had in fact intended him to be a Jewish hero, perhaps in the line of David or Judas Maccabaeus, at a time when Jews living in central Europe were coming under increased persecution. The original comic strip was written in the 1930s by two Jewish Americans, both of whom are included in a book of the one hundred most influential Jews,[6] alongside Henry Kissinger, Steven Spielberg and Moses. Once this Jewish connection has been pointed out, we remember that Superman is sent out by his parents from his dying planet in a tiny space vessel that looks a little like the basket found by Pharaoh's daughter. The cyborg of *Terminator 2* stands in the line of such super-heroes and – as we shall see –also awakens religious echoes.

There is a tradition for preachers to draw their illustrations from classical literature and occasionally from serious films, but those films which could hardly be considered 'art house' are also a rich vein to be mined.[7] A film maker himself, Noel Coward had a firm grasp on the power of stories told on film and on the impact of what we now call 'pop culture'. In *Private Lives* his character Amanda comments, 'extraordinary how potent cheap music is'. He might have said the same about 'cheap' films – although cheap obviously does not refer to the cost of production of *Terminator 2* and *3*. But are the *Terminator* films simply 'pop culture'? Sean French hints that they might be more:

> Some literary professors might even argue that *The Terminator* is a serious work of art because of its religious theme. John Connor shares his initials with that other redeemer of mankind, Jesus Christ, and the film is an obvious allegorical conflation of the Nativity with the story of Eve and the serpent. Reese is a version of the annunciatory angel who impregnates Mary as well as informing her of the glad tidings. The terminator is a Herod, slaughtering the Sarah Connors[8] instead of the first born, and he is also Satan, who by attempting to destroy humanity perversely brings about its salvation (the paradoxical story Milton tells in 'Paradise Lost'). So *The Terminator* must be serious, mustn't it?[9]

Serious or not, the 1984 *Terminator* film – a low-budget B movie – spawned two hi-tech multi-million dollar sequels and projected its former body-building lead actor to superstardom and the Governorship of California. A brief synopsis of the story is required.

The *Terminator* story

Sarah Connor records a message on a cassette recorder to the unborn child she carries in her womb:

> Should I tell you about your father? That's a tough one. Will it change your decision to send him here … knowing? But if you don't send Kyle, you could never be. God, you can go crazy thinking about all this …

This quotation, almost unintelligible on its own, points to the fact that the plot is going to be complicated and that the *Terminator* series of films is based upon the sort of circular premise, involving time travel, loved by the tellers of science fiction stories. Sean French notes[10] that something similar happens in *Escape from the Planet of the Apes* – another sequel, the second in the *Planet of the Apes* series – and also in *Back to the Future*.[11] The latter film narrates a more comic circular incident than in *Terminator*, one in which Marty McFly (Michael J. Fox) has travelled thirty years back in time from 1985. He lands up on stage playing guitar with a group of local musicians. The crowd of fifties young people are whipped into excitement as he plays Chuck Berry's 'Johnny B. Goode'. One of the band gets on the telephone: 'Chuck! Chuck! It's Marvin – your cousin, Marvin Berry. You know that new sound you're looking for? Well, listen to this …'

These examples of 'historical feedback' are simple in comparison with the story behind the *Terminator* series. It might help to explain the characters involved in the first film. Sarah Connor is an ordinary working-class Californian young woman. John Connor is her son, who will grow up to become the leader of a resistance movement that will fight back against the machines who have taken over the world. The Terminator is a cyborg (a flesh-covered machine), sent back in time by the victorious machines. Its mission is to 'terminate' Sarah Connor and so prevent her from giving birth to John. Kyle Reese is John Connor's trusty lieutenant, sent back from the future by the resistance movement that is still fighting against the machines. Reese's purpose is to save Sarah Connor from the cyborg Terminator. Reese loses his life in successfully saving Sarah, but Sarah is already carrying the child that she and Reese have conceived.

Reese has therefore saved Sarah and ensured, in the best possible way, that John Connor will be born.

The first film ends with Sarah Connor having just been photographed by a young lad in a Mexican petrol station just south of the border with the US. The still wet Polaroid photograph, which the pregnant Sarah holds, is the same crumpled one which Kyle Reese, her recently deceased lover and the hero of the film, kept safely with him and through which he fell in love with Sarah. The photograph was given to him in the future by John Connor, the leader of the resistance, and the son that he had himself fathered in the past. One could, as Sarah Connor said, 'go crazy thinking about it'. However, perhaps it is better just to sit back and enjoy the ride.

The middle of the series of three films, the one on which this chapter will concentrate, offers, through a voice-over spoken by Sarah Connor at the start of the film, this explanation of what happened in the first film:

> 3 billion human lives ended on August 29th, 1997. The survivors of the nuclear fire called the war Judgment Day. They lived only to face a new nightmare, the war against the Machines ... Skynet, the computer which controlled the machines, sent two terminators back through time. Their mission: to destroy the leader of the human Resistance ... John Connor. My son. The first terminator was programmed to strike at me, in the year 1984 ... before John was born. It failed. The second was set to strike at John himself, when he was still a child. As before, the Resistance was able to send a lone warrior. A protector for John. It was just a question of which one of them would reach him first ...

It was something of a shock for Sarah Connor, John's mother, when she first received a message from an other-worldly visitor, who said that she would bear a son destined to become the saviour of the world. In a similar New Testament account, such a visitor was asked, 'How can this happen, since I am a virgin?' (Luke 1:34), but this is not a question that seems to occur to the unmarried Sarah. She is not Mary, although we might remember that it was a Sarah who was the mother of a miraculous child in the Old Testament. The first film ends with the Terminator having failed in its task, Sarah accepting her fate, and her child, the potential saviour of the future of humankind having been conceived.

The second film starts with John Connor as a teenager and Sarah having been committed to a psychiatric hospital on account of her 'delusions' that a cyborg from the future had tried to kill her and that she must warn the world that unless it changes its ways 3 billion people will be wiped out by war. This was society's rational response to a woman who had claimed that she had given birth to a son who would grow up to be the saviour of humankind, having been fathered by someone from outside our world. Someone in Sarah's position might deal with such an experience in one of two ways. In the New Testament we are told that Mary kept all these things to herself and pondered them in her heart and that later on she sided with those who believed Jesus to be mad. Sarah Connor's reaction could almost be compared to that of an Old Testament prophet, or of John the Baptist: she speaks and is locked up by those who seek to have her message silenced.

But the machines have not given up trying to stop John Connor growing up and they send another Terminator – a T-1000 – back in time. In the first film, the human resistance sent back a man, but to thwart the new improved cyborg they have reprogrammed the original model of cyborg, which therefore, rather confusingly, looks like a slightly older version of the Terminator in the first film. So in the first film Arnold Schwarzenegger, who plays the Terminator, is the villain, whereas in the second film he has changed sides, is now a good cyborg and is the Terminator who is sent to protect John Connor. He is the good cyborg who, if he were a living being, would lay down his life for John Connor. It is the good cyborg's task to get to John Connor before the T-1000, the bad cyborg, does. This bad cyborg comes only to kill and destroy. In the nick of time, the redeemer Terminator gets to John and they then look to rescue his mother, Sarah, from the psychiatric hospital in which she has been detained.

The T-1000, disguised as a police officer, enters the hospital to search for Sarah Connor. John and the Terminator arrive not far behind and they break in to rescue Sarah, who has chosen this moment to attempt her own escape having overpowered an orderly and stolen his keys. The hospital's security orderlies, the T-1000, John Connor and the Terminator are all trying to find Sarah Connor, who is now on the loose. Who will reach her first?

The answer is that they all come upon Sarah almost simultaneously. Sarah runs down a corridor and, seeing a lift ahead, she believes that she is almost home free. The lift bell rings, the doors open, and the nightmares of the last seven years are a reality again as she sees the Terminator emerge. She knows him only to be the cyborg who had previously been sent back in time to prevent her son being born, and from whom she had escaped. Now he is here again and will surely succeed where before he had failed. But despite appearances to the contrary, this is not the same cyborg, and he has come as her redeemer. John Connor, her son comes next from the lift, but shielded by the bulky frame of the Terminator, Sarah does not see him, until she hears him cry out, 'Mom! Wait!' But Sarah is in no mood to wait and warns the approaching orderlies, 'Goddamnit, it's gonna kill us all!'

She is shouting, pleading, trying to get them to understand what is coming. They grab her thrashing arms and legs, without even looking at where she is pointing – back along the corridor. As the orderlies pin her to the floor, her doctor attempts to inject her with a tranquilizer. Sarah cranes her neck and she sees the silhouette of the Terminator coming up behind them. The Terminator reaches down and grabs an orderly with just one hand and hurls him against the far wall of the corridor. The other two orderlies react instantly, leaping on to the intruder. For a moment they appear to have overpowered the Terminator until they are simultaneously flicked off like flies. The doctor takes flight and Sarah looks up at the Terminator standing over her, clad head to toe in black leather, as her son squats next to her, asking 'Mom, are you okay?' Sarah looks from the Terminator to John and back to Terminator. Is this a nightmare? Or has she finally gone truly mad?

The Terminator politely reaches his hand down to her, offering to help her up: the last thing she ever expected to see. As he does so, the Terminator says to her, 'Come with me if you want to live.' We may recall the comment of Jesus about himself, that 'they will follow him because they know his voice' (John 10:4). In a daze, Sarah takes the huge hand in her shaking fingers, perhaps remembering that the very line that the Terminator uses here is the same as that which Kyle Reese uses in the first film when, in the nick of time, he rescues Sarah Connor from that film's murderous Terminator. For those watching *Terminator 2* for the first time, having seen the original film, there will be a flash of recognition, as well as one of surprise, as the villain of the first film becomes the hero of the second, and as it becomes his turn to speak the redeemer's line, 'Come with me if you want to live.' It was this line that first attracted me to the possibility that this film had something to say about our faith, for it echoes the very heart of the message of Jesus to those who first became his disciples. Can we not hear, through the commandment of the Terminator, resonances of other promises such as 'come to me, all who are weary, whose load is heavy, and I will give you rest' (Matt. 11:28), and 'I have come that they may have life, and may have it in all its fullness' (John 10:10)?

Fatherhood

Fatherhood is a much less common theme in science fiction than either redemption or salvation, but it is one that is important in *Terminator 2*. The cyborg sent back to protect John Connor from the murderous attentions of the T-1000 is programmed to care for the future saviour of the world. The cyborg is completely dedicated to this end and as such is the father that John Connor has never had. Since before John's birth, Sarah Connor had lived with the uncertainty of her situation – a young woman expecting a Saviour child with no husband, not even a confused and reluctant one such as Joseph. Yet in the Terminator, Sarah has found someone who can be the father she has always wanted for her son. Having escaped from the psychiatric hospital, Sarah and John Connor and their cyborg protector head out of Los Angeles to the semi-desert of Hispanic southern California where they join up with a small militia force at an arms dump. Here Sarah finally relaxes and as she watches her son playing the fool with the cyborg, she muses:

> Watching John with the machine, it was suddenly so clear. The Terminator would never stop, it would never leave him ... it would always be there. And it would never hurt him, never shout at him or get drunk and hit him, or say it couldn't spend time with him because it was too busy. And it would die to protect him. Of all the would-be fathers who came and went over the years, this thing, this machine, was the only one who measured up. In an insane world, it was the sanest choice.

It is sometimes in fiction far-removed from reality that we see what is truly real. We can see something of what it means to be human in the story of Pinocchio, or in its modern science fiction equivalent, *Artificial Intelligence: A.I.*,[12] the story of a robot child that wanted to become human. Perhaps there is something similar here in a rather more explicit fashion in Sarah Connor's thoughts on the nature of fatherhood. When we think of divine fatherhood we are in something of a chicken and egg situation: do our ideas about the fatherhood of God come from our understanding of human fatherhood, or is how we behave as human parents derived from our understanding of divine fatherhood?

It is likely that our understanding of God as Father is influenced by the relationship that we have or have had with our own father. Some people will never have known their father and so will perhaps have created an idealized picture of what a father *should* be. Is Sarah's picture just a human idealization? If we change the pronouns from neuter to masculine, Sarah Connor's soliloquy would sound like this: 'He would never stop, he would never leave him … he would always be there. He would never hurt him, never shout at him or get drunk and hit him, or say he couldn't spend time with him because he was too busy. And he would die to protect him.' In an unlikely setting, there emerges here a shadowy picture of the God who is revealed to us through Jesus Christ – always, eternally there. Having promised always to be with us,[13] he is eternally faithful to the people he has made; and he would die to save them.[14]

When Sarah Connor expresses her thoughts on fatherhood, they are informed by the human fathers she has known. We are not told whether the fathers with whom she compared the Terminator – the men who left, who hurt, who shouted, got drunk and could find no time to spend with their children – were men with whom she had relationships while bringing up her son, or whether the cyborg was being compared with her own father. Whatever was the source of these comparisons it is illustrative that the fatherhood of God is rarely considered in a vacuum. People speaking of God as father do so from their own experience, but also from the experience of their culture. One danger of speaking of God as father is to consider one's individual and cultural experience as the norm, yet it is possible also that the image of the true Father has been given to us rather than merely projected out of our experience, and that there is a witness to this even in this piece of popular culture.

Similarly, while fatherhood is not a common theme in science fiction films it does occur elsewhere. Denzel Washington plays the eponymous *John Q*[15], a father who takes the law into his own hands when his son needs life-saving medical care that goes beyond the cover of his health insurance. John Q demonstrates fatherhood by protecting his son with no regard for himself. Jason Robards, Steve Martin, Rick Moranis, Tom Hulce and Keanu Reeves all play fathers in *Parenthood*[16], a comedy which offers insights into the complexities of fatherhood and family life in general.

Fate

One of the joys of the science fiction sub-genre of time travel is that it claims to be logical. Generally, this claim has holes in it and the *Terminator* series has pretty big holes. But one interesting minor theme is how a message has been transmitted. The message was given by the adult John Connor some time in the future to his trusty lieutenant to take back into the past. The lieutenant gave the message to Sarah Connor, who taught it to her son who when he grew up gave it to his trusty lieutenant who went back in time ... and so it goes on. The important point is really the content of the message: 'The future is not set. There is no fate but what we make for ourselves.'

Fate can be a difficult subject for Christians. A belief in fate means that whatever we do or say, the outcome is out of *our* hands. Christians tend to deny a belief in fate, and yet may come close to it in thinking that the outcome is out of our hands, since it is in God's. This is expressed in the words of a worship song that was popular a few years ago:

> I know who holds the future and He'll guide me with His hand,
> with God things don't just happen, ev'rything by Him is planned[17]

But is this what really happens? Is our life mapped out for us before ever we were born? Is the universe like some great game of chess in which the moves have already been weighed and measured ?

The Old Testament story of Joseph and his brothers throws up some interesting thoughts with regard to the extent to which God's plan incorporates human agency. Joseph became Pharaoh's chancellor, having been sold into slavery by his brothers and taken to Egypt by Midianite traders. Joseph's story was a dramatic rollercoaster ride which ended with his being in charge of the nation's grain store in a time of great famine in that part of the world. Joseph's father and brothers came down to Egypt to seek food and when Joseph eventually revealed his identity to them they were given cattle and land on which to settle. In making himself known to his brothers, Joseph tells them that what has happened is God's doing: 'It is not you that sent me here, but God' (Gen. 45:8). In saying this he seemed to absolve them of responsibility for his fate. However, despite Joseph's absolution of his brothers, the story itself makes much of the cost to all parties of what they did to Joseph: Jacob's inconsolable grief, Joseph's wretched imprisonment as well as the brothers' own sense of guilt. This is a good example of the tension that can seem to exist between divine sovereignty and human responsibility.

Wrestling with the idea of how the message about fate first came into being in the *Terminator* series is, in many ways, more straightforward than trying to understand how *our* choice and *God's* choice fit together, and also how they fit into the time-bound human realm as well as in the eternal world which God inhabits. It is hard for us to understand how the eternal and temporal worlds co-exist, although William Blake brought these two worlds together in his poem *Auguries of Innocence*[18]:

> To see a world in a grain of sand,
> and a heaven in a wild flower,
> hold infinity in the palm of your hand
> and eternity in an hour.

Perhaps, however, the mind-boggling nature of the clash of realms of time in *Terminator 2* provides us with a window through which we can see human existence as held by God, but where fate does not control us. The key sentence is: 'There is no fate, but what we make for ourselves.' God does hold the future in God's own hands, in that God holds *all* things together, but it is a future that is changeable. It is a future with countless possibilities and potentials and God allows us to share the responsibility for shaping the future. God *has* a plan – the redemption of the world, for which purpose the Son died – and the Spirit guides and prompts us. Yet choices remain ours, and whatever our choice, God has promised to be with us and to work with us. This is perhaps the point of the story of Joseph, for in another account of Joseph's meeting with his brothers he tells them: 'Even though you intended to do harm to me, God intended it for good, in order to preserve a numerous people, as he is doing today' (Gen. 50:20).

God is able to work with our lives wherever our choices may take us. If this is the case for individuals, could it also be true for communities of God's people and, taking this to its logical conclusion, the whole of God's creation? If the future is not fixed, then nor is the destiny of creation, the fulfilment of all things that was God's purpose in the work of Christ. God cannot be thwarted in bringing about a re-creation of the cosmos, but the nature of that fulfilment could be contingent on creation itself.

Faith

> *Terminator 2* is a nice film in which everybody is saved, including Jesus, as, in a last-minute alteration to the story, the father lays down his life so that the son doesn't have to suffer after all.[19]

So Sean French draws an ironic contrast, as well as parallel, with the Christian story. *Terminator 2* ends with the good cyborg having destroyed the bad cyborg and John and Sarah Connor, the future resistance leader and his mother, safe and sound. There is just the little matter of making sure that no bits of future technology are left lying around for anyone to use as spare parts to build more bad cyborgs. This involves throwing them into molten metal in the steel works where the final chase happened to end up. Then the Terminator says that there is one more computer chip to be destroyed, the one inside him. Until now he has failed to understand the nature of human emotion, the one thing he, as a machine, cannot emulate. But as the teenager realizes the implications – that his friend and father-figure must die in order to secure the future of humankind – tears well up in his eyes. For the first time, the machine with the appearance of humanity understands something of human emotions and he says to John, 'I know now why you cry. But it is something I can never do.' With that the Terminator is lowered into oblivion.

The idea of sacrifice is older than the time of Jesus, but in the Christian story the death of God's Son draws much of its meaning from Old Testament instances of sacrifice, such as the account of the spilling of the blood of the Passover lambs, slain to liberate God's people from Egypt. We are helped to understand the death of God's Son through these other sacrifices, but the one reconciling act of God is the sacrifice to which the others point, and Christ hangs on the cross above these just as he hangs above the world in Salvador Dali's famous painting of St John of the Cross. With that said, our generation is one for whom the Passover story is unknown, and Old Testament sacrifice is arcane religious mumbo-jumbo; perhaps then this film ends in a way which prepares minds of today to understand the Christian story of how one death has saved the world.

Yet there is a significant difference: the crucial final statement by the Terminator that he can never cry. He is not and can never be human. The need for the Terminator to be sacrificed is because he is *not* human – he is a potentially dangerous machine. But the need of humanity was that God should become human – that God knew what it meant to cry – and in God's human death, having taken our sin to the grave, God saved the world.

This popular film offers a kind of proving-ground, to test out certain views of what a saviour must be like. The Terminator appears to be human, but is in reality a machine. This is a version of a view that some early Christians held about Jesus – that he appeared to be human, but was really a skin-covered God. He could no more know the pain of loss than could the Terminator. But the film, in its contrast between a machine and a person, makes us think about what salvation through a person would be like. Christians came to affirm that Jesus, in a way that is a mystery, was both 'fully man and fully God', as without either his humanity or his divinity, God could not have done what God has done. This was one of the important issues debated by fourth century theologians. One of these was Gregory of Nazianzus, sometimes known as Gregory the Theologian. In defence of Christ having a human body and human soul as well as being divine he wrote, 'That which is not taken is not healed, but whatever is united to God is saved.'[20] Here he was building on the thought of a much earlier writer, in the New Testament:

Since, then, we have a great high priest who has passed through the heavens, Jesus, the Son of God, let us hold fast to our confession. For we do not have a high priest who is unable to sympathize with our weaknesses, but we have one who in every respect has been tested as we are, yet without sin (Hebrews 4:14-15)

God has always been forgiving towards us, but in Christ, a human person, God gave God's self to experience the depths of human life. God then offers forgiveness not as a ruler from on high, who simply gives a royal pardon, but as one who has endured the full weight of sin in solidarity with us, experiencing life as we do.

Conclusion

The Terminator series is a story designed for entertainment. Sean French ensures that we don't get too serious about looking for meanings: 'As for the film's religious allegory, it should be remembered that John Connor shares his initials with James Cameron [director of the Terminator series] as well as Jesus Christ.'[21] Casting a cyborg like the Terminator as a redeemer is not particularly surprising, in that the writers of popular literature and films tend to plunder stories about salvation and a redeemer for their ideas. Biblical parallels can be found in the most unlikely places if the searcher has sufficient ingenuity, imagination and desire to find them. But for all that, even in what is frequently called a post-Christian age, there is a deep uncertainty within women and men which often leads to searching for a saviour and place of belonging. *Terminator 2* just might help some people 'join the dots' and make the right connections.

Notes

[1] In New Road Baptist Church, Oxford, on 5th, 12th and 19th October 2003.

[2] *The Bridges of Madison County* and *Sophie's Choice.*

[3] *Field of Dreams* and *The Natural.*

[4] The film that was featured each Sunday had been extensively previewed in a midweek meeting the previous Thursday. This meant that there was an opportunity for some response before clips of the film were shown on Sunday, and the reviews for *Terminator 2* were mixed! Although the midweek clips had not

included blasphemy and sexual swearwords, they did include violence, which some found disturbing. However, it was possible, even with *Terminator 2*, to show a clip in Sunday worship that was neither violent nor used bad language, but still had something useful to contribute to the discussion.

[5] *Terminator* (1984), *Terminator 2: Judgement Day* (1991), *Terminator 3: Rise of the Machines* (2003): all were directed and co-written by James Cameron.

[6] Jerry Siegel and Joe Shuster ranked at 100 in Michael Shapiro, *The Jewish 100 : A Ranking of the Most Influential Jews of All Time* (New York: Citadel Press, 1994).

[7] See, for example, a 1968 essay by Pauline Kael, the American critic, written in support of popular cinema. 'There is so much talk now about the art of the film that we may be in danger of forgetting that most of the movies we enjoy are not works of art. … The romance of movies is not just in those stories and those people on the screen but in the adolescent dream of meeting others who feel as you do about what you've seen. You do meet them, of course, and you know each other at once because you talk less about good movies than about what you love in bad movies.' Pauline Kael 'Trash, Art and the Movies' reprinted in *Going Steady: Film writings 1968-69* quoted in Sean French, *The Terminator*, (London: British Film Institute, 1996) p. 10.

[8] The Terminator finds all the Sarah Connors who are listed in the telephone directory, and sets out to kill them, one by one.

[9] French, *Terminator*, p. 49.

[10] French, *Terminator*, p. 28.

[11] *Back to the Future* (Director: Robert Zemeckis, 1985).

[12] *Artificial Intelligence: A. I.* (Director: Steven Spielberg, 2001).

[13] Isaiah 7:14, Matthew 28:20.

[14] John 10:11.

[15] *John Q* (Director: Nick Cassavetes, 2002)

[16] *Parenthood* (Director: Ron Howard, 1989)

[17] Words and Music by Alfred B. Smith and Eugene Clarke © Universal Songs Bv/Cherry Pie Music UK.

[18] Included in D. H. S. Nicholson and A. H. E. Lee (eds.), *The Oxford Book of English Mystical Verse* (Oxford: The Clarendon Press, 1917).

[19] French, *Terminator* p. 53.

[20] See Aloys Grillmeier S.J, *Christ in Christian Tradition* (London: Mowbray, 1965), p. 210.

[21] French, *Terminator*, p. 54.

12
All-Consuming Holiday Snaps: *Open Water*

Tim Bradshaw

The story: alone in the universe

Chris Kentris' film *Open Water*, released in the UK in 2004, was quickly dubbed 'Jaws meets Blair Witch' because it told a story of a couple faced with shark attack and was filmed by close-up digital camera, giving it a directness and immediacy. It succeeded in producing terror in a gradual, understated and realistic way, deliberately lacking in special effects in its technical ordinariness. In fact this use of digital camera filming cohered with the subject matter of the story, nothing particularly out of the ordinary.

Based on a true story, a couple of Californian 'twenty-somethings', both evidently well paid professionals in hectic demanding jobs, are grabbing a vacation at short notice. Susan is in the film industry, and when we first see her she is on two mobile phones, dealing with a production and also talking to her husband Daniel. She brings her laptop, despite his questioning of the decision. He is packing their holiday bags into the car, and also on a mobile to a friend about installing a new boiler on his return. The camera lingering on a shiny brass door handle and lock on their front door, they drive off. The film regularly puts up the date and time in the corner of the screen. Next we see them arriving in Kingston Jamaica, spending a day shopping, and in their rather unsatisfactory hotel room where the air conditioning is broken. Daniel sits on the bed, interestingly using her laptop, checking his e mails, and she declines to check hers. Their first night portrays a very unusual, explicit 'non-sex scene', our naked young heroine being too tired but on the other hand offering just to talk – he then opting to go to sleep, himself suddenly too tired. The lights go out. Their unsatisfactory hotel room is lit up suddenly again at 3 am with Daniel absurdly trying to swat a mosquito – we have all been there! Our young are perhaps trying too hard to relax after their stressful jobs, and yet life throws up silly problems. Next the alarm clock gets them up to catch their scuba diving boat.

They join a party of twenty people on a boat going out to sea some eighteen miles into the ocean. The cheerful Jamaican in charge of the trip gives instructions in jocular mode. Don't worry about sharks, they are not interested in humans. If any do get into trouble give the 'international distress signal' – that is, shout and wave frantically. A heavily muscled overbearing American fidgets and irritates the others during the jolly instruction session; he has forgotten his mask and so cannot dive. All the others jump into the water off the safety of the platform; they have half an hour and must swim in pairs for safety. The filming of the spectacular fish as Susan and Daniel swim with them is superb. The sun is shining, the water is piercingly blue and hospitable. A heavenly holiday episode unfolds. The screen fills with almost abstract sea-patterns along with relaxing music, and we are in a reverie of happiness.

Meanwhile, on the surface an inexperienced pair swim back to the platform boat early, they are counted back in with two strokes of a pen. The muscular American sees his chance and bossily borrows a mask from them, then he browbeats one of the reluctant pair to be his partner and they dive in, 'God bless you, you have a place in heaven' he calls to the lender of the mask. He becomes the numerical reason for the unfolding counting error, itself the cause of the horror later in the film. It is increasingly obvious that the crewman responsible for counting the divers back on board is now going to be deceived. He marks down the big American and his reluctant partner as back when they finish their dive and return, instead of Susan and Daniel who are taking their half hour to the very limit and have remained aloof from the other divers. Apparently all the divers are back on board. The boat departs. Susan and Daniel surface to find open water and their boat gone.

Floating in their high quality scuba wet suits, air cylinders buoying them up, equipped with all the best kit, bobbing in the water, they are baffled at the lack of their boat. Daniel looks down to check from a piece of coral he noted earlier that they are indeed in the right place. They see other boats not too far off. Susan wants to swim to them, but Daniel tells her not to bother as their boat must surely realize the mistake and return; after all their bags are on board. Also the other craft visible may be further away than they seem. Better to wait. Daniel is not too worried. They do not swim after the other boats. A small aircraft flies overhead, and they do not wave to it. Susan then looks down to the sea bed and sees no coral – they are drifting in a current, afloat and helpless. The pair get less confident as time passes, time regularly notified to the viewers. The sun remains high, and some vessels do hove into distant view, they swim, wave their arms and shout, using that 'international distress signal', to no avail. Back on shore the other divers disembark, but noone notices the remaining two string bags left under the seats of our unhappy couple. Back in open water, Susan says she is getting cold and Daniel jokes as he urinates in the water. The sea pales into a grey colour – and they are startled by the flick of a fin tip showing in the water close to them. Again he jokes, 'you were patting them not long ago' – 'they were catfish', she replies. He gets his knife out, and she is shocked at this sign that he is seriously worried despite his words.

The water grows dark and threatening, changed suddenly from its blue holiday mood. Water laps at the camera lens. The couple seem utterly vulnerable in the vastness of the ocean. A feeling of duration is brilliantly achieved in a short film, the couple shot as objects drifting, and we are cut in to conversations from time to time. They are isolated, alone, truly *scuba* divers in the sense of 'self-contained units of breathing apparatus', afloat in a dirty greyish brown. Susan is getting cold, and indeed the body loses heat fast even in warm tropical water. She is thirsty and cannot drink the salt water. She complains of real hunger, 'I'm starving' – then she cries with pain and Daniel sees the stinging jellyfish; they swim away from it, the first of their injuries from sea creatures treating them as a source of food. She begins to weep, cracks fast appearing in her confidence. Daniel tries to rally her, citing *Dive Magazine* for the view that being abandoned in the ocean is more common than you think. Another boat appears, and goes. Hopes suggest themselves, only to disappear. All the while Daniel's bright yellow waterproof camera bobs on the surface attached to his arm.

'Stay close to me,' Susan entreats Daniel, 'what if they don't know we're missing?' Doubt spreads, but again Travis insists that they must realize the mistake, since their bags are on board. She is feeling ill, and she lets her divers' weights drop to the ocean floor. 'Lie back and sleep,

I've got you', he says. Time passes, the camera scans the ever darker seascape. Then she awakes, alone, terrified; she calls out and Daniel wakes; they swim together but they had drifted quite a way apart. 'Thank God – I'm so sorry' he says. She feels a tapping on her leg at the jellyfish bite; a little cleaner-fish has made a tiny opening in her rubber suit and a little cut. She is sick – 'let's swim out of this puke', he says. Sharks thrash the water very close to them. Fear builds and builds. Storm clouds gather overhead. The rack is turned slowly, the tension and horror grow and grow. Fins surface again.

Daniel now cracks, and rages at his situation, yelling out obscenities, sarcastically cursing the holiday that landed them as shark bait – 'we wanted a view of the ocean, boy did we get it!' She is quiet, and he responds 'Mad at me? Great vacation isn't it honey! You think its my fault?' She does indeed blame him for not staying in the group, for cutting their timing too fine, for refusing to swim to the boats they saw. He turns the tables: 'It was your job that caused us to take this holiday at short notice' …'You picked the date'. 'I wanted to go skiing', she retorts. Sharks swirl close to them prompting terror in them yet again. Seascapes of despair and menace play on the screen. The couple fade in and out of sleep as the water torture draws out so slowly, with nothing actually happening.

A huge tanker suddenly lies on their horizon; they wave and shout, it moves away, and it gets darker. Again they grow quiet, amid the periodic terror of the shark fin appearances. Ashore we see carnival and partying as evening draws on. Above the couple sea-birds circle. 'I love you', she says; 'I love you', he responds. He reassures her again, 'this is a story we're going to be telling for the rest of our lives'. They have a brief measure of relief; she finds a few sweets she has stowed on herself, they feel suddenly refreshed and happy – and then he is shaken violently, and drops his knife. He has been bitten by a shark; the water goes red; there is shock and pain. He yells in agony. She puts a small belt round the wound. He shudders, she keeps him focused. The sky goes red in the seascape shots, the sea goes red, the sun sets spectacularly.

Back ashore the parties are in full swing, dancing and clubbing to Jamaican rhythms. On the open water, 11.30 pm is the time; it is dark, thunder rumbles and lightning flashes on the horizon – no artificial lighting is used by the director. From this fearful seascape we cut to the couple; 'Thy kingdom come, thy will be done' we hear on his lips. Now she rallies him: 'It's good if it hurts, keep going'. Then she cries from her terror-filled heart, 'I love you, I love you, I love you!' in the blackness of the night, as below she knows the sharks swirl and blood is in the water. Weeping she implores him to hold on, 'don't leave me here'. Now we are the high pitch of pain and terror and it is primarily her terror. He is semiconscious; she feels his aorta for his pulse. Morning is arriving, the sharks thrash around. At the harbour a crew man spots their bags. The hotel is contacted, their room found empty. Boats are scrambled, helicopters and sea planes set out over the blue ocean.

Susan floats holding Daniel, now unconscious. She feels his pulse, he is dead. She is grey, drained of energy, beyond despair. After a while she kisses him and pushes him away to float off, face down in the sea. His corpse is pulled and jerked, and goes under. Will she make it? Will there be a happy ending … surely, surely. Sharks are shot swimming by her legs in numbers. She is past terror, past weeping, greyish brown to match the cruel sea. She removes her scuba air cylinders, putting off the remaining supports she has … and sinks below the waves.

The credits form the right hand side of the screen, while the left is taken up by a scene of a shark being cut up on shore. The fins are removed, presumably for soup. Slicing open the guts of this mass of muscle and teeth reveals a stomach sack, inside which is … the yellow waterproof camera. Holiday snaps indeed.

Exploring the story
1. The bleakness of life

Reviews of the film are divided in opinion, but most praise the understated terror and the growing menace of the constant, yet largely unseen, threat below, occasionally breaking surface and very occasionally thrashing fiercely. It is good story brilliantly shot, a day in the life of a very unfortunate couple. Psychologically the move from confidence and humour into abject fear and final despair beyond despair captures something of the human spirit in free fall from hope. The temporary props to keep spirits up each fall away. Susan ends up the stronger character, Daniel a know-all who fails to deliver, even failing to staying awake for his wife. His bad decisions at the critical early phase may have cost them their lives. For most of the film Daniel was the leader and guide, but he is revealed as a less substantial person than she as everything is stripped away from them.

Sheer bleakness marks the long horror of the deaths of Susan and Daniel, terrorized from below and above. This film could easily be interpreted as depicting, through this story, the bleakness of our modern life, apparently confident and in control, yet really afraid and vulnerable. A Sartrean hopelessness gradually takes hold and triumphs as Susan, numbed beyond despair, resigns herself to death, without even a whimper. And yet as this plays out, the musical score plays Jamaican hymns, 'Jesus Promised Me A Home Over There', and 'I Ain't Got Long'. These gospel songs alone point to anything beyond watery absurdity, suffering, isolation and death.

2. The nature of relationships

The film studies the relationship of this pair under the pressure of the elongated horror, and we see what we might expect: much mutual support and mutual need. They love each other, and as the crisis deepens they say so, in the darkness of sea and sky. They need each other desperately in the face of the dawning crisis. To be totally alone would be beyond endurance, as they realized when they drifted apart. Quite naturally they blame each other, although this tragedy really was the result of amazingly bad luck as well as complacency by human tourists of the great deep. Susan and Daniel are not heroes but very ordinary and quite decent people, themselves embodying the fault-lines of western culture.

Signs of something wrong were trailed through the early parts of the story; at every step there were glitches and things rushed, a haste to be 'on vacation' and away from it all. Early in the film we see images of a lighthouse in the dark, and a red sea. Nature chimes in with the events unfolding through the nightmarish experience. The story then probes the two individuals, exploring their relationship quite sympathetically in its realism; the relationship is not perfect but there is a core of love between them as well of some very natural complaining and mutual recrimination. This is the reverse of schmaltz, containing a good deal of credible and very human experience.

3. The relationship with nature

The couple are portrayed in several kinds of context. We have wealthy westerners buying an ocean view, and, as Daniel puts it later, 'boy did they get it'! A major theme here is surely that of taking for granted the power of nature as we seek to view it and get close to it for 'recreation'. Nature is beautiful but remains bigger than we are. However thick our wallets, she is indeed red in tooth and claw, thunder and lightning above and vicious below, in the medium that is not ours. All the hi-tech equipment at our disposal cannot guarantee our safety if we overreach our limits in the hunt for the ultimate beautiful scene, and for experience of something that is not our ordinary, albeit privileged western lifestyle. We are not divine, we are at the mercy of nature even as we seek to harness and exploit her.

Added to this is a kind of carelessness, even arrogance, in the way westerners assume sometimes that there are no limits. In the age of the mobile and internet it is easy to forget that we can be totally cut off and isolated, that we are vulnerable and need to stay together, rather than press towards being 'self-contained units' observing all manner of strange and wonderful contexts, as floating viewers. Once this couple jumped off the safety of their platform, they chose to stretch safety constraints to the limits, failing to budget for any mistakes or problems at all. A hubris and self-centredness contributed to their plight, an insistent egocentric obsession to extract every drop from the scuba trip.

The consumers on holiday were consumed, became 'shark bait'; as the very final shot – the end after the end – revealed, only the floating camera survived. Kentris signals this reversal in several ways besides Daniel's bellow of rage at paying good money for the privilege of becoming shark bait. When Susan first begins to feel cold and says she is very hungry, she is bitten by the jellyfish. Later when she finds some sweets and they enjoy a brief moment of respite eating them, Daniel is bitten in the leg by a shark. Kentris deploys subtle irony throughout his narrative. The story could easily be used as an illustration of the destiny of idolatry: we end up being consumed by our obsessions.

4. Our political world

Is there a wider horizon of meaning in the film, beyond that of the personalities, their relationship to each other, and to the world of nature as tourists? The Oxford poet Tom Paulin, in his contribution to BBC Newsnight Review,[1] found the film full of political symbolism about the place of the USA in the world at the moment. This great nation has jumped, with all manner of hi-tech equipment, into open water and is in danger of finding itself drifting in the water, while below the surface vicious forces of terror wait to attack. Paulin argues that this is the post-Iraq situation, as fanatical insurgents swirl around, impossible to fight off with conventional hi-tech armaments. The cry 'I love you, I love you, I love you!', uttered in deep distress as darkness fell, was one of those cries to loved ones from a hi-jacked aircraft on 9/11, credible evidence that Kentris weaves a scary political message into his film. The confident, wealthy young couple symbolize the plight of the USA drawn into Iraq, going it alone, without sufficiently keeping in touch with other nations, failing to appreciate the risks and how things could go so badly wrong. They are in alien territory and alien cultural environment, very much at risk.

The huge oil tanker suddenly appearing on the horizon resonates with this theme. It indicates the massive presence of oil. Paulin also thinks that Leviathan, the ship of state in Hobbes' political philosophy, is symbolized by the boat off which the couple jump into the water. It seems a plausible layer of meaning, a symbol of political distress symbolized by the over confident couple as they tread water in a current beyond their control, isolated, increasingly vulnerable to untameable hostile forces striking unpredictably and fatally. The 'international distress signal' is a joke made in the boatman's briefing to the scuba divers – the distress signal being to wave one's arms frantically for help. Paulin's political interpretation does have merit.

Once in their plight of abandonment, fear increases and hope gradually ebbs: it is likely that Susan and Daniel will indeed bleed to death and be devoured. The political symbolism could well be a warning that the USA faces a Vietnam in Iraq, or the same experience as the Soviet Union in Afghanistan – entering a very strange new world beyond control and full of hidden menace. Drifting in a current and with no response to its 'international distress signals', a nation can be helpless against the attacks of enemies who have them at their mercy, out of their natural habitat and with no 'plan B'.

Woven through all these areas of meaning, theologically we can hardly avoid the theme of alienation: from others, from nature, from hope. Like Adam and Eve scrabbling around naked and helpless in the dust, no longer relishing the lush and lovely Eden, Daniel and Susan find themselves, because of their hubris, deeply alienated and vulnerable, needing to be saved. Notwithstanding the Christian hymns being sung in the background to the nightmare, salvation does not come, and we get a bleak ending.

The floating camera
Daniel's yellow waterproof camera floats on the surface throughout their ordeal, attached to him by a line, very deliberately put into our vision regularly by Kentris' camera work. This camera emerges, as the credits roll simultaneously, from a dead shark as it is butchered for human consumption. This end, after the official end, triggers the now thoroughly depressed viewer to think about the nature of this film and of all film. Obviously this film is deliberately 'low-budget', shot with a digital camera and with no special effects. Even the shark sequences were shot with real sharks in the water with the actors Blanchard Ryan and Daniel Travis. Kentris intends realism in this web-cam mode. Theme, mood and technique cohere brilliantly.

The viewer's attention seems to be drawn intentionally to the fact of the camera at work in this technique of filming. Water slaps against the camera lens held half above and half below the surface, as if against a scuba diver's mask worn by the viewer. Did Kentris deliberately devise the episode with that overbearing American and his borrowed mask, whose selfishness was ultimately the cause of the tragedy, as another strand in the symbolism of the film? The viewer identifies with the American as someone who is desperate for a mask through which to view the scene, and so is drawn into the project of the film itself. The divide between film-maker and the action of the film is subtly breached or made ambiguous and reflective. We are drawn into the story, and are apprised of the fact that we are watching through a lens. Somehow the maker of the film gets close to the action in the film, declaring his presence as the medium through which *we* watch the lengthening terror play out. We – film-maker and film-viewers – become joint voyeurs of this suffering.

The yellow camera invites us to ponder the place not only of the camera work but of our own place in relation to the 'action' of the film. In that yellow camera are the records of Susan and Daniel's subjective vision of the open water, that holiday vista soon to become a sea of peril and death; like a set of Russian dolls one inside another we see the film, and see in the film the recorder of our tragic subjects' vision of the apparently friendly deep. The cameras in the film, the lens through which we look against which water slaps regularly, and that floating yellow camera, raise the question of film and photography itself. It raises too the question of ourselves as onlookers. What is our context for viewing this film? Why are we watching at all? Indeed, what are we watching and how do we relate to the figures in the film?

On this intriguing issue of the place of the camera, and our place in relation to the camera, the philosopher Stanley Cavell has interesting observations to make.[2] Cavell defines this relationship in terms of presence and presentness. In a theatre the members of the audience are those to whom the *characters* are present, whilst *they* are not present to the characters. Similarly, the viewers of a photograph of an object or set of events see that object but are themselves invisible; they are absent from its world. So they are those to whom that *object* is present whilst *they* are not present to it. This might seem to lead to the view that our relationship to the world of the play and of the photograph are exactly the same, but Cavell brings in an important distinction, concerning space and time. The audience of a play cannot directly approach its characters, since they do not share a space with them; but they can share their time, and they can make the present moments of the characters present to them. By contrast, the viewers of a photograph share neither a space nor a time with the object in the photograph; they are not in its physical presence, and the moment at which the object is captured by the camera is not made present to them and cannot be. The world of a photograph does not exist *now*. In a theatre our absence from the world of the play is conventional, but in a cinema our absence is mechanically assured. We are present in the cinema not at something happening to which we should respond, but at something that has happened, which we must absorb, like a memory.[3]

For Cavell then, the film makes a world present to us, from which we are absent. It causes living human beings, objects and events in actual spaces to appear to us when they are in fact not there. It makes present a no-longer existent world. This, Cavell suggests, exemplifies the way modern scepticism understands our relation to the world itself: 'for the sceptic, what we take to be the world is but an image of it.' Film is a moving image of scepticism as a basic stance of modern western humanity.

We feel absent from our world, isolated in our subjectivity over against the world. By making a world present to us, photography - Cavell suggests – 'satisfies the human wish to escape subjectivity and metaphysical isolation – a wish for the power to reach this world'. At some point in the development of the modern world, our consciousness has become unhinged from the world around; this has interposed our subjectivity between us and our presentness to the world. Then all that is present to us is our own subjectivity, and individuality has become isolation. Photography, maintains Cavell, offers to overcome this lonely subjectivity 'by removing the human agent from the task of reproduction ... Photography maintains the presentness of the world by accepting our absence from it.'[4] Our subjectivity is screened out of the world; the film world makes us helplessly absent viewers.

Photography thus *seems* to achieve an overcoming of the problem of human subjectivity. The sceptic mistrusts the perspective that human consciousness gives us on the world, and so places weight on the subjectivity as a means of establishing our 'presentness' to reality, with the result that only our subjectivity seems to be present to us. Photography, on the other hand, seems to make a whole world present. But the world resulting from the film is one to which no human subjectivity can acknowledge a relation; we cannot be present *to* it; it is a world receding beyond any grasp. For Cavell this illustrates the plight of our western scepticism, as we are transformed into absent viewers of the world, rather than participants in it.

We might say that Cavell ponders on modern alienation from nature, from community, from one another. This echoes the classical biblical and theological view of human sin. Films and photographs, good in themselves, can provide a mere surrogate for genuine engagement; we view the pictures and scenes as if we are viewing 'the real thing' in a genuine participatory relationship. This particular film, *Open Water*, with its digital camera technique, makes us very aware of our looking on, of being voyeurs. Its theme too, of human beings alone in the vast ocean, underlines the sense of alienation.

Cavell, 'the philosopher of the ordinary', thinks we need to recover our sense of having a place in the world. In this way we will regain a perspective on our finite world as something which is in fact real, and in which we share. In particular, sceptical questions conveniently forget the sceptic's own location and connection in the world as a questioning observer; we are already engaged in patterns of life vital to being human. Is Kentris' yellow floating camera not an apt image of this floating subjectivity, attached yet disconnected from us, while transcribing reality for later viewers?

The yellow camera contains the photographs that Susan and Daniel have shot in the water, their last will and testament of scuba diving fun, and yet it reaches over the boundary to us, the viewers, as it emerges from the shark's belly – as the credits roll after the film 'ends'. The camera becomes a theme itself, recalling the digital camera used by the filmmaker, of which we are made so aware as it captures the long ordeal of our two subjects in the water. We the viewers become voyeurs of that water torture through the key-hole, or through the scuba mask, of the film maker's equivalent of the brownie box camera. What is our place in the world as viewers of this appalling story, with all its possible symbolic triggers? This is the question left with us as we get up and walk out of the cinema.

Notes

[1] Newsnight Review, BBC2, 13 September 2004.

[2] For my understanding of Cavell I am wholly dependent on the excellent work of Stephen Mulhall, *Stanley Cavell: Philosophy's Recounting of the Ordinary* (Oxford: Clarendon Press, 1994).

[3] Mulhall, *Stanley Cavell*, p. 228.

[4] Mulhall, *Stanley Cavell*, p. 228.

13
Finding God in the Holocaust:
Schindler's List
John Weaver

Heroes in the Holocaust?

At the end of May 2003 I visited the Baptist Theological Seminary in Warsaw (Radosc), and was taken to the historic city of Krakow and the nearby town of Auschwitz. While Krakow is a beautiful European city, where much of the historical splendour is preserved, nothing can prepare the visitor for the atmosphere created by the Auschwitz concentration camp. Entering the wrought iron gates with its tragically ironic inscription, *Arbeit Macht Frei* ('Work liberates'), and seeing the rows of neat two-storey accommodation blocks and high barbed wire fences, is enough to send shivers up and down the spine of any visitor. It looks so clean and tidy, and even with crowds of visitors seems so quiet and peaceful. There is a silence in which you can almost hear the cries of a previous generation who 'lived' and died here.

The accommodation blocks have been turned into a museum, with rooms displaying various artifacts: one full of bags and suitcases of all shapes and sizes, another full of artificial limbs, another of spectacles, another of shoes, and many others containing different items of clothing and personal possessions of those who were for a short time prisoners in this place. The enormity of the horror that took place begins to dawn even before one visits the 'shower blocks' and ovens. As a Christian you find a question nagging at your spirit: 'Where was God in all this? Where was God in the holocaust?'

Between two of the accommodation blocks is a yard with high brick walls. This is the execution yard, where special prisoners were shot by firing squad. In block 13, the block on the right hand side, there are basement cells, where prisoners awaiting execution were held. Some of these cells, today, have plaques to remember former prisoners, and one is dedicated to Maximilian Kolbe, a Polish Franciscan priest who gave his life for another at Auschwitz.

Maximilian Kolbe is remembered because of his sacrificial act. One day at the end of July or beginning of August 1941 the prisoners were lined up for selection; some would die and some would live. Maximilian voluntarily took the place of a Jewish prisoner, Franciszek Gajowniczek, and was led off to the cells, to be tortured or starved to death, to be shot, or to receive a lethal injection of carbolic acid. After two weeks, an injection was the means by which he was killed. In her book *Candles in the Dark* Mary Craig writes,

> How could a man as morally purblind as Fritzsch [deputy commandant] have understood that he had just witnessed a classic victory of good over evil, a definite routing of the ideology of hate? For in Maximilian's free and loving choice to undergo a horrible death for the sake of a total stranger, love had decisively conquered.[1]

In October 1982, Father Maximilian Kolbe was canonized as a martyr-saint by his fellow Pole, Pope John Paul II. The Pope described St Maximilian as 'our countryman in whom contemporary man may discover a wonderful synthesis of the sufferings and hopes of our age.'[2] When we search for signs of God in the Holocaust, Maximilian Kolbe is one, and Oskar Schindler – though very different – is another.

Oskar Schindler was born on 28th April 1908 in Zwittau, an industrial city in Moravia. After the first world-war Moravia was annexed to the newly formed Czechoslovakia. Through the 1920s Schindler worked as a salesman for his father's farm-machinery factory. When the factory closed in 1935, Schindler joined the pro-Nazi party in Czechoslovakia and in 1938 joined German military intelligence, the *Abwehr*. His involvement with military intelligence excused him from military service. Schindler was a hard drinking gambler, who, although married to Emilie at nineteen, was never without a mistress.

When the Czechoslovakian government ceded the Sudetenland to Germany in 1938, many Jews and Czechs fled to Poland. Before the second world-war three and a half million Jews lived in Poland, which was a relatively safe haven for European Jews. Some 50-60,000 lived in Krakow, where they made up about twenty-five percent of the population. On 1st September 1939 German troops invaded Poland and in October,

Hans Frank, Hitler's lawyer, was designated Reichsführer of Nazi-occupied Poland. From this time on the removal, brutal persecution, imprisonment and murder of Jews began.[3] Jewish property and businesses were either destroyed or appropriated by the Germans and sold to Nazi 'investors', one of whom was Schindler.

Oskar Schindler arrived in Poland shortly after the German invasion. He immediately became involved in the black market and the underworld. His influence with the local Gestapo helped him to acquire and set up an enamelware factory in January 1940 with cheap Jewish labour.[4] When Hans Frank ordered the removal of all but 'work essential' Jews from Krakow in August 1940, Schindler accepted 150 Jews as employees at his factory. Schindler almost exclusively employed Jewish labour throughout the next three years.

Schindler certainly made money, but it is recorded that everyone in his factory was fed, noone was beaten, and noone was killed. 'It became an oasis of humanity in a desert of moral torpor,'[5] although Schindler, himself, continued to live a less than moral life. In 1944 the enamelware factory was closed and the prisoners sent to Plaszow. Schindler established a new factory at Brunnlitz in Czechoslovakia and prepared a list of those workers who would be essential to its operation. Schindler made his money, but in the end he spent it all on preserving the lives of some 1300 Jewish men and women. On 8th May 1945 the *Schindlerjuden* (Schindler's Jews) gave Schindler a gold ring. The gold was extracted from the bridge in a prisoner's mouth, and is engraved with the inscription, 'He who saves a single life saves the entire world.'[6]

After the war Schindler left Germany, in 1949, to set up a nutria factory in Argentina, but in 1957 the nutria farm failed and he became bankrupt. He returned to Germany in 1958 without his wife or mistress and, with the help of money from Jews he had helped, established a cement factory. This also failed and closed in 1961 leaving Schindler bankrupt for a second time. On 28th April 1962 the Jewish government awarded Schindler the honour of 'Righteous Gentile.' He died on 9th October 1974 in Frankfurt, and his body was buried in the Latin cemetery on Mount Zion in Jerusalem.[7]

Depicting the Holocaust

Schindler's List is one of the films that has most clearly presented the nature of the Holocaust in recent years, and has done so to critical acclaim.[8] It is not fantasy but fact; not colour but black and white; not special effects but grim reality; not entertainment but the dark side of fallen humanity. This is the Holocaust told through the story of Oskar Schindler. The film is adapted from the Booker Prize-winning novel *Schindler's Ark,* written by Thomas Keneally.[9]

Oskar Schindler (Liam Neeson) enters Krakow, Poland during the invasion of 1939, with the single aim of making money. He wines and dines and bribes the officers leading the German army of occupation so that they will support his business schemes. The Jews of Krakow are first herded into the ghetto and then into the Plaszow concentration camp, where they come under the control of the sadistic commandant, Amon Goeth (Ralph Fiennes). Schindler uses Jewish slave labour from the camp to work in his enamelware factory, which is run by a Jewish book-keeper/prisoner, Itzhak Stern (Ben Kingsley), who has helped raise Jewish money to buy the factory for Schindler. In return, in such difficult days, Schindler had promised 'payment in kind' rather than money. The factory runs smoothly, under the direction of Stern, who makes sure that Schindler remembers to bribe all the right German officials.

When Schindler's wife, Emilie, arrives, Schindler tells her that he has 350 workers in his factory. She asks, 'To make pots and pans?' 'No,' he replies, 'to make money for me!' She then comments sarcastically, 'Oskar Schindler, he did something extraordinary – he built a factory and made money.' Schindler replies, 'War is the difference between success and fail-ure.'

At the concentration camp Goeth takes delight in random killing of the Jews, in one scene taking pot shots from the balcony of his villa at breakfast. As members of the camp come under threat of death they are placed within the safety of the list of Schindler's employees, camp guards being bribed to effect their transfer. Eventually, in 1944, it is decided that all the Jews must be transferred to Auschwitz, and Schindler is told that he will have to use Polish employees in his factory. At this point Schindler decides that he will take the Jews, 'my children', to his home town to work in an armaments factory. To do this he pays a bribe for every worker and many more who are added to his list, over 1100 men, women and children. He uses all his money, risks his own future, even going to Auschwitz to rescue the women, whose train had been sent there by mistake. When liberation comes these Jews have survived. The film closes with the facts that underline what has been achieved. Before the war there were three and a half million Jews in Poland, but today there are only 4,000. Today, Schindler's Jews and their descendants number over 6,000.

The film is haunting and harrowing with a near-documentary style. There is the horror of the pile of teeth with gold fillings; the intense fear of the naked women in the Auschwitz wash room, wondering if gas or water will come through the shower heads; and the grim truth of falling 'snow' that is the ash of burning human bodies. There are no easy answers given in this film. The impulse for good or evil is not explained; Goeth is hanged, Schindler is free. What moves this German profiteer to a righteous bankruptcy is not explained. His life after the war is of no help either, with a failed marriage and a number of failed business enterprises. But the life of this man as told in this film raises important theological questions.

Three theological issues

A first question we might consider is one of the redemption of human life. Schindler, a Nazi Party member and nominal Catholic, gives up all his money, the making of which seems to have been his sole aim in life, to save the lives of Jews, a race despised by his party. When the camp at Plaszow is to be cleared and the prisoners sent to Auschwitz, Schindler bargains with Goeth to purchase the prisoners to be workers at his new factory in Czechoslovakia. Stern discovers that Schindler is buying each worker and says, 'This list is life.'

At the end of the film, as the war ends, Schindler grieves that he did not do enough. 'I could have got more out … If I had made more money … I didn't do enough … If I'd sold my car … If I'd sold my gold Nazi Party pin … two more people,' he sobs. Lola Orzech, one of the Schindler Jews said in an interview with the film magazine *Empire* (February 1994), that no one realized, at first, that Schindler paid for them with his own money ($2 million). Whether Schindler was good or bad was beside the point. Schindler wasn't a hero – just a human being. They were in short supply in Germany and Austria. What do we feel about a man who gives up all he has that others might live? What about the list of those who will have life - those who are Schindler's Jews? Does this help us to look at the Easter message with fresh eyes?

A second question is about goodness. Schindler is clearly not a man of high moral standards; he is unfaithful in his marriage, grasping in his desire to make money at any cost, and ready to pay bribes to get his own way, right or wrong. But it is his concern and humanity that leads to actions that we will describe as altogether good. The new factory in Czechoslovakia makes artillery shells. Stern tells Schindler that there is a rumour going around that Schindler has altered the calibrations on the machines so that the shells do not work. The conclusion is that for seven months of operation the factory has been 'a model of non-production'. As they learn of the end of the War in Europe, the soldiers guarding the factory have orders to kill the prisoners. Schindler tells the soldiers not to kill the prisoners but to return to their families as 'men not murderers.'

We are left with his closing words to the workers: 'You have thanked me. Thank yourselves. Thank Stern. I am a Nazi Party member, a profiteer, and a criminal. I must flee.' But his activities were recognized officially by the Jewish nation, who in 1958 invited him to plant a tree in the *Avenue of the Righteous* in Jerusalem. What is the source of goodness and what part might we suggest that God has played in the events recorded in this film? There may even be a hint of an answer to the question of where God was in the Holocaust.

A third question revolves around the nature of power. Goeth, the concentration camp commandant is clearly portrayed as an evil man, who takes delight in torture and killing. In one scene Schindler talks with Goeth about the nature of power, and asks him whether power comes as the ability to kill, or in the decision to forgive and let live. Goeth says to Schindler, 'You're not drunk. You are in control. Control is power.' Schindler replies, 'They [indicating the Jewish prisoners] fear us because we have the power to kill. But power is when we have the justification to kill, but don't.' Schindler stands on the side of life, whereas Goeth embodies death and derives sadistic pleasure from the use of force. Goeth tries to live his life in accordance with Schindler's example, but soon reverts to type, once again finding more pleasure in killing. His inhumanity provides a sharp contrast. Can we find echoes of 1 Corinthians 1:23-25 here? 'God's foolishness is wiser than human wisdom, and God's weakness is stronger than human power'.

Searching for God in the Holocaust

In April 1944 Goeth receives orders to evacuate the Plaszow camp to avoid the advancing Russian army. He must exhume and burn the bodies of over 10,000 Jews killed at the camp and in the massacre of Jews in the Krakow ghetto. The ash-flakes from the burning fall as snow. Later, at Auschwitz, when Schindler rescues his workers mistakenly sent there, the smoke billows from the crematorium and again the ash falls as snow. How can God be both good and almighty when there is such evil in the world?

Theodicy meaning 'justice of God' was a term coined by Gottfried von Leibniz (1646-1716) to refer to this very work of defending the idea of a just God in the face of what seems contrary evidence. Traditionally Christian theology has tried to hold together that God is almighty and all loving and that we, as human beings can express some measure of understanding of God's nature.[10] But one of these three aspects has always been lost or necessarily redefined. Nigel Wright in exploring the nature of evil and the character of God in his book *The Fair Face of Evil*,[11] recognizes the challenge of Auschwitz and addresses this central question: If God is so loving and powerful, why does he not prevent suffering or why does he allow suffering in the first place? Wright suggests that the horrors of history and of our current world context might lead us to ask whether God is either a loving Father who is impotent, or a cosmic sadist who lacks love.

In the light, or perhaps we should say 'darkness', of the violence and injustice revealed in events such as Auschwitz, Ronaldo Munoz likewise suggests that there are three possible philosophical positions: God wills or at least allows suffering; God is above all such things and is not concerned about them; or God is unable to prevent such things.[12] The first suggestion presents the picture of a punishing God. The second image is of a God who is indifferent to the sufferings of the world. It is this third alternative, that God cannot prevent injustice and violence, which Munoz insists takes us closer to the experience of the suffering peoples of the world. He believes that the two statements: 'God is almighty' and 'God cannot prevent suffering' are only contradictory if God is placed outside the world. But when we posit an immanent God, who in love is involved with the oppressed, through love, combating evil, then

> the contradiction and scandal are turned into mystery. Then it is no longer we who question God about evil and injustice, but God – voluntarily crucified in Jesus and the crucified of history – who questions and challenges us. Then it is no longer we who have to 'justify' God (theodicy), but the very God who has to justify us, accomplices that we are, through action or passivity, in the sin of the world that oppresses and slaughters the wretched of the earth.[13]

Munoz also alerts us to the fact that the theoretical expression of the theodicy question may not be the most helpful way of wrestling with such a fundamental aspect of human experience. There will always be the sense that any rational answer will be unsatisfactory as we face such a mystery. But if we were to ask fundamentally the same question, but from a personal and existential perspective, we might ask, 'Where was God in the Holocaust?' In his exploration of evil, Wright quotes from Eli Wiesel's book, *Night*, where the author speaks profoundly of losing his faith in God in the face of the horrors of Auschwitz. God stands as the accused. Then more specifically, seeing the slow death by hanging of a young boy in Auschwitz, Wiesel asks where God is, and hears the answer within himself, 'Here he is – He is hanging on this gallows.'[14]

This well-known phrase must be treated with some caution. It is used by Wiesel as an expression of despair and rejection of the God he had served and worshipped and was never intended to have the Christian interpretation that has, sometimes, been placed upon it.[15] But recognizing this, as Christians it is our understanding of the cross that will help us to locate God in the midst of evil and suffering. Jürgen Moltmann also acknowledges that no theological argument can justify the mountain of misery represented by Auschwitz, but recalls that the *Shema* of Israel and the Lord's Prayer were prayed in Auschwitz, indicating something of God's presence there.[16] So he argues that we can affirm that God is present in such extreme experiences as Auschwitz, present as the one who suffers. Paul Fiddes goes on from this to urge that the conviction that God suffers will also prevent the construction of any argument that God directly causes suffering, in any circumstances, although God may allow suffering. This is part of an understanding that God freely accepts self-limitation for the sake of the freedom given to creation,[17] and impinges upon our whole concept of God. For 'the question of theodicy is deeply bound up with the notion of the passibility (capability of feeling suffering) of God.'[18]

Similarly, Frances Young says that 'the effect of evil and suffering is paradoxical; its existence and power call in question belief in God, and yet a religion of redemption from evil, like Christianity, requires its existence.'[19] Young's solution is that:

> God took upon himself the consequences of evil and sin. God accepted the terrible situation, demonstrating that he takes responsibility for evil in his universe, that he recognises the seriousness of evil, its destructive effect, its opposition to his purposes; that it cannot be ignored, but must be challenged and removed; that it is costly to forgive; that he suffers because his universe is subject to evil and sin.[20]

In his book *Love's Endeavour, Love's Expense*, W. H. Vanstone offers a graphic portrayal of this, daring to take as a paradigm the tragedy at Aberfan in South Wales on 21st October 1966 when a coal tip slid down onto a school and caused the deaths of over 100 children. Here God's step of risk in creation led to a step of disaster. Science and technology enabled coal to be mined; human greed seen in the demand for profit led to the siting of spoil heaps where they were; and the result following freak weather conditions was the suffering of the innocent. But our faith, affirms Vanstone, is not in a creator who permits disaster from the top of the mountain, but rather in one who is at the foot of the mountain receiving the impact. His limitless love is evidenced in not abandoning people in their suffering but suffering with them.[21] With such a belief in the self-emptying of God, Christianity should have no hesitation in attributing to God that authenticity of love that it recognizes in Jesus Christ.[22] Limitless love is not incompatible with the existence of evil and suffering in the world, since this is the consequence of the freedom that is given by such loving creativity.

So, reforming the theodicy question from an existential perspective, these various theologians help us to respond to this pressing question which Wiesel asks, although by offering a different answer. We can locate God in Auschwitz, in the cells, showers and crematoria, suffering with those who suffer. Although this may not have been the experience of all those present in Auschwitz, from a Christian perspective this is the significance of the cross.

Our discussion so far has hinted at a number of deeper theological issues, two of which are particularly significant in relation to the film. One such issue is that of power, for we see the exercise of power graphically portrayed in contrasting ways. Similarly, in our attempt to offer a response to the concerns of theodicy we must necessarily consider our understanding of the power of God. We have already noted how Paul Fiddes combines an insistence on the suffering of God with an understanding of God's self-limitation. In his work *Past Event and Present Salvation*, he returns to this theme and asks again, 'Can there be any theology after Auschwitz?' No theology which speaks of the goodness of God in creation will entirely satisfy in these circumstances. But Fiddes says that we may

> *begin* a theodicy by affirming that God has passed over to his creation a radical freedom to be itself, and that he has limited himself in this way because he wants to make and enjoy fellowship with personalities who have, like himself, the ability to create. With their freedom to respond to God's purpose and to make their own contribution to his project, there also comes the risk that such personalities may slip away from the Good. Evil and suffering have thus emerged from creation as things strange to God, a disruption which he has not designed.[23]

Human beings have the freedom to make choices that go against God's purposes and which are damaging and destructive. This is the risk that God takes in giving free will to creation, and God must in some way suffer the sadness of such decisions. Keith Ward presents a similar argument, suggesting that God may not be able to prevent some evils, which arise as the 'shadow side' of the good things that a created universe makes possible. But then he questions whether our world contains too much evil to be explained in this way, and that 'the sheer amount and horror of suffering, at Auschwitz, or in Vietnam, or Leningrad or in the trenches of Flanders, might make the firmest believer waver at times.'[24] Ward appears to favour the view partly held by Augustine, and in recent times by theologians such as John Hick, that the worst kinds of suffering are the result of the free choice of human beings rejecting God and choosing self-centredness. To assert that God truly and radically shares our suffering asks questions about our understanding of God as the 'Almighty'. Schindler comments that 'power is when we have justification to kill, but don't.' Power gives life. To proclaim that God is all-powerful means that God is the one who gives life, and the more God gives life to others the more God limits God's self.

Following on from this, locating God in Auschwitz amongst those who suffer points us to a God, to use Vanstone's image, at the bottom of the pile rather than at the top. Fiddes maintains that the cross of Jesus 'assures us that God himself never directly inflicts suffering: a suffering God is to be counted among the victims and not the torturers.'[25] While suffering can sometimes enrich the character of the one who suffers and lead others to acts of compassion, 'confronted by an Auschwitz even these benefits fall short of convincing us that the risk of creating a free universe was justifiable.' Fiddes continues by suggesting that

> the affirmation that God himself shares the consequences of the risk he took is the most satisfactory theodicy we can achieve, and enables us to think of God and Auschwitz together, as long as we can speak of his transforming the effects of evil and suffering.[26]

This qualification draws us back to a second issue in the film, that of redemption, as Schindler attempts to bring new life and hope out of the midst of suffering and despair.

Redemption and transformation
Suffering is never nullified, but Schindler seeks some kind of transformation. The suffering of God and God's self-emptying/self-limitation are important elements in our discussion. But there can be a problem unless weakness is victorious over evil. Here we might remember Mary Craig's

comment about Maximilian Kolbe that in 'Maximilian's free and loving choice to undergo a horrible death for the sake of a total stranger, love had decisively conquered.'[27] Again we look to the cross, for in suffering with us, God suffers for us and brings redemption.

Jon Sobrino in attempting to explore the suffering of oppressed peoples in the Third World speaks of the general agreement among theologians about the reality of suffering, its negativity, the fact that it is unwanted by God, and that in one way or another it is the consequence of sin.[28] But Sobrino states that for liberation theology 'the major form of suffering in today's world is historical suffering – suffering unjustly inflicted on some by others.' He goes on to say that:

> Historical suffering is massive, affecting the majority of humanity, making it practically impossible for people to direct their own lives, causing a poverty that brings death slowly and violently. In the presence of such suffering, theology must understand itself as an intellectual exercise whose primary purpose is to eliminate this kind of suffering. Briefly stated, suffering in today's world means primarily the sufferings of people who are being crucified, and the purpose of theology is to take these people down from the cross.[29]

He believes that in a world of suffering it is the humanity of human beings and the faith of believers that is at stake, and along with this, the relevance and credibility of theology.[30] Sobrino tightly binds together theology and human suffering, the purpose being to find here some redemption. He concludes:

> The most truth-filled place for any Christian theology to carry out its task is always the suffering of our world, and in the crucified people of our world, theology finds, as part of the Christian paradox, its own salvation, its proper direction, and the courage to carry out its task.[31]

In searching for God in the Holocaust we have wanted to affirm that we find God amongst those who suffer, seeking to bring about transformation and redemption. But the film also makes us grapple with the person of Oskar Schindler himself, and as mentioned above, poses the question of the nature of goodness.

The mystery of goodness

In an interview, Steven Spielberg records going to Poland, where he spoke with the survivors, spending time with Jews who had returned to Poland, but failing to discover what led to the transformation of Schindler from businessman to saviour. 'None of the witnesses could tell me why Schindler did it, even though I asked everybody I met.' And they all said, 'It's not important why he did it, it's only important that he did.'[32]

Spielberg believes that there was no one particular moment when Schindler was transformed, although Schindler did try to suggest, after the war, that he was out to save Jews from the beginning. He was after all one of the richest factory owners in Krakow. Spielberg says:

> He took a lot of that money and he greased a lot of palms, he threw a lot of parties, and he made a lot of people very happy by offering them perishables – black market goods that were impossible to get other than through people like Oskar Schindler – and he ingratiated himself into the lives of very important, high-ranking SS colonels and officials. But he did this, in my opinion, like any good businessman would, for himself. And for those truckloads of money he had dreamt about all his life. He didn't necessarily do that for the Jews in the beginning.[33]

Did God work for God's own good through the activities and mixed motives of this one individual? In our search, can we find God in the activities and life of this man? We live in a world that constantly seeks answers to every problem faced by humankind. In areas of illness, suffering, failure, defeat, someone must be to blame. We are now part of a blame culture in which litigation is often the first thought. But we also like heroes, and was Schindler a hero?

At the beginning of the film, Schindler says to his Jewish accountant, Itzhak Stern, 'My father said there are three things that you need: a good doctor, a forgiving priest, and a clever accountant. I couldn't have done this [set up the Krakow factory] without you.' Thomas Keneally observed that Schindler 'negotiated the salvation of his 1,300 Jews by operating right at the heart of the system using all the tools of the devil – bribery, black marketeering and lies.'[34] However, of his wartime actions Schindler said: 'If you saw a dog going to be crushed under a car, wouldn't you help him?'[35] (Compare Matthew 12:11-12). Perhaps this is what he would have liked his attitude to have been all the time.

In the summer of 1942, it is recorded that Schindler witnessed a German raid into the Jewish ghetto. As he watched people packed into trains to be transported to certain death he was deeply moved. Later he reflected on this event: 'Beyond this day, no thinking person could fail to see what would happen. I was now resolved to do everything in my power to defeat the system.'[36] In trying to answer the inevitable question, why did he do it, one of the survivors is quoted as saying: 'I don't know what his motives were … But I don't give a damn. What's important is that he saved our lives.' Perhaps both the question and the answer become unimportant now, allowing us to focus on his actions, which are testimony that even in the worst of circumstances, the most ordinary of us can act courageously. If Oskar Schindler, flawed as he was, did it, then so might we, and that is reason enough to hope.[37]

Conclusion: the mystery of suffering

Suffering will always have a dimension of mystery, and no explanation, even one that finds God sharing the risk and pain of creation in the cross, will entirely satisfy. But, like Job, 'all believers in God will finally bow before the utter mystery of the divine being, from which all things arise, and to which all things must finally return (Job 42:1-6).'[38] For David Atkinson, the book of Job 'confronts us with failure, and with suffering for which there is no explanation.'[39] He maintains that we have to re-think our theology in the face of suffering and injustice. The book of Job calls us to see things from a divine rather than a human perspective.

There are searching questions for believers in the Holocaust: Why did God allow this? Where was God in all this? Can there ever be belief in God after Auschwitz? Atkinson notes that Job's friends were uncomfortable when face to face with that which defied their theology. 'They insisted on treating suffering only as a problem to be solved, rather than being willing to cope with the uncertainty of facing its mystery.'[40]

As we move toward the close of the book of Job, we find God speaking. We recognize that the writer of wisdom here wants to tell us that divine wisdom is greater than human wisdom. In chapters 38 and 39 God asks Job a series of questions: Did you know this? Did you know that? Do you understand everything? Job is silenced by his ignorance and inability. In Job 41:11 God says that everything under heaven belongs to God. There may be some value in considering Romans 8:28-39 alongside this – 'nothing can separate us from the love of God'. God is able to hold onto us through suffering, pain, torture and death.

In the end, Job is humbled in God's presence (Job 42:1-6). He has been caught up into the purposes of God, of which he knows nothing. He has to trust in the creator. As Christians we trust in God, who loves us and suffers with us and for us. We look to the death of Christ and see the lengths to which God's love will go. We are not promised freedom from suffering, nor do we know the mystery of God, but we are promised grace and hope (Revelation 21:1-4).

With the war at an end and the Allied armies at the gates of the Czechoslovakian factory, the film portrays the workers as giving Schindler two gifts. The first is a letter, 'in case you are captured. Every worker has signed it.' The second is the gold ring with its inscription in Hebrew: *Whoever saves one life, saves the world.*

Notes

[1] Mary Craig, *Candles in the Dark. Six Modern Martyrs* (London: Hodder & Stoughton, 1984), p. 127.

[2] Craig, *Candles in the Dark*, p. 130.

[3] www.historyinfilm.com/schnlist/timeline.htm, accessed 03/11/04.

[4] www.jewishvirtuallibrary.org/jsource/biography/schindler.html, accessed 26/10/04.

[5] www.jewishvirtuallibrary.org/jsource/biography/schindler.html, accessed 26/10/04.

[6] www.historyinfilm.com/schnlist/timeline.htm, accessed 03/11/04.

[7] www.historyinfilm.com/schnlist/timeline.htm, accessed 03/11/04.

[8] *Schindler's List* was nominated for twelve Oscars and won seven. But we are left to ask whether such awards are a true indication of the social value and worth of the film, or simply a measure of the film's entertainment value.

[9] There are details about the production of the film in Franciszek Palowski, *The Making of Shindler's List: Behind the Scenes of an Epic Film* (New York: Birch Lane Press, 1998).

[10] See Charles Taliaferro, *Contemporary Philosophy of Religion* (Oxford: Blackwell, 1998,) pp. 299-349. Here Taliaferro rehearses the arguments for a good God in the face of the existence of evil, concluding that to be able to demonstrate altruism and loving care human beings must have a choice, and therefore the possibility of choosing to do harm. For further discussion see R.L. Sturch, 'Theodicy' in David Atkinson & David Field (eds.), *New Dictionary of Christian Ethics and Pastoral Theology* (Leicester: IVP, 1995), p. 844.

[11] Nigel Wright, *The Fair Face of Evil. Putting the Power of Darkness in its Place* (London: Marshall Pickering, 1989), pp. 73-97.

[12] Ronaldo Munoz, *The God of Christians*. Liberation and Theology 11, (Tunbridge Wells: Burns & Oates, 1991), p. 91.

[13] Munoz, *The God of Christians*, pp. 93-94.

[14] Eli Wiesel, *Night*, trans. Stella Rodway (Harmondsworth: Penguin: 1981) pp. 45, 79; quoted in Wright, *Fair Face of Evil*, pp. 74, 75, 76-77.

[15] See, for example, the discussion in Anthony Clarke, *A Cry in the Darkness: The Forsakenness of Jesus in Scripture, Theology and Experience* (Oxford / Macon: Regent's Park College / Smyth and Helwys, 2002), pp. 3-4, 237-8.

[16] Jürgen Moltmann, The Crucified God, trans. R.A. Wilson and John Bowden (London: SCM Press, 1974), p. 278; cf. Paul Fiddes, *The Creative Suffering of God* (Oxford: Clarendon Press, 1988), p. 31.

[17] Fiddes, *The Creative Suffering of God*, pp. 32-3.

[18] Fiddes, *The Creative Suffering of God*, p.31.

[19] Frances Young, *Sacrifice and the Death of Christ* (London: SCM, 1975) p. 124.

[20] Young, *Sacrifice and the Death of Christ*, p. 125.

[21] W. H. Vanstone, *Love's Endeavour, Love's Expense* (London: Darton, Longman & Todd, 1977), p. 65.

[22] Vanstone, *Love's Endeavour, Love's Expense*, p. 59.

[23] Paul Fiddes, *Past Event and Present Salvation. The Christian Idea of Atonement* (London: Darton, Longman & Todd, 1989), p. 207.

[24] Keith Ward, *Christianity: A Short Introduction* (Oxford: Oneworld, 2000), p. 22.

[25] Fiddes, *Past Event and Present Salvation*, p. 208.

[26] Fiddes, *Past Event and Present Salvation*, p. 209.

[27] Craig, *Candles in the Dark*, p. 127.

[28] Jon Sobrino, *The Principle of Mercy: Taking the Crucified People from the Cross* (New York: Orbis, 1994).

[29] Sobrino, *The Principle of Mercy*, p. 29

[30] Sobrino, *The Principle of Mercy*, p. 30.

[31] Sobrino, *The Principle of Mercy*, p. 46.

[32] www.insidefilm.com/spielberg.html, accessed 26/10/04.

[33] www.insidefilm.com/spielberg.html, accessed 26/10/04.

[34] quoted in www.jewishvirtuallibrary.org/jsource/biography/schindler.html, accessed 26/10/04.

[35] www.jewishvirtuallibrary.org/jsource/biography/schindler.html, accessed 26/10/04.

[36] www.jewishvirtuallibrary.org/jsource/biography/schindler.html, accessed 26/10/04.

[37] www.jewishvirtuallibrary.org/jsource/biography/schindler.html, accessed 26/10/04.

[38] Ward, *Christianity*, p. 25,

[39] David Atkinson, *The Message of Job. The Bible Speaks Today* (Leicester: IVP, 1991), pp. 14-15.

[40] Atkinson, *The Message of Job*, p. 16.

14

Grace of the Valar:
The Lord of the Rings
Stratford Caldecott

Film critics and Tolkien fans, by and large, have responded to the three-part *Lord of the Rings* movie directed by Peter Jackson with ecstatic praise. Some have claimed it as the cinematic equivalent of Beethoven's *Ninth Symphony*, Mozart's *Requiem* or Shakespeare's *Hamlet*. Ludicrous praise of this sort aside, there is a certain magic about the films – a providential convergence of the newly developed CGI technology with brilliant acting, music and cinematography, all at the service of a story possessing unrivalled mythic resonance in the modern world.

For Tolkien's story was an imaginative response of a cultured European soul to the two World Wars that mark the bleak 'coming of age' of the modern experiment. Tolkien served in the First War, in the trenches of the Somme itself, and it was there that his imagination began to explore the darker possibilities of Faery. His son served in the second, and the letters between them written at this time reflect both the intensity of their relationship and the slow progress of *The Lord of the Rings* towards completion. This experience of the Wars brought Tolkien face to face with the greatest evils of our time, and especially with the great temptation of our time, that of technological power, which he dramatized in the form of the One Ring.

The nature of the One Ring
It is notable that movie audiences seem to have had no difficulty at all in recognizing the nature of the Ring, although the film's portrayal of it might easily have been confusing. It is supposed to be a Ring of Supreme Power, yet the only power it seems to grant is that of invisibility and extended life. It certainly brings the creature Gollum little more than that – combined with misery – during the centuries that he possessed it. Furthermore the wearer of the Ring becomes immediately highly *visible* precisely to those he would most wish to avoid. In the flashback where we

see its maker, the Dark Lord Sauron, wearing the Ring three thousand years earlier, we find that it neither renders him invisible nor seemingly enables him to quell the vast army of Elves and Men assembled against him, for the Ring is cut from his hand by the simple blow of a sword. Later we find that possession of the Ring cannot prevent Gollum biting it from Frodo's finger. Yet we see the corrupting effects of the temptation to claim the Ring in each of the main characters who come into direct contact with it, and we perceive it through their eyes as an infinitely desirable thing, the concentrated essence of all that is most lusted after in Middle-earth, like the forbidden fruit proffered by the serpent in the Garden of Eden.

The Ring of Sauron is perfectly smooth, bearing no stone; the famous writing that appears upon it when heated ('One Ring to rule them all ... and in the darkness bind them') is invisible at room temperature. It is a circle of gold representing the self impregnable to others, closed in upon itself. No wonder it makes the wearer invisible to others, unreachable by light! Also it is a ring not received but taken; not placed upon the finger as a gift, but claimed for oneself. As such it seems fitting that the prop used in the movie was an actual wedding ring. The One Ring is the very antithesis of what a wedding ring is supposed to represent; it is the symbol and agent of isolation and domination rather than communion.

In his *Letters*[1] and at various places in the posthumously published twelve-volume *History of Middle-earth*,[2] Tolkien explains the ambiguous power of Sauron's Ring. For him it is the archetypal Machine, and it possesses all the false allure of technology in the modern world. In fact Tolkien explores two different types of technology, two different understandings of science, through the contrast in his story between the magic of the Elves and that of the Enemy: the goal of the former is art, whereas the aim of the latter is 'domination and tyrannous re-forming of Creation'. Technology always offers more power than it delivers, and its real effect is to make us increasingly dependent upon it and therefore in reality *less* powerful in ourselves. Sauron puts a measure of his own spirit into the Ring and cannot take it back; the Ring enables him to bend his evil minions to his purpose, but as he does so his personal power is diminished, 'spread out' among those he controls. The loss or destruction of the Ring means a loss of control, even of his own bodily shape.

The film and the novel

It is perhaps important to note that the film is flawed in several respects. The action is unrelenting, the emotional scenes often sentimentally over-wrought. Cate Blanchett's Galadriel struck me as a misjudged performance – perhaps she was trying to inject some other-worldly mystery into the character. In general the Elves appear too human and insipid, too smug and pompous, compared to the strong yet ethereal, serious yet fun-loving Elves of Tolkien's masterpiece. We generally see them at night or in twilight, whereas Tolkien finds them often (and certainly in Lothlórien) in the broad light of day, brighter and more colourful than anything in the world we know. The Shire, too, is slightly mishandled. Probably only an English director could have understood quite how the balance of humour and seriousness was to be maintained in the case of the Shire. It was, after all, supposed to represent the world of real life within the novel. Tolkien's caricatures of rural English folk were affectionate, but also telling. For Jackson, the caricature ends up uppermost, the Shirelings become too clownish, and much of the complexity of Tolkien's exploration of the English psyche is lost. This matters most at the end of the third movie, when the 'scouring of the Shire' is omitted completely, and the travellers return to a homeland that has been completely unaffected by the great events 'away down south'.

Of course, much can be said in mitigation of these failings. Many of the most moving moments in the film involve visual and musical images originating with Jackson and his team rather than Tolkien – and there are far too many to list here. Even the treatment of the Elves, and the decision to associate them only with mournful, haunting music, is understandable if intended to convey more easily to a cinema audience unfamiliar with the mythic context of the story that the time of the Elves in Middle-earth is coming to an end. There is a sense of the tragedy of history, of cosmic entropy itself, which is powerfully present in the movie, and perhaps it could not have been conveyed so effectively in any other way. The Shire meanwhile becomes a backdrop to the interlinked drama that is taking place in the souls of Aragorn and Frodo.

The film is partly about a man achieving his destiny through self-mastery and service, and that man is clearly Aragorn, who moves from being a somewhat peripheral character when we encounter him in *The*

Fellowship of the Ring to a much more central role in the second and third parts of the movie. This is not the Aragorn of the novel, but a more modern character, initially much more confused, and in the end less majestic. He begins in a state of rejection, having renounced his claim to the kingship long before, fearful of his own weakness, which is the weakness of men and of his ancestor Isildur. The Ring would not be a problem if Isildur had not taken it for his own, against the advice of Elrond. Thus the War of the Ring is Aragorn's war in a very personal sense, and not just because by it he may win the throne of Gondor. The definitive rejection of the temptation represented by the Ring is his task, even more than it is Frodo's.

More than in the book, the force that impels Aragorn into his ultimate transformation is the love of Arwen. Here Jackson develops a theme that for Tolkien was at the heart of the story, though in the novel, which the publisher already thought overlong and over-late, it was largely relegated to an appendix. It was not simply in order to 'bump up the love interest' or to find more lines for Liv Tyler (she does speak Elvish beautifully!) that the romance was moved centre-stage. In Jackson's version, it is Arwen's faith in the destiny of her lover, and in her destiny with him as the mother of his child, that 'mothers' him into existence as king. One of the most poignant scenes in the third movie is that in which Arwen, in the process of departing from Middle-earth, having accepted Aragorn's decision to break off the engagement, has a vision of their future child and rides back to confront and contradict her own father in Rivendell. This must be one of the most powerful 'pro-life' moments in recent cinema history. The decision to link her destiny with Aragorn's is confirmed in a much more complex way than Tolkien ever suggested. She becomes mortally ill, which forces Elrond to recognize the need to re-forge the shards of Narsil into Andúril, the Flame of the West. With the sword finally in his hand, knowing that the life of Arwen depends on the destruction of the Ring, Aragorn is at last able to overcome the fear of his own weakness that had been holding him back, and can summon the dead to fight at his side in the battle for Minas Tirith.

Of course, though the rejection of the Ring is Aragorn's task, Frodo bears the Ring itself: this is why Aragorn's unexpected cry during the final charge at the Black Gate ('For Frodo!'), though Tolkien would never have written it in that way, is appropriate to the film. It comes after a momentary pause in which Aragorn clearly hears an Elvish voice calling him, I imagine, to his destiny as Elessar. This follows an extended scene on the DVD where Aragorn confronts, and decapitates, the ambassador of the Black Tower, refusing to believe the lie that Frodo has been tortured to death. Jackson skillfully interweaves the struggle of Frodo and Sam up the side of Mount Doom with the events at the Black Gate, leaving no doubt that these form the two halves of a single psychodrama. The combined will and self-sacrifice of Aragorn and Sam jointly carry Frodo to the threshold of his mission. Aragorn even lets Frodo and Sam go off alone at the falls of Rauros at the end of the first segment, when he could easily have stopped them. When I first saw this, I thought it a mistake, and one that could have been easily avoided. But in fact it makes sense, as does the scene, again not present in the novel, where Aragorn gently closes Frodo's hand around the Ring. The Ring is his by right of conquest, as the heir of Isildur, and Frodo is taking it where he cannot go, with his permission and support.

A true story
J. R. R. Tolkien created a mythology, not just for England as he had originally intended,[3] but for the whole modern world. 'Mythology', in the sense Tolkien evidently intended it, is not merely a pack of lies dreamed up by men too primitive to be acquainted with scientific truth. It is a way of capturing truths that cannot be adequately expressed except in story, and which need to be communicated on several levels at once. Peter Jackson has faithfully captured enough of the original story to achieve an impact on the popular psyche that few film-makers could hope to emulate.

The actor Viggo Mortensen, who plays Aragorn in the film, was asked in various interviews why he thought the film, like the book, had proved so incredibly popular. 'Because it is a true story,' he replied simply. It is indeed a true story, not a 'fantasy' at all, despite the CGI monsters and other special effects. At its heart it is a re-telling of the One True Story, the story we find made fact in the Gospels. *The Lord of the Rings*, both book and film, is a story about light and darkness, heroism in the face of what Théoden calls 'overwhelming hate', life affirmed in the face of death. It is the story of our civilization, and the great speech of Aragorn to the Men of the West before the Black Gate, entirely an invention of the film-makers, yet fully in the spirit of the book, is a direct challenge to our own time to stand fast and give battle for the sake of our civilization, of which Gondor represents the mythological ideal. We too need the 'king' to take his throne. For then we can go back to our own polluted landscape, with its mean brick houses and its small-minded officials, its devastated orchards and missing avenues of trees. We can return endowed with the authority of servants and friends of the King, to commence our own task, the task which awaits us here at home: the 'scouring of the Shire'.

This important final climax of the War of the Ring, the purification of Hobbiton by the returning heroes, was sadly omitted from the theatrical version of the film, even from the extended version. Nevertheless, Tolkien's message survives all this remarkably well. *The Lord of the Rings* embodies a sense of reverence for the living whole to which humanity belongs. That 'whole' may be taken in three senses: it is the world of nature, the world of tradition, and the spiritual world of providence. Modernity, in its negative aspect, is a rebellion against these three worlds. Peter Jackson's team captures enough of these concerns in the movie to remind us of something that had almost been lost to our civilization.

Reverence for the world of nature
Reverence for the world of nature is present not simply in the care with which her moods, her weathers, and her elements are lovingly described throughout the novel, and of course vividly represented in the film, but in their portrayal as spiritually animated, sometimes (as in the case of the Ents and eagles) even speaking with human language. Yet this is no godless 'bucolic paganism'. Tolkien's elvish 'Bible', *The Silmarillion*, makes it clear that Middle-earth is the creation of Eru Ilúvatar, the God beyond all gods, whose care extends to the smallest details of the great drama even when it is exerted through the intermediary of creatures. Hints of this are scattered throughout *The Lord of the Rings*. The film, too, conveys glimpses of transcendence through nature. Two tiny scenes that admirers of the book will be glad to see restored to them by the DVD make the point well: the crown of flowers on the fallen head of the old King's statue illuminated momentarily by the dying sun in Ithilien, and the heart-

piecing moment when Sam notices a star shining through the cloud-wrack of Mordor, speaking of a beauty high above the world that evil can obscure but never touch. Tolkien knew that monotheism, and ultimately Christianity itself, is perfectly compatible with a strong sense of a sacred presence within nature, and indeed provides the only secure basis for believing in the inherent value of the natural world, which the God of Genesis repeatedly pronounces 'good'.

Reverence for tradition

Reverence for tradition runs directly counter to the modern obsession with equality. As G.K. Chesterton wrote, tradition is the 'democracy of the dead', in which a group of the living are not allowed to overrule their ancestors just because they happen to be alive.[4] Customs and cultures are hallowed by time, whether for good or ill. In the novel, when the Men of Gondor under Faramir's command eat together, they first stand in silence and face the west: looking 'to Númenor that was, and beyond to Elvenhome that is, and to that which is beyond Elvenhome and will ever be.' Living in remembrance of the past, celebrating it, rehearsing it, is an essential part of keeping any culture alive and growing – or of renewing it when it has almost failed. Thus when Aragorn is crowned king, he echoes the words of his forefather Elendil as he stepped on to dry land from the ruin of Númenor thousands of years before: 'Out of the Great Sea to Middle-earth I am come. In this place will I abide, and my heirs, unto the ending of the world.' In the film, the actor sings the words to music he has himself composed, such is his identification with the part. All the more pity, then, that the film-makers insist on placing immediately afterwards in Aragorn's mouth a banal and unnecessary extra speech about 'rebuilding our world'.

From first to last, the civilizations of Middle-earth, whether these be the warrior-societies of Rohan and Gondor or the peaceable farming and trading communities that make up the Shire, are built up through remembrance and custom. It is a modern mistake to think that great personalities can grow without being rooted in the rich soil of the past, in the memory of great deeds and in fidelity to promises made across the generations. Civilization is founded on covenants that cannot be broken without consequence. The great army of the dead will fight to regain its honour in the service of the king.

Reverence for the spiritual world

Reverence for the spiritual world underlies the reverence Tolkien shows for nature and for tradition. The world of nature and the world of culture have a significance beyond themselves. They possess a *form*, a meaning. They reveal something, a beauty, that lies not simply beyond them, but within them. The world is a story, as a master story-teller could not but recognize. Stories have a beginning, a middle and an end; and they have a Teller. There is a pattern to the story of the world beyond the knowledge or grasp of the characters who play a part within it, as Gandalf, Aragorn, Sam and Frodo in their various ways become aware at different points in the adventure. Every event that takes place, no matter how trivial or seemingly accidental, has a purpose within the whole, and forms a thread or a colour within a tapestry that is being woven by the choices and decisions we make or are forced to make moment by moment.

It is not merely, as Aragorn says to Éomer in the book, that we walk both in legends and in the broad daylight because 'those who come after will make the legends of our time'. Rather, some things are *meant* to be – as, for example, we are told in both book and film, Bilbo was '*meant* to find the Ring, and *not* by its maker'. The whole pattern is obscure until it can be viewed *sub specie aeternitatis*. It may not be clear to us why we are here, what we are accomplishing on earth, or what we doing wrong, for we have not yet entered the world of vision that lies 'out of memory and time'. But when we do, our faith tells us that even the most apparently pointless suffering will be seen to have a sufficient reason and a place in the whole.

A call to arms

Nature, tradition and spirituality are all under attack in the modern world. If Tolkien has succeeded in evoking a nostalgia for these things in the world of the imagination, that is not escapism but therapy. There are three possible responses to such nostalgia. One is retreat. That would be the true escapism, the escapism of the grim 'realist' who wants to bury his face in the modern world to hide from the deeper truths stirred into life by

The Lord of the Rings. Another response is to rekindle the embers of this triple reverence in our own lives, by trying to preserve nature, by respecting the worthy traditions of our culture – call this, if you like, a 'discerning conservatism' – and finally by deepening our spiritual life. For Christians this will mean a participation in the sacraments that celebrate and renew the meaning of the story.

The third response, which is equally necessary if we have been 'awoken' by Tolkien, is to discern the ways in which our modern way of life undermines the second response, which is the return to religion. In his published letters, for example, Tolkien refers to what he calls the 'tragedy and despair' of our reliance on technology.[5] In the story, this tragedy is vividly illustrated in many ways, not least by the corrupted wizard Saruman, with what Treebeard, the voice of nature, calls his 'mind of metal and wheels'. To emphasize the point, Jackson has Saruman meet his death impaled on the very machinery of Isengard. In the modern world, with its ecological disasters and its factory farms, we have seen the devastating and dehumanizing effects of Saruman's purely pragmatic approach to nature.

The English Romantic movement, from Blake and Coleridge to the C. S. Lewis' Inklings, believed there must be an alternative. At the end of his essay on education, *The Abolition of Man,* C. S. Lewis writes of a 'regenerate science' of the future that 'would not do even to minerals and vegetables what modern science threatens to do to man himself. When it explained it would not explain away. When it spoke of the parts it would remember the whole.'[6] The goal of our present science, by and large, is power over the forces of nature. Of course, the quest is also for understanding, but since Bacon the identification of knowledge with power has become ever more complete. According to Lewis, the 'magician's bargain' tells us the price of all such power: nothing less than our own souls. The conquest of nature turns out to be our conquest *by* nature, that is to say by our own desires or those of others; and the one who aspires to be the master of the world becomes, in the end, a puppet.[7]

People have remarked on the fact that the Enemy is not portrayed in *The Lord of the Rings,* except by allusion and symbol. The trappings of his power are described, along with his minions, such as Orcs and Wraiths, but he himself remains indistinct, elusive. The film represents him as a giant eye of fire brooding over Mordor, like the searchlight in some hideous concentration camp. Readers of *The Silmarillion* will know that Sauron himself is merely a minion, being the former lieutenant of the fallen angel Melkor, who has been expelled from the visible world by the other Ainur in a great battle at the end of the First Age of the Sun. Sauron's lack of bodily form makes the novel more realistic than it might have been were Evil to have been visibly one of the main characters – a pantomime demon. For in the real world, evil is similarly elusive; we rarely confront it in its concentrated, archetypal form.

Tolkien always insisted that his fantasy was not an *allegory*. Mordor is not supposed to *be* Nazi Germany or Soviet Russia. 'To ask if the Orcs "are" Communists is to me as sensible as asking if Communists are Orcs', he once wrote.[8] But at the same time he did not deny that the story is 'applicable' to contemporary affairs; indeed he affirmed this.[9] It is applicable not merely in providing a parable to illustrate the danger of the Machine, but in showing the reasons for that danger: sloth and stupidity, pride, greed, folly and lust for power, all exemplified in the various races of Middle-earth. Against these vices he set courage and courtesy, kindness and humility, generosity and wisdom, in those same hearts. There is a universal moral law, he demonstrates, but it is not the law of a tyrant. It is the one and only law that makes it possible for us to be free.

Achieving the quest

The temptation that besets the righteous is to employ an evil means in a good cause. This was how the great had fallen, how Denethor and his son Boromir were deceived, how Gandalf and Galadriel might easily have fallen, and how we ourselves can still fall. Aragorn triumphs over this temptation. Evil must not be done for the sake of the good. Even the Orcs, who appear utterly evil and 'must be fought with the utmost severity,' Tolkien writes in one of his notebooks, 'must not be dealt with in their own terms of cruelty and treachery. Captives must not be tormented, not even to discover information for the defence of the homes of Elves and Men. If any Orcs surrendered and asked for mercy, they must be granted it, even at a cost.'[10] The only true power is spiritual, and is exercised primarily over oneself.

Aragorn illustrates Tolkien's understanding of real authority. The ruler who first rules himself is also able genuinely to represent his people. He is not a man isolated and alone, but a man loved and supported by others. If he does not impose his own will upon others, thereby dissipating it, the will of his subordinates will flourish and support him. In the long run, a society built on respect and mutual support is always going to be stronger than a pseudo-society built on fear and self-interest.

The might of Mordor is not defeated by Aragorn, however, who in the end provides only a diversion, nor by Frodo, for his dramatic moral failure on the edge of the fire is also part of the intense spiritual realism of both novel and film. The quest is achieved despite this failure, although the Hobbit who was broken by the Ring nevertheless is rightly honoured for taking it to the brink. The destruction of the Ring is not achieved by Frodo's strength of will in casting it away, for he has no such strength left. It is brought about by his mercy towards Gollum, and his desire to redeem even this most wicked and corrupt of creatures. He has earlier shown this intention in a way that is full of theological meaning: by restoring to Gollum his original name, Sméagol, long forgotten, and offering a relationship that might have led the poor creature out of the prison of isolation and despair into which he had thrust himself by wearing the Ring. (The dialogue between Gollum and Sméagol is one of the most powerful and moving, as well as funniest, scenes in the film).

As an Englishman, Tolkien might have hated the film's overt manipulation of his emotions in a few places, even though he freely admitted weeping at certain moments during the writing of the novel. One of those moments, of course, was omitted from the film entirely. It is when Gollum teeters on the brink of repentance, looking down on the sleeping Frodo as they climb the stairs to Cirith Ungol. Disturbed and insulted by Sam, he loses what may have been his one chance of salvation. The film substitutes for this the moving rejection by Frodo of Sam, at Gollum's instigation. (In Jackson's new version of the story, it is Frodo's apparent betrayal of Gollum to Faramir, confirming his belief that he can trust no one except himself, that causes him to set his path towards an evil end).

The Ring that corrupted Gollum, of course, remains with us. The task of un-making it is a quest to undertake in our own day, if we have the courage. We must form a new Fellowship, and take the path that the Evil

One will least expect: having obtained the Ring through theft and murder (Gollum) and by legitimate inheritance (Frodo) – a metaphor of original sin passing down the generations – we must resist all the temptations it represents. Our only ultimate safety lies on the path of foolishness and humility. That path, however, is impossible to follow to its end without help from beyond ourselves, 'graces' that may come from the most unexpected places and people.

And death is not the end, as Gandalf (who has passed through it already, and returned) tells Pippin on the eve of battle. After death the 'grey rain-curtain' of this world is 'turned all to silver glass' and rolled back to reveal 'white shores, and beyond them a far green country under a swift sunrise'. These words (borrowed from the novel, where they describe Frodo's haunting vision of the distant west) echo in the song that closes the movie.

> *And all will turn to silver glass*
> *A light on the water*
> *All souls pass*
> *…What can you see*
> *on the horizon?*
> *Why do the white gulls call?*

The Great Sea, with the sound of its ceaseless waves and the crying of the white gulls, represents for Tolkien the spiritual world that enfolds Middle-earth. Across that sea the angelic Valar preside over the Land of the Blessed, and the music of the sea echoes a Great Music that was before time, and was the archetype of time. The light of the stars that falls upon the waves is beautiful in part because light and music are deeply akin in Tolkien's cosmology: vibrations in time that convey the harmony of the One. Sung beautifully by Annie Lennox, the closing song succeeds in capturing the essence of Tolkien's concern with death, shot through with Christian hope. Such moments of creative fidelity to Tolkien raise the film far above ordinary film-making, to the level at times almost of religious art.

Notes

This paper is based on material developed in the author's book *Secret Fire: The Spiritual Vision of J. R. R. Tolkien* (London: DLT, 2003) and an article in the fourth issue of the journal *Second Spring* (see www.secondspring.co.uk).

[1] See, for example, Letter 211 in Humphrey Carpenter (ed.), *The Letters of J. R. R. Tolkien* (St Leonards, NSW: George Allen & Unwin, 1981), and the discussion of technology in my *Secret Fire: the spiritual Vision of J. R. R. Tolkien* (London: Darton, Longman and Todd, 2003), pp. 44-9.

[2] Christopher Tolkien, *The History of Middle-earth*, Vols 1-12 (St Leonards, NSW / London: Allen & Unwin / HarperCollins, 1983 – 1996); see especially the volume entitled *Morgoth's Ring*.

[3] See Letter 131 in *Letters of J. R. R. Tolkien.*

[4] This famous phrase of Chesterton's occurs in the second chapter of his *Orthodoxy* (1908), 'The Ethics of Elfland': 'Tradition means giving votes to the most obscure of all classes, our ancestors. It is the democracy of the dead. Tradition refuses to submit to the small and arrogant oligarchy of those who merely happen to be walking about.'

[5] Letter 75 in *Letters of J. R. R. Tolkien.*

[6] C. S. Lewis, *The Abolition of Man or Reflections on education with special reference to the teaching of English in the upper forms of school* (London: Fount, 1978), p. 47.

[7] Lewis, *The Abolition of Man*, Chapter 3, especially p. 43.

[8] Letter 203 in *The Letters of J. R. R. Tolkien.*

[9] Letter 203 in *The Letters of J. R. R. Tolkien.*

[10] The quotation is from the section 'Myths Transformed' in *Morgoth's Ring*, a volume of *The History of Middle-earth*. The 'applicability' to Guantanamo Bay and Abu Ghraib is obvious.

15
The Trouble with Paradise:
Pleasantville

Chris Holmwood

The seventeenth-century poet George Herbert wrote:

A verse may finde him, who a sermon flies
And turn delight into a sacrifice.[1]

Successive generations have flown from both verses and sermons and the cinema is one of many areas to which they have turned for delight. In this chapter I aim to explore the various delights of the film *Pleasantville* and to suggest ways in which it aims to engage its audience through initial pleasure towards a more profound experience. As with most of the films discussed in this book, there is a huge difference between the 'verse or 'sermon' that Herbert had in mind, both constructed for a spiritual purpose, and the purpose of this film, constructed for a social one. Although many writers and directors would see this distinction between social and spiritual as a clear one, the narrative, imagery and themes of *Pleasantville* show to what extent this distinction can be a false one. What may be a firm dichotomy between the two from a secular perspective may become a fruitful dialectic of the two from a spiritual one.

Released in 1998, certificate 12, *Pleasantville* was written and directed by Gary Ross. It was described by *Empire* magazine as 'a smash hit comedy' and by *Time Out* as 'imaginative and ingenious.' Ross was best known previously for the film *Big* in which Tom Hanks changes bodies with a teenage boy. *Pleasantville* is similarly witty in taking a seemingly ridiculous premise and exploring it both humorously and seriously in such a manner as to appeal cleverly to both a teenage and an adult audience. In this respect *Total Film*'s review of the film as '*The Truman Show* meets *Back to the Future*' is a pertinent one. Not only does it bridge the generation gap with its humorous mix of 1950s nostalgia and modern teenage characters in the way of the latter film, but it also has the intelligence and profundity of the former. The film also owes something to these two predecessors in its substance as well as its style and as these two films are better known than *Pleasantville* they may serve as a useful reference point. Now that readers have perhaps been helped to get their bearings, we need next to examine the journey of the characters of *Pleasantville*, and explore this absorbing, enjoyable and visually stunning film more fully.

Putting you in the picture

Pleasantville clearly declares itself as a contemporary fable with the white words 'Once Upon A Time ...' on a black background as it begins. We are presented with a TV screen upon which a range of satellite channels are being flicked through, and it is through this selection of diverse and dissonant images of modern society that we arrive at the homely black and white nostalgic world of the programme 'Pleasantville'. It soon becomes clear that the programme is a 1950s American sit-com in which life is simple, and people are perfect.

David (Tobey Maguire) is a huge fan of 'Pleasantville,' and we soon see why as the camera cuts from his viewing of the calm, caring mother on the television with her perfect family to his stressed single mother anxiously arranging a weekend away with her boyfriend. His sister Jennifer (Reese Witherspoon) clearly has interests other than preparing for the 'Pleasantville TV marathon' and we see her in high school impressing her friends by arranging a date at her house that same night. That evening brother and sister argue over the use of the television and break the remote control without which the TV will not operate. A mysterious TV repair man arrives, quizzes David on 'Pleasantville' and gives him a new remote control promising him, 'It will put you right in the picture.' It does exactly that, and David and Jennifer are sucked through the TV screen into the black and white world of Pleasantville itself. They have become Bud and Mary Sue, the children of the perfect family that David had so enjoyed watching.

The TV repair man communicates with them through a 1950s TV set in their new world, only to become angry that David and Jennifer do not share his excitement that they find themselves in 1958. The sassy and sexually precocious Jennifer is left to berate her brother for stranding them in 'nerdville', and we are introduced more fully to the pristine world of Pleasantville in which firemen only ever rescue cats from trees, every basketball flies through the hoop, and husbands return home from work with the words, 'Honey I'm home' to find their dinner ready on the table.

The discrepancy between the attitudes and sensibilities of the modern characters and the naïveté of those around them provide some deft comic touches, but the more serious legacy of planting these characters with their modern experience in a world of such innocence is at the centre of the film's narrative. Up to this point, Pleasantville's black and white perfection has known no complexity. There has been no passion, no questioning, no self-knowledge and no appreciation of beauty. As Jennifer and then David engage with the characters of Pleasantville and deviate from the script of the episodes, the black and white world gradually becomes colour. And as the film progresses the tension between the world of black and white and that of colour shifts as it becomes clear that the world of colour, what we may call 'real life,' also has its dark side.

'This Other Eden'[2]

As well as being ambitious in terms of its script the film is visually stunning as it merges black and white cinematography with the slow introduction of colour. It is refreshing to see a film in which both narrative and visual effects complement each other so purposefully. In portraying this progression of events Gary Ross clearly intends the film to be of moral and social relevance and I believe offers us something also of spiritual interest. In looking more closely at his intentions in the film I intend to quote him directly from the Director's commentary supplied on the DVD version of the film.[3]

Many viewers would read the film's exploration of the consequences of the way Innocence becomes Experience in Utopia as a clear biblical reference to the fall of Adam and Eve in Eden. Indeed, the film's imagery does much to support this. An apple wrapped in a serpent appears on the important mural towards the end of the film, the TV repair man shows David a repeat of the scene in which he is offered an apple by a young woman, and the first colour painting that the art loving Mr Johnson is shown is Masacio's 'Expulsion of Adam and Eve from Paradise.' Nevertheless, as writer/director, Gary Ross is keen to dissuade us from

too rigid a reading of the film. 'People who says it is just an Edenic allegory are missing the point. It's about the getting of all knowledge, the
consequences of knowledge and the liberating nature of knowledge. It's
also about what free will gives you and what free will can also disturb.'

Any allegorical reading is impoverished by too strict an exercise in
hermeneutics, but this emphasis on knowledge and free will clearly aligns
the film's narrative with the themes of Genesis chapter 3. Ross himself
describes the film as 'a hailstorm of mixed metaphors'. We are showered
with an eclectic range of ideas and images and this contributes to aspects
of the film's ambiguity. However, it is difficult not to feel that it is Ross
himself who is missing the point. He is only exploring what he describes
as 'the liberating nature of knowledge' within the limitations of the fallen
state of humankind. And in doing so, he is blind to a deeper truth. By
virtue of writing about 'the getting of *all* knowledge' the film should
surely not exclude an exploration of spiritual knowledge. This seems to
have been divorced from the self-knowledge and social knowledge that
the characters develop. It may be unfair to criticize a work of art for not
accomplishing what it does not set out to do, but the seeds of this spiritual
dimension are within the film. They are, however, tantalisingly scattered,
rather than allowed to take a firmer root.

Ross makes many comments in the Director's commentary that reveal
why he has taken this particular stance and they explain the thoughts
behind his decision to dramatize the tension between the certainty of
black and white and the complexity of colour:

> Some people need to drown out doubt, uncertainty and fear of change,
> but embracing that uncertainty is the only thing that will fully let us
> engage with our social structure, the society around us, and live a more
> fruitful, full and fulfilled life. So the personal and the social were fused
> for me in the film, because I don't know another way to look at life.

Given this, it is not surprising that Ross says that *Pleasantville* is one
of the few films that has been described as amoral and moralistic all at the
same time'. It is moralistic in seeking to depict the personal and social
merits of living 'a more fruitful, full and fulfilled life', but amoral in
believing that embracing uncertainty is enough to achieve that. He says, 'I

think we can handle the pluralism, the conflict, the complexity. I don't think that driving them away in some sort of pious fury is some sort of answer, which is what the movie says.' Ironically, given the technical skill with which he achieves this, Ross is happy to handle the pluralism of a world of many colours, but not the pluralism of a world of many colours that includes black and white. We are not truly shown perfection or pluralism but polarization. And when 'pious fury' is displayed it is in the guise of the TV repair man who is angry with David. Communicating through a TV screen he chastises David, showing him the scene in which a girl presents him with an apple plucked from a tree in Lovers' Lane.

> Do you think this place is a toy? Your own God damn colouring book?
> You don't deserve this place. You don't deserve to live in this paradise
> … You're coming home. I'm turning this place back to how it was.

This would suggest that God is on the side of simple certainty rather than a satisfying complexity. Yet if the film perhaps is unresolved in its conclusion that we should embrace the unpredictable nature of the universe, it raises questions about how what Ross describes as 'a more fruitful, full and fulfilled life' might be achieved. Perhaps complexity (colour) should not be simply contrasted with certainty (black and white). Perhaps complexity should be approached *with* certainty. Ross says about his film's conclusion, 'Life isn't tidy, life isn't neat and that's the good news.' The Good News itself says, 'I have come in order that you might have life – life in all its fullness'.[4]

If Ross' visual imagination were to be attracted to such a spiritual understanding of life, in addition to his personal and social view of 'life in all of its fullness', then perhaps his depiction of this world would require an even more impressive cinematographic language. Perhaps what would be required would be a world in which the one dimensional comes into conflict with the two dimensional and results in the three dimensional. We would probably need silly glasses to watch it and no doubt we would have problems about the theology too! In short, as Christian viewers we should be aware of the limit of Ross' vision, but also find this perspective a helpful secular starting point for spiritual debate. It is interesting that he chooses biblical imagery, since this is helpful in highlighting the degree to which we can regard what is either 'lost' or 'regained' in the film as paradise.

'We're supposed to be in colour!'

The film challenges our thinking in a number of ways as we unravel the significance of the imagery used and the narrative developed in the light of a Christian perspective. Firstly, I have touched upon the idea that the film does not portray an accurate representation of either the 'real world' or of 'paradise'. Indeed, the back and white world of Pleasantville is presented as a caricature of perfection from the very start, yet despite this still holds attraction for David and still contains elements of truth for us. There is a fascinating tension between David and his sister on their arrival in Pleasantville that leads us to the heart of the question of whether our view of perfection is of something that can only be seen as a static state, in which nothing can ever change, or whether it can be challenged and changed.

David's chief concern on arrival in Pleasantville is not to stray from the script of the episodes and to keep the perfect world as he has seen it. He and Jennifer have an interesting argument in which he says, 'We're supposed to be at school,' and she replies 'We're supposed to be in colour!' It is revealing to take these lines as indicating the starting point of their individual journeys in the film. Jennifer ends her part in the story by staying in the world she has kick-started into colour in order to continue going to school. David's journey is to learn to embrace her view, and to come to accept that his black and white view of perfection can be challenged and to champion the world of colour. We understand that the film is arguing that a type of personal redemption occurs through embracing change. It is therefore interesting for us to consider to what extent our own views of both creation and redemption may be termed as coloured and not as black or white.

Two events in the film begin the slow rippling effect of bringing Pleasantville into colour. One is to do with the sharing of knowledge through temptation, the other with the discovery of free will. Jennifer is unhappy with the sexual constrictions of her new world, but soon turns this to her advantage when she discovers that her character Mary Sue is admired by Skip, the basketball captain. She takes him to Lovers' Lane and he experiences a sexual awakening that later results in him seeing the first coloured object in Pleasantville, a single red rose. To some this might cast Jennifer as Eve, and Eve as a temptress who unleashes a sexuality that is the root of all evil. Ross' interpretation is more measured. 'Sexual awakening is the first thing that occurs because it is the most primal. Sex isn't the only thing that's liberating but it gives rise to a whole world of nuance and beauty that's non sexual.' So in an inversion of what we may have expected, Pleasantville's sexual revolution gives rise to more than parked cars in Lovers Lane, the birth of rock 'n' roll and groups of young people bursting into colour. It also leads to queues outside libraries and an appreciation of literature and art and a depth of questioning hitherto unknown. It transpires that all of Pleasantville's books are blank, until they too suddenly burst into life. The first book to do this is 'Huckleberry Finn', whose characters' own experiences David relates as: 'in trying to get free they see that they're free already.'

This connects with the other aspect of the fall, the discovery of free will. Whereas Jennifer's sexual acts are conscious, David's first contribution is unwitting. By rushing off early from work at the soda shop to see where Jennifer has gone he leaves the owner Mr Johnson to pack away on his own. For the first time Johnson does this in a different order. This small and independent act calls into question not only why he has only ever seen his world in one particular way but how this small change might transform his ability to make more of his own choices. This moment is the beginning of his artistic self-expression which not only becomes the focus of much of the clash of values in the film, but also the provider of much of the film's biblical imagery.

The biblical aspects of imagery and narrative in the film are once again used in a secular way. These two instances initiating the exploration of knowledge and free will are not presented as acts of direct disobedience, but as moments of liberation from a static view of perfection. In this way in particular, it seems that the film will not do as an interpretation of Genesis 3 because there is no concept or discussion of sin. The film falls short of a Christian understanding of the fallen state of humankind in this key respect. On the other hand it could be read as a subversive response in as much as it argues that giving freedom to our personal passions liberates us from a pre-ordained and anodyne existence. The film is certainly socially subversive, for the caricature of 'Pleasantville' portrays what some would regard as 'traditional American values', especially in respect of the nuclear family.[5] But, particularly in its cultural context within more conservative Christian communities in the United States, the film also has an element of spiritual subversion.[6] Fundamentalism will be offended by the way in which the film uses Biblical imagery to suggest that the fall of Adam might be seen as a good thing.

An important moment in transforming the entire world of Pleasantville into colour is when David argues to the Judge who defends the world of black and white that the cause of what brings colour into their world is 'within us'. But perhaps we need to move away from a view of personal growth as human-driven, towards one that is God-given. In this case we might assert that creation is coloured because God created us with room to grow and develop, to add our own creativity and colour to the world. We are created with the room to do good, but with the risk of doing evil. Redemption is coloured because there is still space for discovery, journey and growth. Perfection need not be static and unchanging, but can contain its own complexity and movement. Paul Fiddes, drawing on the vision of the book of Revelation, describes another, future city, full of life and vitality where we are able to participate in God's own life, which he presents as a true biblical image of perfection, one that we might also suggest is full of colour.

> The city is an image of busy activity and creativity as well as fellowship. So the gates of this city are open, promising that there are journeys to be made, adventures to be had, strangers to be welcomed and homecomings to be enjoyed. This is no static eternity, no simultaneity, but a healing of time. It is closure with openness at its heart. City and dance, dwelling and movement, are complementary images for the promised end which is nothing less than to move and dwell in God.[7]

This is very different from what some might see as the God-like view represented in the film, quoted earlier in the TV repair man's objection to the world being treated as a 'colouring book'. We recall that he threatens, 'You don't deserve to live in this paradise … You're coming home. I'm turning this place back to how it was'. However, he does not do this. And when we see him next it is on David's return to reality from a Pleasantville that is fully colour. He drives off in his van from outside David's house with a smile. It is only at that point that we read what is on the side of the TV repair man's van. Beneath the logo of a 1950s family looking into a television is the slogan, 'we'll fix you for good'. The TV repair man, perhaps the 'God' figure in the film, obviously felt that sending David and Jennifer to his paradise would achieve this. Yet as he drives away with a smile perhaps he too has been changed by what has happened. Perhaps he is now happier with the complexity of colour rather than the static perfection of black and white that he previously wished to protect.

And we could certainly drive away from the film with some thoughts about a God who creates the world with colour, yet with its own freedom so some can choose to see things in black and white whilst others add colour of their own, and with the space for us to change from one view to the other. And perhaps we might consider a God who will redeem the world so that all of the colour that we have added is included and cherished in a new creation. For God has contributed to this colourful redemption by God's willingness to change and to suffer in Jesus. The colours of free will have come at a cost and are paid for by the colours of redemption, namely white and red, flesh and blood, bread and wine. George Herbert writes, 'Man stole the fruit and I must climb the tree'[8] and this clearly links Adam and Christ in a traditional view deriving from the Apostle Paul.[9] In a film in which there is only a portrayal of secular redemption it is hard to apply the truth of Herbert's words, though we might think that the world of the film would do well to heed them.

Perhaps we should conclude that God's willingness to change and to suffer means that we can be involved in the shaping of the future paradise. This is well expressed in the terms of neither sermon, verse or film, but in the words of a song:

I believe in the Kingdom Come
Where all the colours bleed into one.[10]

Pleasantville reveals that Gary Ross may still not have found what he is looking for, but I believe the film may certainly assist others in exploring the tensions between social and spiritual views of 'fullness of life', as well as the dialogue between theology and film.

Notes

[1] George Herbert, 'The Church Porch', lines 5-6.

[2] Shakespeare, *Richard II*, Act II, scene 1, 42.

[3] Director's Commentary, *Pleasantville* DVD, New Line Home Video.

[4] John 10:10 (Good News Bible).

[5] Gary Ross, in the director's commentary, suggests that his choice of books was deliberately subversive: *Huckleberry Finn*, *Catcher in the Rye*, and *Lady Chatterley's Lover* have all have been banned books in USA.

[6] The comments on some websites suggests that some viewers rejected the film because they found it too subversive. See, for example, www.christiananswers.net/spotlight/movies/pre2000/i-pleasantville.html and www.hollywoodjesus.com/pleasantville.htm , accessed 14/12/2004.

[7] Paul S Fiddes, *The Promised End: Eschatology in Theology and Literature* (Oxford: Blackwell, 2000), p. 287.

[8] George Herbert, 'The Sacrifice', line 202.

[9] See, for example, Romans 5:15.

[10] U2, 'I Still Haven't Found What I'm Looking For'.

15
Interpreting the Gospel:
The Passion of the Christ
Stephen Holmes

'On a scale of one to ten, no one ever gave it between two and nine.' So ran an advert for Laphroaig, my second favourite brand of single malt whisky. Oddly, this is also generally true of films seeking to depict the life of Christ in some way: from the (woodenly?) literal *Jesus of Nazareth*, to the imaginative *Jesus Christ, Superstar* and *Miracle Maker*, the allusive *The Last Temptation of Chris* and *Jesus of Montreal*, or the intentionally bizarre *The Life of Brian*. These films are either loved uncritically or hated irredeemably, particularly by the Christian community. Reviews of Mel Gibson's phenomenally successful film, *The Passion of the Christ*, seem to have taken this rule to extremes: on a scale of one to ten, most reviewers have given it either minus two or fifteen. Positive or negative, the responses have been, well, *passionate*.

Perhaps, some time after the media frenzy, we can begin to step back and explore the cultural event with – if not less passion, at least more detachment.[1] Cultural event it was. No film in history had grossed more receipts in British cinemas in its first week on general release. Amazingly enough, *The Sun* ran two double-page spreads, asking theologians to comment, and giving prominence to their wisdom.

Most of the churches embraced the film as a mission opportunity: tracts explaining the context of the film were produced and handed out to cinemagoers; other churches bought up tickets en masse, and offered them free to all takers, in return for attending a 'seminar' discussing the relevance of the sufferings of Jesus. A few dissenting voices were heard: articles in the *Evangelical Times* inveighed against the film on the (dubiously) biblical grounds that 'faith comes by hearing' – and therefore not seeing – and that any depiction of Jesus falls under the ban on idolatry in the second commandment.[2] The seventh ecumenical council and its thoroughly evangelical defense of icons, seems to have passed these authors by. Largely, however, Christian communities realized that this film provided 'a blip on the radar' of popular culture and so a chance to make known the gospel. Powerful stories of repentance and conversion being caused by the film were recalled in conversation and in the Christian and secular press. If there is joy in heaven over a repentant sinner, even contributors to the *Evangelical Times* might perhaps manage a cautious smile.

An accurate retelling of the Gospels?

A large part of the reason for this cultural impact was the repeated accusation of anti-Semitism. Record takings were recorded in Arabic countries[3] where *The Passion of the Christ* was allowed to be released, presumably on the morally dubious grounds that my enemy's enemy might just be a friend. In the West, some condemned the film severely, claiming it made the (allegedly already anti-Semitic) Gospel accounts even harsher on the Jewish people than they in fact are. Others defended it as no more than an accurate repetition of the Gospel stories – a recurring and revealing phrase, to which we will return – and insisted that, as the gospels are not anti-Semitic, neither could the film be. Either way, the allegations made it hot news. This, more than any interest in the Gospel narrative, was what got *The Sun* interested, or so it seems.

Just in case any reader did not see the film, it is a slow, graphic and astonishingly violent meditation on the last hours of Christ's life, beginning in Gethsemane and following through to the crucifixion and a (brief and allusive) coda depicting the resurrection. It is almost no exaggeration to say that, from the moment of Jesus' arrest, ten minutes or so in, the only breaks to the continual acts of sadistic violence perpetrated against him are occasional flashback scenes, mainly to the Last Supper, but once or twice to earlier events, notably a couple of imagined scenes from Jesus' childhood. The famous twenty-eight minutes of brutal flogging capture the tone, with special effects depicting Jesus' body being lacerated and torn in ways perhaps more lingering and graphic than any previous cinematic depiction of physical violence. As a (Jewish) friend of mine put it, this is the gospel for a Quentin Tarantino generation.

The violence has been justified, and the film sold, on the claim of authenticity. 'It is as it was,' the Pope is reputed to have said and, although there seems to be some uncertainty about the Holy Father's opinion, many senior Christian leaders were invited to special preview screenings, and their endorsements were the main marketing tool. Evangelical spokespeople in particular were queuing up to assert that here, at last, we had a faithful retelling of the gospel story in cinematic form, with little or nothing added or taken away. It should be seen, by Christian and non-Christian alike, as an accurate repetition of the gospel accounts, that told the story truthfully and powerfully, without addition or dilution.

This, it seems to me, is the most interesting thing about the cultural event that was *The Passion of the Christ.* It may have been many things, but an accurate repetition of the Gospel accounts it was not. Indeed, it simply could not have been, since there are four canonical accounts of the death of Jesus, which are notoriously resistant to harmonization. One may, as many have done through the centuries, produce an attempted harmony, but it will follow each Gospel at certain points and depart from it at others. It may, if constructed with sufficient skill, turn out to be a more or less accurate reconstruction of the history that underlies the fourfold Gospel, but that makes it a fine piece of biblical criticism, not a faithful retelling of the text. A conscious decision was taken at the time of the settling of the canon of Scripture: Greek, Latin and African churches alike chose to retain the fourfold tradition of the Gospels, despite the option, embraced by the Syriac church, of using instead Tatian's second century harmony, the *Diatessaron*. The canon settled variously by Athanasius's Festal Letter of 367, The Council of Carthage of 397, and papal decree in 405, deliberately retains the unharmonized gospels. This is no doubt theologically interesting; dramatically, it makes the idea of a single retelling being an authentic repetition simply impossible.

One might, I suppose, produce a film or play that attempts to be a simple retelling of one or another of the Gospels – Gibson apparently focused on John for his main narrative structure. However, issues of visual depiction and historical reconstruction mean that the retelling will still be an act of interpretation: the gospels give us no hint of what Jesus, or any of the other main characters, looked like, so even casting is a hermeneutic act – here is the force of what truth there is in the criticisms printed in the *Evangelical Times*. Period detail such as architecture, clothing and even language are reconstructions, interpretations, guesses – or worse. The film is performed in Latin and (stilted) Aramaic; most New Testament scholars agree the *lingua franca* would have been Greek.Given

Gibson's very public support for the maintenance of the Latin mass, it is difficult to suppose that his visual depiction of Jesus speaking Latin is completely devoid of polemic intent.

Much more than that, however, assertions of accuracy to Scripture are simply astonishing. The film depicts many events that are not found in any of the canonical gospels. Mary the Blessed Virgin and Pilate's wife are portrayed as friends, and this friendship drives the plot in places. Demons appear to torment Judas the betrayer and drive him to suicide. The various traditional 'stations of the cross' along the *via dolorosa* are represented one by one, and whether, as tradition would teach us, St Veronica did in fact wipe Jesus' face as he stumbled, and come away with a miraculous impression thereof on her cloth, it is not an event the canonical gospels chose to report. As already mentioned events from Jesus' childhood are imagined and depicted in flashback scenes. I did not run a stopwatch, but would guess that around a third – perhaps even up to a half – of the film is showing things that no gospel writer records.

Here is the decisive point: the film is an interpretation, a telling of the story in a particular way to emphasize particular themes and ignore others. There is no shame in this, of course. The sermons I preached over the Easter weekend that the film was showing in British cinemas were also interpretations. I did not pretend otherwise. However, the massive and carefully orchestrated publicity campaign devoted to promoting the film portrayed it as a plain telling of the facts as recorded. (To be fair, Mel Gibson did not make these claims himself, but one assumes he approved of the marketing campaign.)[4] This brings us back to the violence and to the accusation that the film is anti-Semitic.

An anti-semitic retelling of the Gospel?
I am quite sure that Gibson did not set out to produce an anti-Semitic film; I assume that he is no more a hater of the Jewish people than I am. But the question can be asked: if the film is inevitably and obviously an interpretation, is it an interpretation that is generous to the Jewish people, or one that is otherwise?

The accusations began when a leaked copy of the script reached a group of Christian and Jewish scholars in the United States.[5] Their statements, whilst weighty, were susceptible to the obvious responses that film scripts change throughout production, and that a movie cannot be judged on its script alone, as visual and performance factors influence the interpretation of any particular line of dialogue. The accusations did not cease after the film was released, however, and some very senior public figures made some very blunt comments. Gerald Kaufmann, chair of the House of Commons Select Committee on Culture, Media and Sport, was reported as saying on ITV:

> What you are in for is sadism, gratuitous violence, ugliness, wallowing in blood and, it has to be said, crude anti-Semitism. That is what this movie is about. I am not accusing him (Gibson) of being a deliberate and overt anti-Semite but there is no doubt that the message of the film is seriously, damagingly anti-Semitic. If this is the film that Mel Gibson has always wanted to make then so much the worse for Mel Gibson.[6]

The Council for Christians and Jews was more measured, but hardly supportive:

> Most of the difficulties can be accounted for in terms of traditionalist reading of the texts, dramatic license, and a considered degree of ignorance, but the film does not target Jews collectively, aiming at specified individuals and groups rather than Jews in general. It is, however, a close run thing. Gibson left out the famous 'May his blood be upon ourselves and upon our children' only in response to Jewish pressure. Its inclusion would have brought the film into the realm of anti-semitism as it is clearly read as applying to Jews in general, and it does remain in the Aramaic dialogue. Gibson is surely well aware of the impact of some of his scenes on Jews down the ages, but he does not hesitate about intensifying them; clearly they will rekindle prejudices in at least some of his audiences, and Jewish leaders have every right to be concerned. While Gibson's Jesus is clearly Jewish, Jewish content is played down – the crucial Passover context is treated en passant in a very perfunctory aside, and all we see of Jews in general are violent mobs and the villainy of the High Priest and his colleagues. Even Jesus' final prayer – 'Father forgive them...' – is directed solely at the High Priest by an unscriptural addition. This denigration and inaccurate portrayal is bound to have a

subliminal impact on the audience and will, alas, confirm and rekindle ancient stereotypes of Jews and Judaism.[7]

The release of the film on video/DVD brought a resurgence of criticism. Typical was a 'Statement by Concerned Christians' entitled *'The Passion of the Christ,' Jewish Pain, and Christian Responsibility*.[8] This revisited the various charges, and urged Christian viewers of the film to be aware of the interpretation it was offering. In all these various discussions, the same two lines of criticism can be discerned. On the one hand, it was suggested that the film is (as was claimed) no more than an accurate portrayal of the gospel accounts, which accounts are irredeemably anti-Semitic, leading to the film's inevitable guilt on the same charge. On the other hand, many Christian discussions insisted that the film was an interpretation which verged on anti-Semitism precisely in those aspects in which it deviated from the canonical gospels. These are of course two different charges, and deserve to be explored separately.

First, then, there is a suggestion that the handling of the biblical material supports a charge of anti-Semitism; it is claimed that the gospel accounts are already anti-Semitic, and that Gibson makes this worse in his interpretative decisions. The response, for example, of the Council for Christians and Jews and the joint Catholic-Jewish Scholarly Group illustrate how some feel that Pilate was painted more sympathetically, and Caiaphas more evilly, than in the Bible. Current biblical scholarship debates whether the gospels invite a legitimizing of the long and sorry history of Christian anti-Semitism; that there is such a history and that texts from the Gospels have been deployed to defend it, is not in doubt. The verse at the heart of this history, Matthew 27.25, used for centuries to justify the persecution of Jewish people, appears in the film, although it is not translated in the subtitles. Here is the central problem, perhaps, of pretending that the film can be justified as no more than a retelling of the original stories: even if we believe, as I happen to, that this text can be read as not being anti-Semitic in its original context, to pretend that after all the vile and bloody history these words, 'let his blood be upon us and on our children', can be repeated without inviting suspicion and offence is to misunderstand the nature of the way text fundamentally works.

This brings us back to questions of authenticity and interpretation. To make a good postmodern point, texts do not exist outside of a cultural and hermeneutic history. It is an important scholarly question whether a text is itself anti-Semitic (or oppressive to women, or legitimatizing of violence), or whether such associations are later accretions resulting from the history of the interpretation and use of the text. The answer to this question does not affect the present hearing of the text, however; no (informed) person can hear Wagner or read G. K. Chesterton without the spectre of anti-Semitism being present. The same is true of the gospels, and particularly Matthew 27:25.

Within the history of artistic performance, and indeed of liturgical theology, there are well-established practices to cope with this problem. The preacher faced with Matthew 27:25, or some other texts, will own the issue and work at it during the sermon, demonstrating the possibilities of reading the text against its history of interpretation, thus facing up to the problems of that history and seeking to overcome them. Acknowledging that the text comes with a weight of interpretation, or a particular hermeneutical spin, there is a responsibility to offer a counterbalance, or to work at re-spinning the text. It certainly seems to me that the postmodern mindset has shown us that there is no possibility of an unspun text. The mythology of a pure or straight retelling invites a repetition of flawed or offensive interpretations. If Gibson believes, as his publicists certainly do, that he is merely depicting what happened, and not interpreting it, then his film is going to appear anti-Semitic.

Second, there is a suggestion of 'guilt by association'. A number of writers have sought the origin of some of the extra-biblical material in two writings by Roman Catholic nuns: *The Dolorous Passion of our Lord Jesus Christ* by Sister Anne Emmerich, and Mary of Agreda's *City of God*. Both works have been accused of being anti-Semitic, although from my own reading of them there is little evidence that the film draws exclusively from them.[9] Rather, they and it belong to and draw on a long tradition of broadly Catholic devotion, meditating and elaborating on the passion narrative. Grünewald's *Crucifixion*, Donatello's *Lamentation over the Dead Christ*, the great fifteenth century *Pietàs*, Pergolesi's *Stabat Mater Dolorosa*, Bach's great Passions, even Stainer's *Crucifixion* – these are the historic comparisons, alongside any number of similarly intentioned, but less significant, pieces. They are artistic works of devotion, deploying imagination to seek to comprehend the depths of human sinfulness and the heights of divine love by focusing on the extent of Christ's suffering. One might even see the film as a work that is faithful to the method of St Ignatius Loyola's *Spiritual Exercises*, or that stands in continuity with the mysterious gift of stigmata, the ultimate devotional participation in the sufferings of the Christ.

Of course, alongside this tradition is another, more Protestant one, of criticizing such depictions for focusing on the physical sufferings of Christ as if these were central to his passion. François Turretin is only one theologian in a long Reformed tradition who asks if the physical sufferings of Christ were the essence of his passion and replies in the negative[10] (a point made also by the articles cited above from the *Evangelical Times*). Perhaps the most telling example of this line of interpretation is John Calvin's exposition of the credal affirmation that 'he descended into hell'. Calvin, rejecting any linkage with obscure texts from I Peter, instead taught that the *descensus* referred to Christ's suffering of the spiritual torments of hell, notably the pain of separation from God, on the cross.[11] If this line of interpretation is correct, then vivid depictions of the physical sufferings of Christ reveal nothing of the gospel.

I suppose that there must be a mediating way here: as Turretin acknowledges, it is not that the physical sufferings of Christ are irrelevant, but that they are only a part of the whole.[12] We might suggest, then, that their depiction can alert people to the fact of Christ's suffering, causing them to question its nature and purpose. A film like *The Passion of the Christ* might be a *preparatio evangelica*, even if it cannot be a proclamation of the gospel in itself.

Is the film anti-Semitic? I have no ability or desire to settle the question: I am sure that it does not set out to be, and if through foolishness or failure it crosses a line unintentionally, that is serious but perhaps not very interesting. Those who wished to dismiss the film as worthless, awarding it a resounding minus two out of ten saw this as their trump card, surely wrongly. *The Merchant of Venice* and *Die Meistersinger von Nürnberg* are both regularly accused of the same fault, and yet are generally regarded as having some artistic merit. At worst, some people seemed to want to see the whole film as no more than an extended attempt to vilify the Jewish people. Those who wish to see the film as an ultra-realistic and faithful retelling of the gospel narratives will say it is not anti-Semitic, because the Gospels are not. I see the film as a contribution to a tradition of Christian imaginative spirituality; some specimens of this tradition have indeed been anti-Semitic, but by no means all.

Finding a context for the film
As the spokespeople of the Christian community seem condemned to either uncritically love, or irredeemably hate, films about the life of Christ, so they seem destined to misunderstand them. I well recall scandalized Christian leaders being reported in the press as wanting to ban *The Last Temptation of Christ* because Martin Scorsese dared to suggest imaginatively that Jesus, who, Hebrews 4.15 tells us, 'was tempted in every way, just as we are', might have been tempted sexually too.[13] Perhaps most interestingly, *The Life of Brian* was careful to indicate to those who watched attentively that it was not about Jesus – his ministry was depicted as going on in the background to the film.[14] Once this is grasped, the whole film can be read as a satirical look at the incurable stupidity of human attempts to discover or construct religious meaning apart from the grace of God, which is a profoundly theological theme.[15] As such, it stands in continuity with Isaiah's mockery of the idolaters (e.g. Isa. 44.9–20); it could have been a key weapon in the polemic of the Christian churches against new religious movements and all the New Age spiritualities. As it was, however, it was vilified as mocking Jesus. So we could go on through the other films that I began with. Passion in responding to artwork – even *The Passion of the Christ* – is commendable, for art indeed *matters*, but it should be a passion for the truth, not a misunderstanding. If we do not comprehend what a film is about, we are unlikely to judge it adequately.

As usual, however, local churches were wiser than their (often self-appointed) public voices. If, as I have suggested, the film is best understood as an extended meditation on the passion of Christ, then what it demands is context. Somehow, those who see the film and are shocked, sickened or numbed (as many or most viewers will be), need to be helped to understand the meaning of these sufferings. Something needs to be done to take the viewer beyond what might be the single most graphic

depiction of sadistic violence ever seen in a cinema, to understand that it
accomplished something. Bach's Passions were incorporated within Holy
Week liturgies; the Pietàs took their places within church buildings; St
Ignatius' students have a spiritual director. Gibson's greatest failing was
not in the way he made the film, but in the way he distributed it: it
belonged within churches on Good Friday, where the liturgy, lectionary
and preaching could give context; in the public square it was in danger of
being merely meaningless and sickening. The (many) churches who
offered tracts, seminars and other attempts to give the context, to do what
Gibson should have done, had grasped both the nature, and the failure, of
the film and responded rightly.[16]

On a scale of one to ten? *The Passion of the Christ* is a magnificent
technical achievement. It depicts the sufferings of Jesus more graphically
– if not more powerfully – than any of the medieval painters or sculptors.
I found the violence excessive, and was numbed rather than moved, and
so, for me, the film did not work as well as Stainer's oratorio or
Grünewald's altarpiece, but then I do not habitually watch violent films.
Perhaps for those who find *Pulp Fiction* and *Kill Bill* entertaining, this
level of graphic brutality works. The narrative form of the film does not
follow any one of the canonical Gospels, unlike, say, Bach's *St Matthew
Passion*, and indeed introduces many elements that are not found in any
of them, but it is a powerful and coherent imaginative retelling stressing
the spiritual opposition ranged against Jesus. Where it really falls down is
in failing to give the viewer any context for understanding the suffering it
depicts. On a scale of one to ten, perhaps six: interesting, challenging, but,
in my humble opinion, not as good as *The Life of Brian*.

Notes

[1] This is an expansion of an article that originally appeared in a Bible
Society periodical, *The Bible in TransMission* (Summer 2004 issue), under the
title 'Getting Passionate with Mel Gibson'. I am grateful for permission to draw
on that piece. I should also record my thanks to the Revd Darren Hirst, for some
comments about the original piece which have helped my revising.

[2] See Don Fortner, 'Passion of Christ – the Movie' and Ken Wimer, 'What
you won't learn from "The Passion"' (both *Evangelical Times* April 2004).

[3] The same might be true of non-Arabic Muslim nations, but I saw no data from any such nations.

[4] I have heard the defence that the publicity campaign was no more than ICON (Gibson's production company) showing early cuts of the film to various people and inviting whatever comments came. It so happens that I attended one of these preview screenings of the film, and this is not what I felt was happening.

[5] The following long quotation from a member of the group explains the circumstances well: 'The joint Catholic-Jewish scholarly group convened by the Secretariat for Ecumenical and Inter-religious Affairs of the United States Conference of Catholic Bishops and the Department of Inter-religious Affairs of the Anti-Defamation League originally examined the script of the film in use at the time of the original filming in Rome. We did so because of the public claim by one of Mr. Gibson's associates, Fr. William Fulco, SJ of Loyola Marymount University in Los Angeles, who provided the Aramaic translations for the film. He indicated that the script was in total conformity with the Catholic Bishops' Guidelines on Passion Plays issued in 1998. The script was leaked by an employee of Mr. Gibson's production company, ICON. Each of us read it individually before we compared notes. When we did begin a group discussion of the script, we quickly concluded that it was one of the most troublesome texts relative to anti-Semitic potential that any of us had seen in 25 years. It must be emphasized that the main storyline presented Jesus as having been relentlessly pursued by an evil cabal of Jews headed by the high priest Caiaphas who finally blackmailed a weak-kneed Pilate into putting Jesus to death. This is precisely the storyline that fueled centuries of anti-Semitism within Christian societies. This is also a storyline rejected by the Catholic Church at Vatican II in its document *Nostra Atate* and by nearly all mainline Protestant churches in parallel documents. And modern biblical and historical scholarship has generally emphasized that Pilate was a horrible and powerful tyrant, eventually removed by Rome from his position because of his extreme brutality; a tyrant the occupied and politically powerless Jewish community was in no position to blackmail. Unless this basic storyline has been altered by Mr. Gibson, a fringe Catholic who is building his own church in the Los Angeles area and who apparently accepts neither the teachings of Vatican II nor modern biblical scholarship, *The Passion of the Christ* retains a real potential for undermining the repudiation of classical Christian anti-Semitism by the churches in the last 40 years.' John T. Pawlikowski, 'Christian Anti-Semitism: Past History, Present Challenges: Reflections in Light of Mel Gibson's The Passion of the Christ' *Journal of Religion and Film* 8.1 (3-4) This whole issue is devoted to discussing the controversy around the film, and is a useful source.

[6] Reported in *The Guardian*, March 16th 2004; see http://film.guardian.co.uk/news/story/0,,1170487,00.html

[7] From a statement published on
http://www.ccj.org.uk/Downloads/Mel%20Gibson.doc, accessed 11/1/05

[8] Most conveniently on http://www.jcrelations.net/en/?id=2353, accessed
11/1/05

[9] Gibson has been quoted as acknowledging a debt to Emmerich. See Peter
J. Boyer, 'The Jesus War: Mel Gibson's Obsession' in *The New Yorker*
15/9/2003.

[10] Francois Turretin, *Inst. Elenc. Theol.* XIV.14, (Phillipsburg: P. & R.
Publishing, 1993) 'Did Christ suffer only corporeal punishments for us ... [or]
did he in truth also bear the spiritual and infernal punishments of sin themselves
... ?'

[11] John Calvin, *Institutes.* II.xvi.8-12 (London: SCM, 1961).

[12] 'In the body indeed, he endured corporeal pains and agonies and a temporal death most cruel above all others; and in the soul, he endured spiritual and
internal agonies ...' (Turretin, *Inst. Elenc. Theol.* XIV.14.III)

[13] I am aware that there was much to criticise in this film, artistically and
theologically, but the criticisms of the Christian community seemed focused on
this one point, which is not just unobjectionable, but necessary, theologically.

[14] For example, when someone before the revolutionary council announces,
'What this Jesus doesn't understand is that the meek are the whole problem.'

[15] Martin Luther and Karl Barth would have approved.

[16] One colleague on whom I tried this interpretation suggested that the
flashbacks to the Last Supper provided the necessary context; this may be what
Gibson intended, but it is still only helpful for the initiated. The (painfully obvious) linking of the unrobing of Christ to the removal of the cloth from the bread
at the supper can only make sense to one who knows the liturgy or theology of
the Eucharist. Even if this were Gibson's intended commentary, much more was
needed if the film was not to be merely preaching to the converted.

Part III
Resources

Introduction

The material in this section arose out of a desire to find more creative ways to engage in interesting and culturally relevant Bible study, and was devised and used with a variety of small groups, ranging from youth groups and church fellowships to newly-accredited ministers, through work done at Regent's Park College and the South Wales Baptist College. The material is based on the premise of this whole book that there is much value in watching and reflecting on secular films, so that, by entering into dialogue with the world of the film, we may be able to gain fresh insights into our own faith. The aim of this section is to provide a structured opportunity of examining some classic and cult films to discover what they might show us about our Christian faith and commitment to a kingdom-lifestyle. Few would dispute the importance of cinema for our contemporary world and we hope that modern films will be used creatively within the church to bring people to a greater appreciation of their life in Christ.

All the films in this section are secular films rather than intentionally Christian ones, and so it is important that we approach these films from the right perspective. The first section of this book raises significant issues about the 'reading' of films and it is recommended that these chapters be read. They discuss the difficulty of finding meaning in films, the variety of response that one film will provoke, and suggest that there is no simply 'right' way to understand a film. It is important that we allow a film to speak for itself, and – especially in a church context – not simply to read Christian allusions into the events we see on the screen. The chapter on 'Gaining Fresh Insights' works through a number of these issues, and in addition highlights the fact that film offers us a glimpse of a different world, sometimes full of sex, violence and bad language. Sensitive decisions will always need to be made about which films are most suited to which audiences.

This section contains studies of eleven films that have been released for general viewing within the last fifteen years and all are readily available on videocassette and DVD. They cover a range of subjects and run the gamut of human experience: from the destructiveness of prejudice to the inhumanity of war, from family breakdown to the all-consuming power of jealousy, from the harshness of political reality to the imaginative world of science fiction. A number contain some violence and swearing, although all but one carry no more than a '15' rating. The exception, *The Killing Fields*, carries an '18' rating because of its graphic presentation of war, although *Saving Private Ryan*, while a '15' film, offers similar graphic images of war.

The intention is for the film selected to be viewed within the confines of a small-group setting. A suggested worksheet is provided for each film and contains materials which we hope will challenge the viewers, whether they be committed Christians or not, with the relevance of the message of the Christian gospel. Each chapter includes introductory details about the film together with some possible further resources, an in-depth synopsis about the film itself, and a series of questions and topics for discussion based upon the film.

In the synopsis for each film we have identified what we have felt to be the main themes and issues raised within it. One suggestion is that the group leader might read the synopsis to the group before watching the film, although there is the danger that this may give away too much of the ending; perhaps it is best used in this way if only clips are to be viewed. The questions provided could be used by the group leader to raise controversial and thought-provoking questions for open discussion within the group. We would expect that the individual members of the group would bring their own experiences and insights of life to the discussion.

The materials provided would then only be a first step in an engagement with the film, as they are not intended to be the definitive guides to the film and its meaning. No doubt there are going to be many other ideas and insights not mentioned within the synopsis or worksheets which will arise out of the study of the film in a small-group setting. When shared these can enhance an appreciation of the film and enrich the understanding of both it and the Christian faith.

17
The Mission:
Some Missiological Dilemmas
Portrayed

Film details

The Mission (1986)

Directed by Roland Joffe.

Starring Robert De Niro as Rodrigo Mendoza, Jeremy Irons as Father Gabriel and Ray McAnally as Altamirano.

Screenplay by Robert Bol.

Music by Ennio Morricone.

BBFC certificate 'PG'.

Duration 121 minutes.

Released on video-cassette and DVD by Warner Home Video (2002).

The film is based on the book *The Mission*, by Robert Bolt (Harmondsworth: Penguin, 1986). The soundtrack of the film is also available, distributed by Virgin Records (1986).

The film was nominated for several Film Academy Awards and won an Oscar for Cinematography. It also won the Palme D'Or at the Cannes Film Festival in 1986.

Synopsis

The film is set in South America on the borders of Argentina, Brazil and Paraguay, during the turbulent 1750s as Spain and Portugal vie for control of a disputed territory occupied by native Guarani Indians. The story that unfolds is being related by the Pope's delegate, Altamirano, and is set within the narrative framework of a letter he writes to the Pope in 1758. Altamirano had been sent by the Pope, at the request of the kings of Spain and Portugal to investigate the activity of the Jesuit missions in the area around Asuncion. The Jesuits have established a mission in the area and are attempting to protect the people from the slave-traders who occasionally make raids into the area, killing some people and making off with others to sell on the open market. The Jesuits are also helping the native people to make their own plantations, all to the financial detriment of the Spanish and Portuguese colonials.

The martyrdom in 1750 of a Jesuit priest who was seeking to take the gospel to the Guarani Indians living on the plateau above the Iguaçu Falls brings Father Gabriel to his first encounter with the Indians there. 'So the Guarani,' writes Altamirano in his letter, 'were brought to the eternal mercy of God and to the short-lived mercy of man.' Father Gabriel is the Jesuit priest in charge of the San Carlos mission among the Guarani. As he seeks to live out the gospel with the Indians, they are attacked by slave-traders led by Captain Rodrigo Mendoza. Gabriel confronts Mendoza, who subsequently withdraws.

Back in Asuncion Mendoza kills his brother Philippe in a fit of anger over a woman they both love. When Gabriel returns to the city he finds that Rodrigo has been in a state of despondency for six months, living in a cell in the mission. Gabriel is directed by his Superior to counsel Rodrigo. Rodrigo is not immediately open to this. 'Leave, priest! You know what I am!' he says to Gabriel. 'Yes,' replies Gabriel, 'A slave trader. You killed your brother and you loved him, although you showed it in a strange way.' Gabriel tells Rodrigo that he is running away from the world. But Rodrigo counters that there is nothing else for him. 'No penance is hard enough for me!' he says. 'Do you dare try it?' asks Father Gabriel. Rodrigo now finds himself on a spiritual pilgrimage which leads him to live and work among the Guarani he formerly persecuted.

Rodrigo joins three Jesuits, Father Gabriel, Father John and Father Ralph, on their return to the high plateau, climbing the escarpment of the falls. Behind him he drags all of his armour in a rope net behind him. The other Jesuits tell Gabriel that Rodrigo has done penance long enough. 'But he doesn't think so,' says Gabriel. When they reach the Guarani on the plateau it is one of the Indians, whom Rodrigo had sought to capture as a slave, who cuts him free from his burden, and pushes it over the cliff. It falls into the river below and an emotional scene of reconciliation takes place.

Rodrigo becomes involved with the Jesuits in the San Carlos mission and gradually grows in love and care of the Indians. He refuses even to kill a wild boar being hunted by the Indians; he appears to have renounced all forms of violence. The picture of the Guarani, both children and adults, is one of paradise. Rodrigo is given a Bible to read. After reading 1 Corinthians 13 he asks Father Gabriel about becoming a Jesuit. Meanwhile the Papal delegate, in his narrative letter, comments that the Spanish and Portuguese rulers do not like the idea of the poor Indians finding paradise on earth as it undermines their world-view.

It is at this point in the story that Altamirano arrives to investigate the activity of the Jesuits. He is told by the Spanish and Portuguese governors that the Jesuits have too much power. There follows an audience of all the interested parties with Altamirano. Father Gabriel finds, to his horror, that the Treaty of Madrid has turned the territory over from Spanish to Portuguese control. This means that the Guarani will be at the mercy of the Portuguese slave-traders and that they will not, in all probability, be able to survive. In private Altamirano tells Gabriel that it is the future of the Jesuit order in the whole of Europe that is at stake, not only the future of the Guarani. Before reaching a decision on the matter Altamirano, at Gabriel's suggestion, decides to visit all of the missions. He writes in his letter, 'I had come as a surgeon to cut off a part of the body, but nothing had prepared me for the beauty and the power of the limb I had come to sever.'

He sees the beauty of the scenery, hears the singing of the Indian mission choirs, sees the plantations and their produce, sees the scars on the back of a runaway slave from a European plantation. When he hears that the money from the plantations is shared among the workers he says, 'There was a French radical group that did that.' One of the Guarani comments, 'The early church did it first!' Altamirano is torn by what he sees and the political pressure that he is under. 'Back in Spain they are determined to destroy the power of the church,' he says.

Father Gabriel convinces him to come to see the San Carlos mission before making his final decision, yet in truth it appears that his decision has already been made. After being almost overwhelmed by the paradise-like nature of the San Carlos mission and its members, Altamirano tells the Indians that they must leave the mission. The Indian chief replies, 'It was God's will that we leave the jungle and build the mission ... Why has God changed his mind? ... I do not believe that you know the will of God

... You do not speak for God. You speak for the Portuguese.' Altamirano
warns the Jesuit priests against joining the Guarani in resisting this decision, because to do so would result in excommunication. Father Gabriel
says that he must stay with the Indians.

The Guarani retrieve Rodrigo's armour from the river, and Rodrigo,
John and Ralph join the Indians in planning to defend the mission.
Gabriel is sad and tells Rodrigo that he cannot give him his blessing in
these matters. He says, 'You promised your life to God, Rodrigo, and God
is love.' Meanwhile the soldiers of the Portuguese forces are being blessed
by their own priest. This army slowly climbs up to the plateau, bringing
cannons and gunpowder. When they are camped for the night Rodrigo
leads a raiding party to steal powder and rifles. During this raid Rodrigo
kills a soldier to keep him from crying out and warning others.

Before the final, climactic battle Rodrigo asks for Gabriel's blessing.
The priest replies, 'No. If you are right you'll have God's blessing ... If
might is right, love has no place in the world ... I can't bless you.' They
embrace and Gabriel gives Rodrigo the cross that had belonged to the
priest who was martyred in the opening sequence of the film. Against the
overwhelming numbers of the colonial soldiers the Jesuits and the Indians
are killed one by one and driven back to the mission. Here Rodrigo is
among the last to fall. Lying on the ground he watches Father Gabriel and
the Indian worshippers carrying a cross and religious icons as they walk
out of the burning church into volleys of rifle fire. Rodrigo watches until
Gabriel finally falls over under the unrelenting hail of bullets. It is all over
– the mission has been totally devastated.

Altamirano receives the news and says to the Portuguese governor,
'You have the effrontery to tell me that this slaughter was necessary!'
'Given the legitimate purpose that you sanctioned ... in truth, yes!' is the
reply. The governor continues, 'You had no alternative, your Eminence.
We must work in the world. The world is thus.' Altamirano retorts, 'No!
Thus we have made the world. Thus I have made it!'

The final scenes of the film show us naked Guarani children sal-
vaging musical instruments from the mission, leaving crosses and icons
behind as they paddle off in a canoe back into the jungle. Meanwhile
Altamirano concludes his letter to the Pope: 'So, your Holiness, now your
priests are dead and I am left alive. But in truth it is I that am dead and

they are alive. For, as always, your Holiness, the spirit of the dead will survive the memory of the living.'

Topics for further thought and discussion
1. Heroes and villains: a missiological Who's Who?
A. Who would you say are the 'Heroes' and the 'Villains' in the film? Does Altamirano play a Pilate-like role? Would he have been better to adopt Gamaliel's advice in Acts 5:38-39? Are any of the characters free from self-interests?

B. Do any of the characters manage to disentangle themselves from the competing demands of church and state? Is it desirable, or even possible, for us to do so? How do you respond to the suggestion that church leaders should not meddle in politics?

C. What modern parallels can you think of for the hypocritical squabble between Spain and Portugal over the definition of slavery portrayed in the film?

D. Do we have our equivalents of the 'jungle of the Jesuit order'? How can the very human tendency to want to speak for God in a church situation be checked and administered properly?

E. When the Papal representative Altamirano asks Father Gabriel 'What do you think is at issue here?', how would *you* answer? Is Father Gabriel's answer correct, simplistic, or simply naïve?

F. With which of the two responses to the final confrontation with the forces of commercial interests do you sympathize most, Father Gabriel's or Rodrigo Mendoza's? How would you apply the traditional 'Just War' theory to this case? In what ways is Dietrich Bonhoeffer's action against the Nazism of his native Germany a comparable case?

2. Conversion and the missionary impulse
A. In *The Mission* (1986), the book upon which the film was based, Robert Bolt describes Father Gabriel's thinking about establishing the San

Carlos mission above the Iguaçu Falls with these words: 'Come what may, the Guarani above the falls could not be abandoned to their ignorance.' In what ways is this particular theme developed within the film as a whole? How does it compare with Romans 1:20-32 and Acts 17:22-34?

B. Again in the book, Bolt makes much of the desire of Rodrigo Mendoza to enter the Jesuit community as a lay-brother as the catalyst for the Guarani Indians to accept Christianity and accept communion at the Mass. Note the following passage involving Hacugh, chief of the Guarani:

> Gabriel had taken good care to explain to the Guarani that at their Masses the brethren consumed the blood and flesh of Christ himself. As a result they held the Jesuits in awe, watching in strict silence when they administered the sacraments to one another, but they could not be persuaded to take the Mass themselves.
>
> 'Why will you not take the Mass?' he asked Hacugh. 'It is a joy. It is an honour.'
>
> 'Why does not he?' Hacugh pointed to Mendoza.
>
> 'Because he has committed a crime against God, and he does not believe he is forgiven. Is that not true?' He appealed to Mendoza.
>
> 'Yes, that is true. And it is nobody's concern but mine.'
>
> Hacugh's expression became watchful. 'I will take it when I see you take it.' He nodded and turned away. The other men followed him.

What lessons does this passage intimate about the role of sacramental symbols as expressions of our Christian faith? Is it right for Hacugh to make his own conversion to Christianity dependent upon Mendoza's spiritual struggle in this way? What about the tribe following Hacugh's example and becoming Christians once he does so: is there a place in missions for such a 'tribal conversion'? Why or why not? What role does the sacrament of baptism similarly play in the task of Christian mission?

C. Music as an expression of the human spirit plays an important part in both the film and the novel, particularly as it serves not only as an instrument for the conversion of the Guarani, but a declaration of their native spirituality. Yet, how significant is it that most of the music in the film is typically 'western', drawn from composers of Catholic masses, for instance? What lessons can we learn from this and apply to our own setting?

D. How can Mendoza's penance and the journey of Christian in Bunyan's *Pilgrim's Progress* be compared? What does the load Mendoza carries represent? What is the significance of the load being cut off by one of the Guarani? Who determines a penance? Who can accept an act of repentance? Is it right that the load must be carried until Mendoza himself thinks that it has been long enough?

3. A Controversial Ending
A. The final scene of the film shows the surviving children of the Guarani Indians getting in a canoe and paddling down-stream into the unknown that awaits them. Yet, as we watch this scene we hear the voice of the Papal representative Altamirano powerfully expressing a message of ongoing hope:

> So, your Holiness, now your priests are dead, and I am left alive. But in truth it is I who am dead, and they who live. For as always, your Holiness, the spirit of the dead will survive in the memory of the living.

This takes us back to one of the opening sequences of the film, where a Jesuit priest is tied to a cross and sent down the river over the falls to his martyrdom by the Guarani. In other words, the whole of the film is set very much within a martyrdom context, where the ultimate cost of missionary activity is presented in stark fashion.

In the commercially-available version of *The Mission* this speech by Altamirano is followed immediately by three paragraphs of written text on the screen, which are in turn followed by the film credits. These words help to up-date the message as well as provide the biblical basis for hope in the midst of pain and loss. The three paragraphs are:

> The Indians of South America are still engaged in a struggle to defend their land and their culture.

Many of the priests who, inspired by faith and love, continue to support
the rights of the Indians for justice, do so with their lives.

'The light shines in the darkness and the darkness has not overcome it'
(John 1:5).

However, in the televised version of the film the three paragraphs are cut,
and we move straight from Altamirano's speech to the film credits. What
difference does this change make to the overall message of the film? Does
it rob it of a message to the modern world? Why do you think that this
editing was done?

B. As the film reaches its climax, we see the Portuguese troops receive a
blessing from the priest before setting out to destroy the mission. By contrast Father Gabriel refuses to give a blessing to Rodrigo with the words,
'If might is right, love has no place in the world.' Under what circumstances do you think it is right for Christians to participate in a war?

C. The Portuguese governor tells Altamirano, 'We must work in the
world. The world is thus.' Altamirano replies, 'No! Thus we have made
the world. Thus I have made it.' Who is right in this exchange of opinions? Where do the boundaries of individual responsibility and corporate
responsibility begin and end?

D. Alan MacDonald in his *Films in Close-Up* (Leicester: Frameworks,
1991) discusses the film on pages 105-9, and criticizes it as being incomplete, for not ending with a clear message about the resurrection hope
which awaits Christians. Do you agree with his criticism?

18
Blade Runner:
On the Definition of Humanity

Film Details
Blade Runner (1982)
Directed by Ridley Scott.
Starring Harrison Ford as Rick Deckard, Rutger Hauer as Roy Batty and Sean Young as Rachel Rosen.
Screenplay by Hampton Fancher and David Peoples.
Music by Vangelis.
BBFC certificate '15'.
Duration 114 minutes.
Released on video-cassette and DVD by Warner Home Video.

The film is loosely based upon the story in Philip K. Dick's *Do Androids Dream of Electric Sheep?* (New York: Doubleday, 1968), which has been republished under the title *Do Androids Dream of Electric Sheep? : filmed as Blade Runner* (London: Millennium, 1999).

A soundtrack of the music from the film is also available, distributed by WEA International, Ltd. (1982).

The film has been the subject of considerable discussion among science-fiction specialists. Of special note is Annette Kuhn (ed.). *Alien Zone: Cultural Theory and Contemporary Science Fiction Cinema* (London: Verso Books, 1990), which contains several articles dealing with the film. There is also an interesting article entitled 'Back to the Future' by Mark Salisbury in *Empire* magazine (December, 1992), pp. 90-7, which discusses the 'Director's cut' of the film.

Synopsis
The film is set in Los Angeles in the year 2019, and abounds with images and technology so as to represent American life at that time. The city is crowded, polluted and dangerous. Deckard is an ex-cop, ex-killer, ex-Blade Runner, recently retired from his job as a bounty hunter. Deckard

specialized in tracking down and 'retiring' (that is, exterminating) 'replicants', genetically engineered beings who, for all practical purposes, were indistinguishable from normal humans. For obvious reasons, such replicants were banned from Earth and were forced to live 'off-world', where they fulfilled the menial and often dangerous jobs that humans could not or would not do. A group of six of the latest and most advanced replicants, the Nexus-6 model, have hi-jacked a space-shuttle, killing its occupants, and have come back to Earth. They are led by Roy Batty, a combat-model Nexus-6 whose abilities far exceed those of normal human beings. The replicants are searching for Dr. Eldon Tyrell, head of the multi-national corporation which has developed and manufactured them.

The film opens with a worker at the Tyrell Corporation being given an eye-reaction test. This diagnostic test is used to identify replicants: their pupils do not react to emotion or stress with the same responses as do normal humans. The worker under investigation is one of the renegade replicants, and he kills the investigator because he fears he has been discovered. News of this murder requires Deckard to be brought out of retirement in order that he might track down and 'retire' these replicants before they destroy the fabric of the society which has created them.

At the Tyrell Corporation, Deckard is introduced to Rachel, whom he discovers through the eye-test to be a replicant. Tyrell tells Deckard that he has given the latest models a memory, which has the effect of helping them to control their emotions: "'More human than human' is our motto," Tyrell declares triumphantly. He also tells Deckard that the Nexus-6 model has a built-in life span of four years, as a precautionary safety measure. In pursuing the replicants Deckard is forced to examine his own beliefs about human life: 'A replicant with feelings? But then Blade Runners are not supposed to have feelings either!' Life is further complicated when Deckard falls in love with Rachel.

As Deckard begins to find and 'retire' the replicants we learn of their fear of their 'incept date', symbolizing their four-year long longevity. As Pris, one of the replicants explains, the replicants have a problem with 'accelerated decrepitude'. They are therefore anxious to find their 'creator', Dr Eldon Tyrell, to overcome the problem of their imminent termination date.

When Roy Batty meets Tyrell, he exclaims: 'Death! I want more life!' Tyrell tells him that there is an in-built DNA code which cannot be reversed. In a scene which is strikingly reminiscent of Mary Shelley's *Frankenstein* wherein the creation turns on the creator, Roy says to Tyrell, 'You are the god of Biomechanics!', kisses him and then brutally kills him in frustration. In the film's climax, Deckard comes face to face with Roy Batty. Roy begins to lose his motive force and pierces his wrist with a nail in an attempt to keep consciousness: 'You only play the game if you're alive!' he shouts to Deckard. Having cornered Deckard, who now hangs precariously suspended on a girder high above the city streets, Roy says, 'Quite an experience to live in fear. That's what it is like to be a slave!' He then saves Deckard by lifting him off of the girder. The film closes with Deckard and Rachel travelling off into the bright, blue future and the voice of Deckard saying about Rachel, 'Tyrell had said that there was no termination date on this model'. He asks of us rhetorically, 'I don't know how long we'll have together, but who does?'

Topics for further thought and discussion
1. Playing God: who has the power of creating life?
A. According to Genesis 1-3, what is it that is special about the creation of human beings? Are there any differences in emphasis between the two creation stories contained in the book, 1:1-2:4a and 2:4b-3:24?

B. How would you define 'a human being'? By this definition would the replicants of *Blade Runner* be classified as human?

C. Is there a difference in kind between the manufacture of a 'Tyrell Corporation' replicant and the scientific technology now available for genetic research and *in vitro* fertilization?

D. Deckard looks at some of Leon's family photographs and asks rhetorically, 'Replicants don't have family photographs because replicants don't have families?' How important is memory for the continuity of personality in people? In what ways did the implantation of memories help constitute personality for the 'replicants'? In what ways might the reverse (the loss of memory and the subsequent disintegration of personality) be seen in people suffering with afflictions such as Alzheimer's disease?

2. Issues of life and death
A. Why do you think Deckard wanted to retire from his life as a Blade Runner, a bounty-hunter who pursues and 'retires' the offending 'replicants'? What is it that causes Roy Batty to reach out and save Deckard's life?

B. What is the significance of J.F. Sebastian's having 'Methuselah syndrome'? Why were the Nexus-6 'replicants' given a four-year life span? How might this 'in-built limitation on longevity' be likened to the theological idea of original sin? In what ways is it different? Does the confrontation between Batty and Tyrell reflect the human desire for immortality?

C. Roy Batty, speaking to Deckard who is struggling to keep himself from falling off of the girder to certain death, says, 'Quite an experience to live in fear. That's what it is to be a slave.' In this situation, what is freedom and who is free?

D. 'I think, therefore I am,' says Pris. Is this a sufficient definition of our existence? How does this compare with Rachel's mechanical response in repeating Deckard's words after him: 'Love me?' – 'I love you.' 'Trust me?' – 'I trust you.'

3. Shadows of the Christian faith?
A. Do you think that Roy Batty's self-inflicted pain by punching a nail through his wrist is intended to invoke recollections of the crucifixion of Christ? If so, what point is director Ridley Scott wanting to make within the story-line of the film?

B. What is the significance of the release of the dove by Batty as he dies at the end of the film? Might this be taken as a neo-Pentecostal motif? Is this an image of freedom and immortality?

C. In what ways is Batty attempting to 'redeem' his people from the genetically-engineered death to which they will succumb? Is it significant that Batty quotes Ecclesiastes 3:2: ' ... a time to die'?

D. Deckard's thoughts about Batty's impending death are given as follows:

> I don't know why he saved my life. Maybe in those last moments he loved life more than he ever had before. Not just his life ... anybody's life ... my life. All he'd wanted were the same answers the rest of us want: 'Where do I come from?' 'Where am I going?' 'How long have I got?'. All I could do was sit there and watch him die.

Re-read the account of Jesus' crucifixion in Mark 15:22-38 in light of this scene and dialogue from the film. Imagine yourself as an eye-witness to the crucifixion of Jesus Christ. What similarities are there between the questions raised here about Batty and those you might raise about the death of Jesus? What are the major points of contrast?

E. The film closes with a series of voice-overs: Deckard's colleague Gaff says of Rachel, 'Too bad she won't live, but who does?' Again, Deckard is heard to say of his relationship with her, 'I don't know how long we'll have together, but who does?' In spite of all the technological expertise death is the final victor. Does the film offer any hope at all? What then is the gospel for the modern world? Is it simply eternal life in the hereafter?

19
Witness:
'In the World but Not of the World'

Film details

Witness (1985)

Directed by Peter Weir.

Starring Harrison Ford as John Book and Kelly McGillis as Rachel Lapp.

Screenplay by Earl W. Wallace, William Kelley and Pamela Wallace.

BBFC certificate 'PG'.

Duration 112 minutes. Released on video-cassette and DVD by Paramount.

A book entitled *Witness*, based upon the screenplay is also available, by William Kelley and Earl W. Wallace (London: New English Library, 1985). The film won an Oscar for best screenplay.

Synopsis

Pennsylvania, 1984: within an Amish community there is a funeral for Jacob Lapp, who leaves an attractive widow, Rachel, and a son, Samuel. Images of corn fields, horse-drawn wagons, physical labour and sunset seem to be saying 'Paradise!' Rachel and Samuel travel to the big city – 'You'll see many things!' says Grandfather Lapp. Waiting for a connection at the railway station in Philadelphia, Samuel goes to the toilet where he is the witness to a murder. A black man kills a white man, with another unidentified man looking on. Enter John Book, a detective with the Philadelphia police department, who is responsible for investigating the case. Samuel is questioned by the police and is taken to look for suspects: the police car, drug-pushers, the rough and violent city streets, even the police station itself, all appear as alien to him. Rachel tries to explain to Book, 'We have nothing to do with your laws. We don't need to know anything about you.'

Samuel identifies the killer as another police-officer, named McFee. Book shares this information with his captain, Paul Schaeffer. Shortly thereafter, when Book is shot by McFee he realizes that Schaeffer is also involved. Seeking to protect Samuel and Rachel, Book drives to the Amish community where he collapses and needs to be cared for by Rachel and her people. Now Schaeffer tries to find them; he knows that they are Amish and that their name is Lapp. Book slowly recovers from his gunshot wound and is given some of Jacob's clothes – without buttons, only hooks and eyes. 'Buttons are proud,' explains Rachel. Book goes into town to use the telephone; his manner marks him out as different: 'He's an Englishman,' they say, and that explains everything.

Samuel shows Book the farm, a counterpart to Samuel seeing the city. There is a developing relationship between Book and Rachel; they listen to a (forbidden) radio and dance. This is seen by the grandfather and there is a scene that develops the idea of community rules. Rachel is warned about the Amish boundaries of propriety and cautioned that she could be put out of the community. Meanwhile we cut to Schaeffer, still trying to locate Book and the Lapps. 'Can you see John at a prayer meeting? We're like the Amish, a cult with our own rules, and John has broken those rules.' The two worlds are juxtaposed, set in sharp contrast.

There follows another scene of 'Paradise': a barn raising, the building of a barn for a newly-married Amish couple. The whole community is involved, working together, talking together, eating together, singing together, laughing together. That night Book and Rachel come face to face as she is bathing. She is naked to the waist, a storm is breaking outside, perhaps symbolizing the storm that is raging in their lives. She turns away and he returns to his room. In the morning Book says to her, 'If we'd made love either I would have had to stay or you would have had to leave.' The two worlds collide again.

Another visit to the local town involves Book in a fight with local youths who are taunting the peace-loving Amish folk. This leads to a police report of the incident, and so to the whereabouts of Book, Rachel and Samuel being discovered by Schaeffer. Book prepares to leave and in a farewell scene, Rachel lays aside the veil-covering for her head, a symbol of her acceptance of the Amish world, and passionately kisses Book.

The film reaches its climax with the arrival of Schaeffer and two other corrupt policeman, including McFee, at the Lapp farm. They are bent on killing Book. Book manages to kill the two officers, but not without

Rachel being taken hostage by Schaeffer. The alarm bell, rung by Samuel, brings the whole community to witness Schaeffer holding a gun to Rachel. 'Are you going to shoot them all?' asks Book of Schaeffer, 'Enough! Enough!' Book takes the gun away and soon more police arrive to arrest Schaeffer. Now we see many police cars and police officers surrounding the Lapp farm. Book is smoking a cigarette – his world has arrived in the Amish community.

The final scene sees Book dressed in his modern-day suit saying good-bye to the Lapp family. The last word is with Grandfather Lapp: 'You be careful *out there* among them English.'

Topics for further thought and discussion
1. What's in a title?
A. Why is the film entitled 'Witness'? Who or what do you think is being described in such a way? As you watch the film, to what are *you* a witness?

B. How far does our world-view shape our values? How far do our experiences determine our beliefs?

C. What are some of the problems associated with living in the modern world? Can we ever find good reasons for being completely separate from the world? Is it possible to be a witness while being separated from the world in such a way?

D. As Samuel and Rachel leave for Baltimore, Samuel's grandfather says to him, 'You will *see* many things.' To what would Samuel be a witness if he came to your town or city?

2. The collision of cultures
A. Is the Amish world-view confirmed by the experience of Rachel and Samuel? What do you think that John Book finds attractive about their way of life? What do you think that Samuel and Rachel find attractive about Book's way of life?

B. When a local policeman is asked to locate the Lapp family and to use the local telephone directory to do so, he says, 'Amish doesn't live in the

20th-century. Amish doesn't think in the 20th-century.' Compose a list of distinctive attitudes and features of daily life which would characterize the Amish community as portrayed in the film. Compose another list of distinctive attitudes and features of daily life which would characterize big-city Philadelphia as it is portrayed in the film. Would you like to live within an Amish community (or a British equivalent)? Why or why not?

C. It is tempting to see the Amish community of Pennsylvania as a miniature Paradise, a place of peace, tranquillity and social harmony. Do you think the film romanticizes the Amish way of life? Is it realistic to 'retreat to Eden' in this way?

D. Following the death of Carter, Book asserts on the telephone that Shaeffer has 'lost the meaning' of being a policeman. Can we infer from this that Book has 'found the meaning'? Or has he known it all along?

3. Does might make right?
A. Is the use of guns portrayed positively or negatively within the film? In what ways could we describe this as a film against violence? Would it be possible to make the essential point of the film without scenes of graphic violence?

B. What is John Book trying to prove when he attacks the 'ice-cream mugger'? Is Book being self-indulgent, unable to cope with his own emotions? Do you think that the mugger got what he deserved and were you elated when you saw it happen? Yet, what were the consequences of Book's actions in beating up the man? What do the answers to these questions tell you about your own attitudes to violence and aggression?

C. When Samuel rings the alarm bell the community rushes from the fields to the farmhouse and are 'witnesses' to the confrontation between Shaeffer and Book. Here we see the pacifist community disarming the man of violence. Without the presence of the larger community would Shaeffer have killed Book and the Lapp family? What lessons does this teach us about the nature of a community and how might we apply them to the community of which we are a part?

20
Amadeus:
The Destructiveness of an
All-Consuming Jealousy

Film details

Amadeus (1984)

Directed by Milos Forman.

Starring F. Murray Abraham as Antonio Salieri, Tom Hulce as Wolfgang Amadeus, and Elizabeth Berridge as Constance Mozart.

Screenplay by Peter Shaffer.

BBFC certificate 'U'.

Duration 158 minutes.

Released on video-cassette and DVD by Thorn EMI.

The film is based on the award-winning play, *Amadeus*, also by Peter Schaffer (Harmondsworth: Penguin, 1981) which contains a Postscript on the making of the film adaptation.

Excerpts from the soundtrack of the film are available distributed by London Records Limited (1984 & 1985)

The movie won a total of eight Academy Awards, including Best Actor (Abraham in the role of Salieri), Best Picture, Best Director, Best Screenplay, Best Art Direction.

Synopsis

The film is a highly fictionalized account of the life of the classical composer Wolfgang Amadeus Mozart (1756-1792) and his relationship with the Italian composer Antonio Salieri. The film begins with Salieri's attempted suicide and his removal to a mental asylum. Here he is visited by a priest, to whom Salieri tells the story of his relationship with Mozart. It is, of course, the story as Salieri sees it, from his own envy-ridden viewpoint. Salieri is consumed with jealousy. He can speak of Mozart's music as 'hearing the voice of God', yet sees Mozart as a 'giggling, dirty-minded youth.'

Mozart is taught and encouraged by his father, and as a child prodigy composed his first major works at the age of five. Salieri has neither had the encouragement, nor does he possess the gifts, to match this. This leaves Salieri both envious and depressed, summed up by his words: 'All I wanted was to sing for God. He gave me the longing and made me mute.'

Mozart's affair with Salieri's star singer increases Salieri's anger. The envy and bitter longing to succeed lead Salieri to plot against Mozart. To God he says: 'From now on you and I are enemies. You chose a smutty boy!'; and 'I will ruin your incarnation.' This path of destruction takes shape in Salieri's mind when watching a performance of Mozart's opera *Don Giovanni* , wherein Salieri realizes that Mozart has summoned up the ghost of his dead father Leopold. 'And so, the madness began in me,' Salieri tells the priest at the asylum. He begins to plot revenge. While the exact way that Salieri determines to 'kill' Mozart remains vague, it is evidently going to involve driving him to overwork and excessive consumption of alcohol.

Dressing up in a costume that Leopold had worn at a masked ball, Salieri goes to visit Mozart in order to commission a Requiem Mass. This unnerves Mozart, who begins to drink heavily, and we see the gradual destruction of the composer. His wife recognizes what is happening and tries to stop Mozart from working on the Requiem, but Mozart seems to be driven on by a sense of fear and guilt.

Salieri is planning Mozart's funeral, where this Requiem will be presented as Salieri's own composition and this 'divine' music will break over Mozart's coffin, 'God made to listen!'. All of this comes to a climax in a fictional night scene with Salieri acting as a scribe for the dying Mozart, in an endeavour to see the manuscript of the Requiem completed. It is all too much for the frail Mozart, who dies in mid-composition. The final irony is that even here Salieri meets defeat, for Mozart is taken away and buried in a pauper's grave in the middle of a rainstorm – there is no state funeral, no Requiem, and no glory for Salieri.

At the close of the film we return to the asylum. Salieri laughs at the priest and says, 'Your beloved God killed Mozart and kept me alive to torture me for 32 years ... my music becoming fainter all the time, while his becoming more and more.' Salieri recognizes that he has been responsible for the death of Mozart, as well as the destruction of the 'divine' music that he recognized Mozart to have composed. Even with the death of Mozart, Salieri's envy, bitterness and depression continue, but are now added to by the torture of guilt.

Topics for further thought and discussion
1. The gifting of God and self-worth
A. The film opens with a conversation between the priest and Salieri in which the priest asserts that 'All men are equal in God's eyes.' Salieri questions this with bitter disbelief: 'Are they?'. How does this set the scene for the central theme of the film?

B. Salieri says, 'All I wanted was to sing to God. He gave me that longing and made me mute.' Does this sum up Salieri's view of his own worth? How does this contrast with Mozart's brash declaration: 'I may not be the only composer in Vienna, but I am the best!'

C. Compose a list of instances within the film where the gifts of Mozart and Salieri are attributed to God. Is there a difference between natural ability and special endowment by God portrayed within the two characters? When Salieri describes Mozart's music as 'the voice of God' what do you think he means? (You might want to consult 1 Corinthians 12-14 on this question).

D. In Peter Shaffer's *Amadeus*, the play upon which the film was based, the final line of Salieri is 'Mediocrities everywhere, now and to come, I absolve you all. Amen.' What do you think he means by this offer of absolution?

2. The metamorphosis of admiration into envy
A. Identify the scenes in which we see Salieri's admiration for Mozart's music being expressed. How does this clash with the impression that Salieri has about Mozart himself when he describes him in terms such as 'that giggling, dirty-minded youth', 'the creature', 'a conceited brat', 'an absurd instrument'?

B. Is Salieri's struggle with jealousy and envy one that he has with Mozart or with God?

C. Peter Shaffer writes of the clash between Salieri and Mozart in this way:

> To me there is something pure about Salieri's pursuit of an eternal Absolute through music, just as there is something irredeemably impure about his simultaneous pursuit of eternal fame. The yoking of these two clearly opposed drives led us finally to devise a climax totally different from that of the play, a night long encounter between the physically dying Mozart and the spiritually ravenous Salieri, motivated entirely by the latter's crazed lust to snatch a piece of divinity for himself.

In what ways might this also characterize the tensions we feel in Christian ministry?

D. 'Mozart's 'self-centredness' manifests itself in pride whereas Salieri's self-centredness manifests itself in envy.' Can this film help us to cope with our God-given humanity as it indicates where self-centredess might lead? Does this flag up a warning for our churches?

3. 'That was God laughing at me!'
A. Why does Salieri help Mozart in transcribing the *Requiem Mass*? What does Salieri's plan to use this commissioned work, arranged so surreptitiously under cloak of disguise, tell us about his understanding of God?

B. In the film, laughter plays a prominent role but who has the last laugh? What effect has Salieri's obsessive jealousy of Mozart on his own relationship with God?

C. In what ways does this story serve as a warning light to our own personal relationship with God when faced with the success or accomplishments of others?

21
Gandhi: The Strength of Weakness

Film details
Gandhi (1982)
Directed by Richard Attenborough
Starring Ben Kingsley as Mohandas Gandhi, Candice Bergen as Margaret
Bourke-White, and Edward Fox as General Dyer.
Screenplay by John Briley.
Music by Ravi Shankar and George Fenton.
BBRC certificate 'PG'.
Duration 181 minutes.
Released on video-cassette and DVD by Columbia Pictures.
The original soundtrack of the film is available from RCA.

In 1925 Gandhi published his own story, a book which has recently
been re-issued as *An Autobiography, or, The Story of My Experiments
with Truth* (Harmondsworth: Penguin Books, 1982).

Richard Attenborough has written a book detailing the making of the
film entitled *In Search of Gandhi* (London : The Bodley Head, 1982).

The film won a total of eight Academy Awards, including Best Actor,
Best Picture, Best Director, Best Screenplay, Best Cinematography. It also
received 5 BAFTA Awards.

Synopsis
'No man's life is encompassed in one telling.' This film is essentially the
story of the life of Mohandas K. Gandhi (1869-1948), founder of the
modern state of India and one of the great figures of the twentieth century.
It begins in New Dehli in 1948 with the assassination of Gandhi, and follows immediately with the funeral procession through the packed streets
of the city. We hear the newscaster saying, 'the object of this massive tribute died as he lived, without property ... no leader of armies ... and yet
dignitaries have come from all over the world ... he spoke for the conscience of all mankind ... will future generations believe that such flesh

and blood ever walked this earth?' So the scene is dramatically set for the story of a truly remarkable human being.

The film then moves to South Africa in 1893 with Gandhi, a fledgling lawyer, coming into conflict with apartheid. After being thrown off a train for daring to travel first class, he gathers with leaders of the Asian community and persuades them to oppose the Pass Laws. Gandhi is beaten and arrested, but does not resist; here we see the start of peaceful non-cooperation. He is soon joined by a clergyman, Charlie Andrews, and together they oppose unjust laws, set up an ashram, and publish a journal.

The Finger Print Law brings further conflict, and Gandhi encourages the whole coloured community to an opposition that involves no violence, but does involve marches and strikes. Gandhi is imprisoned, but Charlie tells him that he has given the people a way to fight. With reaction around the world calling for a change in this policy, General Smuts concedes the repeal of the hated laws and Gandhi is released.

The film now moves to India, as Gandhi arrives in Bombay in 1915 to a welcome from the crowds and from the Congress Party who are calling for Home Rule. Instead of joining in this debate, Gandhi travels the whole of India to see how the people live. When he returns he tells the Congress Party that the people need bread rather than the demands for independence; they need to know that the politicians stand with them.

Again Gandhi sets up an ashram and publishes a journal. His reputation is country-wide, and a request from a village elder takes him to investigate the poverty of the people. The village railway station is surrounded by a seething mass of people. A British army officer asks what is happening; a soldier tells him that a telegram had arrived saying, simply, 'He is coming!'

Gandhi organizes the people to boycott the sale of English cloth, as the economic conditions of its manufacture and sale is a cause of much poverty. He is again arrested and eventually set free. In the Governor's residence, there is comment, 'He is one lone man armed only with honesty and a bamboo staff … what can he do to us?' The Governor says, 'Children back home are writing essays about him!' Ultimately, the Government is forced to compromise over some of Gandhi's demands. Laws against sedition lead to a demand for violent opposition by some of the leaders in the Congress Party. Gandhi calls for the day when the law comes into force to be a national day of prayer and fasting. Challenged with the words 'You mean a strike!', he replies: 'No, a day of prayer and fasting for 350 million Indians'. Gandhi is yet again arrested for selling his journal, there are riots, and we witness the terrible massacre at the Golden Temple of Amritsar which took place in April of 1919. 'Maybe we are not ready,' laments Gandhi. Later, in a meeting with the British authorities, he says, 'You are masters in someone else's home ... you must humiliate us to control us ... it is time you left.'

The boycott of English cloth becomes the focus of peaceful protest, but riots lead to the killing of policemen and Gandhi says that the protest must stop. When the leaders question his suggestion, he begins a fast which he vows he will only end when the protest has ended throughout the whole of India. As Gandhi explains, 'All through history the way of truth and love has won.' The protest stops, Gandhi is arrested again on the charge of sedition and is sent to prison for six years. Out of prison some years later, and still preaching non-violence, Gandhi finds another way of peaceful protest – salt, for which there was a royal monopoly of production. Gandhi leads a march to the sea, to make salt. By now he attracts the interest of the world's press in all that he does.

The Congress Party leaders begin selling salt. One by one they are arrested; soon 100,000 are in jail. 'Any violence?' the Governor asks, only to find that apart from one police officer losing his temper, there was none. This is followed by the march on the Dharasana Salt Works, watched by the American press. The men march, the police club them down, the women bandage the wounded; it continues all day. The reporter phones in his report, 'Whatever moral ascendancy the West held was lost here today!' The result of this protest, and the press coverage of it, leads to Gandhi being invited to London for a meeting with Prime Minister Ramsay MacDonald to discuss independence. Over this meeting hangs the threat of war with Germany.

The declaration of war in 1939 again sees Gandhi under house arrest, largely because he will not cease from preaching pacifism. A *Life* magazine journalist, Margaret Bourne-White, comes to interview him and photograph him toward the end of the war. 'Could Hitler be defeated with non-violence?' she asks. 'Not without defeats,' replies Gandhi, 'but are there not defeats?' Soon afterwards Gandhi's wife dies of a heart attack.

The Second World War ends and Viscount Mountbatten arrives to oversee the transition to independence for India. Now Moslem and Hindu rivalry come into the open as the possibility of real power arrives. Gandhi persuades the Hindu majority-leader Jawaharlal Nehru to stand down in favour of the Moslem minority-leader Mohammed Ali Jinnah, but is told, 'Not everyone is a Mahatma, Gandhi.' The fear of rioting leads to the agreement for separate states of Moslem Pakistan and Hindu India to be formed. The moving of religious groups into these two countries leads to a violent confrontation on the Pakistani border in 1947, and ethnic rioting which spreads throughout the whole of the Indian sub-continent. Gandhi initiates another fast, again to the point of his death, before the fighting has stopped.

The film now moves to the same scene with which it opened – the assassination of Gandhi. He is planning to go to Pakistan 'to prove to Hindus here and Moslems there, that the only devils are those running around in our own hearts.' Mirabel, Gandhi's faithful follower, says, 'When we needed it he offered the world a way out of madness. But he doesn't see it.' 'Nor does the world', responds Margaret Bourne-White, the reporter from *Life* magazine.

Gandhi is assassinated by a disaffected Hindu, and his ashes are scattered over the Ganges. We are left with his words ringing in our ears, 'When I despair, I remember that all through history the way of truth and love always triumphs ... and wickedness falls.'

Topics for further thought and discussion
1. A Modern Messiah?
A. 'Will generations believe that such flesh and blood ever walked on this earth?' Does Richard Attenborough use these words, spoken at the funeral of Gandhi, to frame the whole film as a tribute to a human messiah?

B. While in South Africa, Gandhi says to Charlie Andrews, 'Doesn't the New Testament say, "If your enemy strikes you on the right cheek, offer him the left?" ' 'I think that the phrase was used metaphorically,' says Charlie. Ghandi replies:

I am not sure. I have thought about it a great deal and I suspect that he meant that you must show courage and be willing to take a blow, several blows, to show that you will not strike back, nor will you be turned aside. And when you do that it calls on something in human nature, something that makes his hatred decrease and his respect for you increase. I have seen it work.

This is the basis of Gandhi's peaceful non-cooperation, but is Gandhi's non-violent direct action what Jesus had in mind?

C. The British Governor describes Gandhi as 'One lone man armed only with honesty and a bamboo staff.' Charlie Andrews says to Gandhi, 'They call you Bapu, which means "Father" '. The leaders of the Congress Party say, 'They're calling you Mahatma, which means "world-soul" ''. In such descriptions and titles, what similarities and differences would you draw between Jesus and Gandhi?

D. The crowds flock to Gandhi, they throw flowers in his path, they respond to his words of wisdom and leadership, but eventually he is assassinated. Does 'Palm Sunday' always turn into 'Good Friday' for those whose lifestyle is too hard to follow? Can you think of other instances in history where this has happened?

2. 'The gates of hell shall not prevail'
A. In response to the Pass Laws in South Africa, Gandhi says, 'If you are a minority of one, the truth is the truth.' Should this be our Christian stand?

B. 'Gandhi was only able to achieve what he did because he operated within the British legal and democratic system.' Do you agree with this often-expressed view? What does this say to us about the importance of Paul's teaching in Romans 13 or the teaching in the Apocalypse about the attitude to the Roman state?

C. Addressing the boycott of English cloth, Gandhi says, 'There must be Hindu and Muslim unity. We must remove untouchability from our hearts and from our lives.' Where do we find similar teaching in the Gospels and how should we apply it today?

D. 'Poverty is the violence that India suffers,' says Gandhi to the *Life* magazine reporter. Was Gandhi's life-work focused on eradicating this violence? If so, does this alter the popular perception of Ghandi?

E. One of the Hindu men involved in the ethnic rioting tells Gandhi that he has killed a little Moslem boy, and says, 'I'm going to hell!' In reply Gandhi says, 'Only God decides who goes to hell. I know a way out of hell; find a little boy and raise him as your own, but make sure that he is a Moslem and that you raise him as one.' Is Gandhi right? Or is this simply a humanistic view of self-achieved redemption?

3. Christian ethical teaching
A. Gandhi once wrote: 'I have nothing new to teach the world. Truth and non-violence are as old as hills.' In his belief, non-violence was the only means whereby one could discover Absolute Truth. Are you comfortable with this as a philosophy? How reminiscent is it of Pilate's question to Jesus (John 18:38)? How would you compare and contrast it to Jesus' teaching in the Golden Rule (Matthew 7:12)?

B. The last words of the film are: 'When I despair I remember that all through history the way of truth and love always triumphs ... and wickedness falls.' Is this true?

C. One of the leaders of the Congress Party remarks about the violence in which a policeman has been killed, 'It's only an eye for an eye'. Gandhi replies, 'But if we go that way the whole world will become blind!' What words of Jesus could we have used to answer this remark, and how do they affect our words and actions?

D. It is often suggested that the Baptist leader Martin Luther King, Jr might be described as a follower of Gandhi. Indeed, James A. Colaiaco in *Martin Luther King, Jr.: Apostle of Militant Nonviolence* (London: Macmillan Press, 1988) writes: 'King's philosophy of nonviolence was a synthesis of the teachings of Jesus Christ and Mohandas K. Gandhi. While the Sermon on the Mount provided the motivating ideal of love, Gandhi provided the method of mass nonviolent direct action' (p. 25). Do you agree? Does such a weakness exist in Jesus Christ's teaching so as to need to be supplemented by Gandhi's approach?

E. We recall that in the beginning of the film Gandhi is reading the New Testament prior to being ejected from the train. He obviously had an interest in Christianity. Do you think that Gandhi might have become a Christian himself if he had found Christ in the Christians he met in South Africa and India?

4. Gandhi and the power-politics of his day
A. 'The children back home are writing essays about him,' complains the British Governor. The commentator at Gandhi's funeral is full of admiration for one who was neither a king nor a leader of armies. What is the difference between admiration and discipleship?

B. General Dyer was responsible for over 1500 casualties at the Amritsar Temple massacre. Why do you think that he felt justified in his actions?

C. In his meeting with the British Governor, Gandhi says, 'You are masters in someone else's home.' One of the Governor's aides says, 'India is British.' What does this have to say to us about political struggles taking place in the world today?

D. Over the general strike (the day of 'prayer and fasting') the British Governor says, 'I've no intention of making a martyr out of him.' But what does 'being a martyr' mean?

E. The selling of salt leads to 100,000 imprisonments. The British Governor is disappointed to find that there has been no violence in the opposition. Why is he disappointed? Is there an answer for us in Romans 12:18-21?

22
The Killing Fields:
The Extreme Limits of Friendship

Film details
The Killing Fields (1984)
Directed by Roland Joffe.
Starring Sam Waterston as Sydney Schanberg, Haing S. Ngor as Dith
Pran, and John Malkovich as Al Rockoff.
Screenplay by Bruce Robinson.
Music by Mike Oldfield.
BBFC certificate '18'.
Duration 148 minutes.
Released on video-cassette and DVD by Warner Brothers.

The film is based upon the Pulitzer Prize-winning article by Sydney
Schanberg entitled 'The Death and Life of Dith Pran'.

The book based upon the screenplay of the film is Christopher
Hudson, *The Killing Fields* (London : Pan Books 1984).

A book by Haing Ngor and Roger Warner, *Surviving the Killing
Fields: The Cambodian Odyssey of Haing Ngor* (London: Chatto &
Windus, 1988) is also available.

The soundtrack of the film is available through Virgin Records
(1984).

The movie won a total of three Academy Awards, including Best
Supporting Actor (Haing S. Ngor in the role of Dith Pran), Best
Cinematography, and Best Editing.

Synopsis
The film is set in Cambodia during the turbulent 1970s as American
involvement in Viet Nam is winding down and communist-led forces
come to power in the countries of South-East Asia. The story told is a true
one, based upon the memoirs of the New York Times correspondent
Sydney Schanberg in which he tells of the remarkable friendship he had

with his Cambodian interpreter/assistant Dith Pran. Most of the film centres upon the siege of the capital Phnom Penh and its aftermath.

The film begins as Schanberg flies into Phnom Penh joining the host of western journalists covering the tense political situation that exists in Cambodia in August of 1973, as the Khmer Rouge troops attempt to topple the government of President Lon Nol. His plane has been delayed in Bangkok due to an increased number of American military flights into the airport. We learn later that there was an 'accidental' bombing of a Cambodian city by the USAF, a fact which Schanberg tries to discover by questioning US military officials who refuse to cooperate. Schanberg joins the café-and-hotel lifestyle of the various reporters covering the war. While ordering breakfast in a café with a fellow reporter a bomb explodes in the street outside, killing and injuring civilians nearby. The pair leap to their feet, the photographer Al Rockoff capturing images of dead and mutilated bodies.

At this critical juncture Dith Pran arrives with news of the USAF bombing of the Cambodian city. The US military officials attempt to prevent press coverage of the event, blocking their passage to the city. A US Embassy official admits, off the record, that the bombing was due to 'pilot error' and that casualties in the hundreds have been sustained. Eventually Pran illicitly arranges a ride to the area on a military launch for himself and Schanberg. They see the carnage, they hear the stories, and everyone seems to be crying for help. They witness the execution of some captured Khmer Rouge troops by the Cambodian soldiers and are promptly arrested. 'Don't leave me, Sydney!' shouts Pran as the two are taken into custody. 'I won't leave you!' Schanberg replies; and the film then moves on to March of 1975.

The fall of Viet Nam is imminent and the future looks bad for Cambodia. Pran fears for both his country and his family. Yet we see Pran's obvious admiration, even love, for Schanberg as the pair go about their job of reporting the war together. The streets and highways are filled with refugees and soldiers, evidence of the Khmer Rouge advance upon the capital. Schanberg and Pran are caught up in the fighting, and there is a great fear that the road to the Phnom Penh airport will be cut off. There are over 2 million refugees in the city and chaos reigns. At the American

Embassy staff are shredding documents in preparation for an ignominious retreat. 'We either stay, or we're living!' says one of the officials.

Schanberg, true to his promise, arranges for Pran and his family of five to be evacuated along with the American nationals. Schanberg asks Pran, 'Do you want to stay or leave?' After a pause Pran replies, 'I am a reporter too.' The film portrays the fear and urgency of the evacuation by American military helicopters: the frenzied activity of those who are getting out and the utter desperation of those who fear they are going to be left behind. Eventually Pran gets his family to the helicopters, but decides to send his wife and children on, waving to them as he stays with his friend Schanberg.

'If the going gets tough, our best bet is the French Embassy,' remarks one of the British correspondents. 'Who told you that?' asks Schanberg. 'The British Embassy,' he replies. The Cambodian government troops eventually surrender to the Khmer Rouge. 'It's peace!' says Pran, happy that the agonies of his nation are over; but Al and Sydney know that it doesn't feel right. The confirmation of their feelings comes with their arrest by the Khmer Rouge. They are taken to a holding centre where they see a number of Cambodians being summarily executed. Throughout the day Pran pleads for the release of Schanberg and the other western journalists and their party. Eventually they are freed and escape through crowded and refugee-clogged streets to the French Embassy. Meanwhile the city is being systematically emptied of civilians by the Khmer Rouge. The order comes to the Embassy that all Cambodians housed in the grounds must by handed over to the Khmer Rouge – a fate virtually equivalent to death. They try and forge a passport for Pran, but fail and Schanberg is left to tell Pran the bad news. Pran brings Schanberg a morning cup of tea; they pack his bag together and embrace, saying their farewells since the Khmer Rouge soldiers are waiting to take Pran away. One of the French journalists shouts at Schanberg, 'Why didn't you get him out while you had the chance? You've got a funny sense of priorities!' But Pran interjects, 'I love him like a brother ... Tell my wife that I love her, and look after my children.' Schanberg looks on silently.

The film moves on to 1979, in New York, with Schanberg trying to find out the whereabouts of Dith Pran. He is also in contact with Pran's family, who live in a graffiti-covered tenement building. Back in his own luxury apartment Schanberg watches a newsreel of President Nixon from 1973 denying American involvement in Cambodia. Meanwhile Pran is one of the thousands of forced labourers in an agricultural camp, terracing fields and preparing them for cultivation. His life is one of constant indoctrination: God is dead, no love, no family, no private thoughts, no corruption from the past, no thought is allowed except that of the Party. The guilty are told to confess their past and thereby receive the forgiveness of the Party, but when they do they are secretly whisked off and executed. To confess is to die, and there is no forgiveness; there is only a need to keep silent. Suspected traitors are identified by their fellows, and after yet another killing in the rice-paddies, Pran decides to make his escape. As the workers finish a day planting rice and begin to return to the camp he hides in the water-flooded field and makes his way across the open country. After some travelling we find Pran in a bomb-cratered landscape, and join him in horror as he sees that the whole area is a carpet of decaying corpses and dried bones. This is one of the 'Killing Fields' of the film's title.

The film cuts to Schanberg receiving the '1976 Journalist of the Year' award in New York. In accepting the prize Schanberg speaks movingly of Pran, of the death and suffering of innocent people, of the White House decision (now admitted) to invade Cambodia so as to relieve pressure in Vietnam and eliminate a Viet Cong training ground. 'Dith Pran and I brought home the reality of those actions ... I receive this on behalf of Dith Pran and myself,' he says. After the presentation Schanberg is challenged by Al, whose interpretation of the events is different. 'It bothers me that you left Pran in Cambodia to win this stinking award!' he says.

Back at home with his sister Schanberg explains, 'I've sent over 500 letters. I've contacted the Red Cross, the World Health Organization ... but I never discussed leaving with Pran. He stayed because I wanted him to stay. I stayed because ...'. His voice trails off and we cut again to Cambodia where Pran is acting as a servant to a Khmer Rouge official in an unnamed village, taking care of the official's son. The official suspects that Pran is an educated man, a suspicion confirmed when he catches Pran listening to the BBC World Service. The official is frightened because the insurgent Vietnamese forces are nearby and his own position as a leader is tenuous. 'I love my country. The leaders of the Party no longer trust the people. I no longer trust them and they do not trust me. I think you love my son. For his sake, look after him', he pleads with Pran.

The Party official provides Pran with money and a map to the Thailand border. He himself is killed trying to prevent the senseless killing of 'traitors' by some of the gun-happy soldiers. Following a Vietnamese air raid Pran makes his move to escape and we follow him, together with the official's son and some other servants, as they move through an ancient temple, a recently destroyed village, and miles of jungle, constantly in danger of being caught by patrolling soldiers of the Khmer Rouge. On a jungle trail one of the servants steps on a land mine and is killed, and the young son of the sympathetic official is mortally wounded. Pran attempts to go on with him to the safety of the Thailand border, but the young boy dies. Pran cremates him and continues on his lonely trek eventually coming over the crest of a hill and looking down into a Red Cross hospital and refugee camp across the border into Thailand. Against all odds, he has managed to escape and survive.

The film returns now to New York where Sydney Schanberg receives news the Pran is alive. He runs through the offices of the *New York Times* relating the good news to all of his newspaper colleagues. He telephones Pran's family and tells them that he has a message from their father. The final scene in the film has Schanberg arriving at the Red Cross camp in Thailand where Pran is tending the wounded who have streamed into the facility. Pran is called to the door by a worker and sees Schanberg arriving in a taxi. To the background sounds of John Lennon's song *Imagine* they embrace. Schanberg says, 'Forgive me?' 'There's nothing to forgive, nothing,' replies Pran.

Topics for further thought and discussion
1. The extremes of life in the midst of war
A. 'To stay is to die'; 'to confess is to die'; 'to love a friend is to sacrifice for him.' How are these three statements worked out in the lives of Sydney Schanberg and Dith Pran?

B. Jesus says in Matthew 26:52 that 'He who lives by the sword, dies by the sword.' What illustrations of this principle can you detect within the film? Is there any group which seems to rise above 'living by the sword'?

C. Were Pran's friends right in trying to forge a passport for him and deceive the Khmer Rouge authorities? How does one decide when it is right to lie and when it is not?

D. The actor who portrayed Dith Pran, Dr Haing S. Ngor, was himself incarcerated in rehabilitation camps of the Khmer Rouge following the fall of Phnom Penh. How do you think this has contributed to his performance in the film? Would you want to relive such an experience as this for the benefit of others' understanding?

2. Duty and responsibility: the expression of character
A. Pran's concern for his family leads to him seeing them safely onto an evacuation flight to the USA, but he remains behind. Why? What were Pran's priorities? Was he simply being selfish? Should he have put his family first and stayed with them?

B. There is a fine line between news-reporting and sensationalistic voyeurism. Can photographs of mutilated bodies and grieving relatives be justified in an attempt to portray the truth in war? In what ways did *The Killing Fields* address these questions?

C. When Pran is finally given up to the Khmer Rouge, Schanberg is rebuked by a fellow journalist: 'Why didn't you get him out while you had the chance? You've got a funny sense of priorities!' Pran rises to Schanberg's defence, 'I love him like a brother. Tell my wife that I love her, and to look after my children.' What were Schanberg's priorities? What do you think his priorities should have been? What would *you* have done in such a situation? How do we decide on our priorities in life?

D. When Schanberg receives the '1976 Journalist of the Year' award he gives a speech that contains high moral invectives against the US policy pursued under President Nixon of clearing the Viet Cong troops from their hiding places in Cambodia. Schanberg utters noble words of praise about the role that Pran had in making the reporting of the situation in Cambodia possible. After the ceremony Schanberg is rebuked by a fellow reporter, 'It bothers me that you left Pran in Cambodia to win that stinking award.' Has Schanberg behaved differently from his own government?

E. Why do you think Schanberg wanted to stay in Phnom Penh? Has reporting the truth become an excuse for selfishness and the desire for critical acclaim by his profession?

3. When is forgiveness needed?
A. Forgiveness plays a part in the film in a number of scenes. In the scene where the Cambodian forced-labourers are being indoctrinated they are offered forgiveness if they confess to a previous life of luxury and capitalistic wrong-thinking. Those who confess are welcomed in an embrace of apparent forgiveness by the Party official, but they are then taken away and are never seen again. What lessons might this teach us about the place that public confession has in life?

B. Following their embrace at the end of the film, Schanberg asks Pran to forgive him, only to be told that there is nothing to forgive. Why does Schanberg feel that he needs Pran's forgiveness? Why does Pran feel that forgiveness in not in order here?

C. Senator Hiram Johnson once said, 'The first casualty when war comes is truth.' How is this statement exemplified in the film? Are the journalists discovering and reporting the truth? Who needs to seek forgiveness from whom?

D. What lessons does the film give us about the nature of forgiveness and how do they inform our understanding about the forgiveness provided for us in Christ's death?

23
The Color Purple:
Breaking Through the Barriers
of Prejudice and Violence

Film details
The Color Purple (1985)
Directed by Steven Spielberg.
Starring Whoopi Goldberg as Celie Johnson, Danny Glover as Albert
Johnson, Margaret Avery as Shug Avery and Oprah Winfrey as Sofia
Johnson.
Screenplay by Menno Meyjes.
BBFC certificate '15'.
Duration 152 minutes.
Released on video-cassette and DVDE by Warner Home Video.

The film is based on the Pulitzer Prize-winning novel *The Color
Purple* by Alice Walker (London: The Women's Press, 1983).

Synopsis
The film opens with two young black girls, Celie and Nettie, playing in a
field of purple flowers. It is 1909, in the state of Georgia, and we are following Alice Walker's acount of life amidst a fairly poor, but land-owning
black community.

The next scene takes place in winter and we see Celie, who is fourteen years old, giving birth to her second child, a daughter. Both this child
and her previous child, a son, are sold to an interested third party. The
children are the result of Celie's being abused by her father. As Celie
explains: 'My daddy said, "You're going to do what your momma would-
n't." ' Celie suffers the humiliation of being abused, her children cruelly
taken from her, and we next find her being married off to a neighbouring
widower so that she can look after his children and needs. This man,
Albert Johnson, or 'Mister' as Celie calls him, actually wants Celie's sis-

ter Nettie for his bride. However, Celie's father refuses to agree to this and eventually seals the bargain for Celie's marriage by throwing a cow into the bargain. Now Celie suffers more sexual abuse, rape within marriage, as she strives to care for his children and build a home for him.

In the summer of 1909 Nettie moves in with Celie to avoid the advances of the sexually aggressive father. Celie warns Nettie of the danger of abuse at the hands of 'Mister'. Recognizing that sooner or later the sisters will have to part under this threat, Nettie begins to teach Celie to read and write. While the two sisters play (for they are still very young), 'Mister' watches lustfully. It is not long before he attempts to rape Nettie while she is on her way to school. Nettie hits him and runs away, only to find herself literally thrown out of the house. As 'Mister' tears the sisters apart Nettie shouts to her sister, 'Nothing but death can keep me from you!' From this point onwards Celie is forever watching out for the mailman, hoping that her lost sister will write to her. But 'Mister' refuses to let her see the letters that are delivered to the house. He tells her that nothing ever comes for her.

We move to the summer of 1916, where a former lover of 'Mister', a Miss Shug Avery, enters the scene. She is a singer, with a dubious reputation. Albert is like an excited schoolboy, frantically trying to get ready so that he can see Shug perform in town. Celie has all of his clothes ready for him, helping him to dress. Even before he asks, she knows his every need. All the while Celie is waiting for a letter from her sister Nettie. 'She said she would write, but she never does,' she says to herself.

Meanwhile, Harpo, Albert's son, wants to marry a strong-minded woman, Sofia, since she carries his child. 'Mister' is not at all happy about this 'shot-gun wedding', and when he sees that Sofia is the one who controls their relationship, he tells Harpo to give her a sound beating to take her down a peg or two. After another episode of domination by Sofia, Harpo asks Celie what he should do. 'Beat her,' says Celie, who seems to have accepted this as a way of life. After a number of quarrels Sofia leaves Harpo.

Albert brings Shug Avery, drunk and sick, to the house to stay. He tries to prepare some food for her with disastrous results. Eventually Celie prepares food for Shug, bathes her, and brushes her hair. We see a growing relationship between the two women. Meanwhile Albert's father arrives at the home to criticize his son's handling of the women in the house. In his opinion, the women are not nearly submissive enough.

The film moves on to the summer of 1922, and we find Harpo building a bar, with Shug booked as the major attraction. There is a considerable amount of drinking, dancing and singing as the camera pans across the fields to the local church where the minister is preaching a fiery sermon against such sinful behaviour. When a fight develops in the bar Shug takes Celie back to the house where she encourages the homely Celie to dress in her clothes. Shug attempts to get Celie to recognize that she is not ugly, as everyone tells her, and that she has a beautiful smile. Shug makes a pass at Celie. There is a touching episode of love shared between the two downtrodden women. As Celie narrates it to us, 'Shug! She like honey and I like a bee.'

Shug goes to the church, but the preacher ignores her. She then decides to return to Memphis and Celie wonders whether to go with her, to make a break from 'Mister Jail'. In the end, Celie does not have the courage to break free, and she passes out as the bus drives off carrying Shug away. Back on the home front, Sofia gets into a fight with the mayor and his wife, who are the first white folk we have seen in the film. The mayor's wife requests Sofia to be her servant. 'Hell no!' replies Sofia. This is seen to be against the accepted rules of white/black relations; Sofia is slapped by the mayor and she hits him back. The white population are staggered by this social indiscretion and Sofia is promptly beaten over the head and arrested by the town sheriff.

It is the fall of 1930 and we see a dejected and beaten Sofia who has been in jail for eight years. She now becomes the maid of the mayor's wife, in spite of her protests in years gone by. In the spring of 1936 Shug turns up at the house of Albert and Celie with her new husband Grady. While Albert and Grady are talking and drinking Shug goes to the mailbox and finds a newly-arrived letter for Celie from Nettie. She takes Celie upstairs where they read the letter together, discovering that Nettie has written scores of other letters and that she is at present in Africa looking after the children of a missionary couple. Nettie writes, 'I love you and I am not dead.' She writes that the missionaries could not have children of their own and that the children they adopted are in fact Celie's long-lost son and daughter, named Adam and Olivia. 'It is a miracle! Your family are all together.' Celie and Shug search the house to see if they can find where Albert has hidden the other letters. Eventually they find them secreted under a floorboard.

We follow Celie around the house, in church, in the fields, as she reads letter after letter, with images of Nettie in Africa interspersed as illustrations of what she reads. 'Mister' strikes Celie when he finds her in a field reading, not having answered his call to come and shave him. Celie prepares to shave him, but the look in her eyes is murderous. 'Mister' complains that she is getting slower and dumber as the years go by. We watch her sharpening the razor blade on a leather strap and it is clear that she intends to slit his throat. At the last moment Shug runs in to prevent Celie from murdering him.

A little later there is a family meal and Sofia has returned home. Shug announces to the assembled group that she and Grady are moving on and that Celie is going with them. 'Over my dead body!' says 'Mister', and turning to Celie he asks, 'What's wrong with you now?' Celie stands up for herself for the first time in the film. 'You're a low-down dirty dog! It's time to get away from you ... You took my sister Nettie away from me. You knew she was the only somebody in the world who loved me ... She's coming home ... we'll all get together and we'll whip your ass! She's got my children and they know other languages.' The family are all amazed at Celie. Albert's father puts into words what everyone must be thinking, 'My God! The dead has risen!' As the emotional climax of the scene is reached and Celie, Grady and Shug prepare to leave, 'Mister' shouts at Celie, 'You're black, you're ugly, you're a woman, you're nothing at all!' As the car drives away with Celie in the back she shouts back at 'Mister', 'I may be black, poor. I may even be ugly. But I'm here!'. Then she waves goodbye.

It is now the fall of 1937 and we see Albert drunk, his home and farm a mess. He is arguing with his father and drowns his sorrows in Harpo's bar. Life seems to have taken a definite turn for the worse now that Celie is not there to hold the home together. She returns to town for the funeral of her father, only to discover that he was in fact her step-father. She had lived under a mistaken belief all of her life. She is relieved to find this out for it means that the children she bore him are not her half-brother and half-sister, and that (biological) incest had not taken place. Now that he is dead she discovers that the family house and the land upon which it sits now legally belong to her, as they were the property of her real father who died while she was but a child. Celie settles down into the house and opens a seamstress shop in the town. As Celie walks through a field of purple flowers with Shug the pair engage in conversation. Shug compares people's indifference to the flowers to their indifference towards God: 'You just walk past the color purple and don't notice it.' 'You mean that God just wants to be loved,' says Celie in amazement. 'Everything wants to be loved,' answers Shug.

Shug is back singing at Harpo's bar, and once again the camera pans across the fields to the church where the preacher is addressing his congregation. The song that Shug is singing carries the words, 'God is trying to tell you something, right now!' In the church one of the women of the congregation tells the preacher that maybe the Lord is trying to tell him something as well. On the porch of the house, Albert is also listening to the words of the song. Shug leads the clientele of the bar in a procession to the church – 'God is trying to tell you something, right now.' The preacher moves forward and Shug embraces him, whispering into his ear, 'See, Daddy, sinners have a soul too!'

Albert goes to the mailbox and finds a letter for Celie from the Immigration and Naturalization Department. He gets out the money he has hoarded over the years and goes to the government offices, where he sponsors Nettie and Celie's children to enter the country. In the final scenes of the film a car arrives at Celie's home carrying Nettie and the children. Celie runs and embraces Nettie in a field of purple flowers. She is introduced to her long-lost children, Adam and Olivia, together with their own spouses. From a distance Albert watches happy at the reunion he has effected. The film closes as it began, with Celie and Nettie playing a clapping game against a background of the color purple.

Topics for Further Thought and Discussion
1. On the treatment of women
A. What does Celie's treatment at the hands of her 'father', and at the hands of 'Mister' demonstrate about the status of women within the community portrayed in the film? What do 'Mister's' words to Harpo concerning Sofia indicate about the attitude of men to women?

B. What do Celie's words to Harpo about how to treat Sofia – 'Beat her!' – indicate about her understanding of the position of women in relation to men? How does she come to have this understanding?

C. Comment on the general attitude to women indicated by 'Mister's' words to Celie as she prepares to leave him: 'You're black, you're ugly, you're a woman, you're nothing at all!'

D. What scenes demonstrate prejudice within the film? Who is prejudiced against whom within the film and why?

2. On the nature of true love

A. How is sex without love portrayed within the film? How is it demonstrated in Celie's relations with her 'father'? How is it demonstrated in her relationship with 'Mister'? Note Celie's comment about her 'father': 'My Daddy said, "You're going to do what your Momma wouldn't." ' What do you think is meant by this?

B. When Shug Avery seeks to help Celie to see her own self-worth, she asks her about her relationship to 'Mister'. Celie explains, 'He beats me for not being you.' Who is the victim in such a situation? What do you think Shug means when, later in the film she says to Celie, 'You're still a virgin.'

C. When Celie and Nettie are parted, Nettie cries out, 'Nothing but death can keep me from you!' During the years that follow Nettie writes frequently to Celie, although she never receives a reply. In the first letter that Celie receives, some 27 years later, Nettie still writes, 'I love you and I am not dead.' What about the character of love is revealed through these scenes?

D. How do we interpret the growing relationship between Celie and Shug? Is it understandable to you that care and compassion, particularly under such oppressive circumstances, might contain an element of sexual attraction?

3. On the nature of God

A. What do you think is significant about the title of the film? What is 'the color purple'? Alice Walker begins the book upon which the film is based with a line spoken by Celie's 'father' to her: 'You better not never tell nobody but God. It'd kill your mammy.' Given this attitude, is it any wonder that Celie confides her deepest feelings to God, asking him for a sign?

B. Nettie describes the reunion of Celie's family as a miracle. Could this be the 'sign' that Celie prayed for? Is this characteristic of the way that God deals graciously with people?

C. As they walk through the fields of purple flowers Shug Avery remarks to Celie how easy it is to walk past the color purple and never notice it, and that it is just like that with God. What do you think she means? Celie in reply says, 'You mean that God just wants to be loved?' Has Celie understood the meaning of 'general revelation' which leads us to the possibility of discovering and worshipping God through his creation (see Acts 17:24, 28; Romans 1:20)?

D. Shug Avery says to her father, the preacher, 'Even a sinner has a soul!' What do you think that she means by this? Does Shug have a better grasp of the true nature of God than any of the other characters in the film?

E. Who do you think the words of the song, 'God is trying to tell you something, right now', are directed at?

4. On redemption and human responsibility

A. 'My God, the dead has risen!' cries 'Mister's' father after Celie's outburst at the dinner table and the response to it given by Sofia. Who and what has played a part in the redemption of Celie's personhood?

B. Albert has clearly changed by the end of the film. He is emerging out of the depths of drunken self-pity. Who or what has brought about this change of character? What are the indications of this change, the sign-posts along the way?

C. Shug Avery has a number of encounters with her father, the preacher. List some of the scenes involving the two within the film. By his attitude to his daughter has the preacher fully understood the nature of God's forgiveness?

D. Which character in the film do you identify with most? Who do you think has suffered the most? In what ways is this suffering crucial to the formation of the character's identity? What can we see of the possibility of redemption through suffering in the life of Sofia, for example?

24
1984:
Controlling the Past and
Determining the Future

Film details

1984 (1984)

Directed by Michael Radford.

Starring John Hurt as Winston Smith, Richard Burton as O'Brien, and Suzanna Hamilton as Julia.

Screenplay by Michael Radford.

Music by the Eurythmics.

BBFC certificate '15'.

Duration 122 minutes.

Released on video-cassette and DVD by Virgin Video.

The film soundtrack is also available through Virgin Records.

The film is based upon George Orwell's classic novel *Nineteen Eighty-Four*, first published in 1949 (Harmondsworth: Penguin, 1967).

Synopsis

The film puts onto screen George Orwell's frightening vision of the future, where the state controls every aspect of the lives of people. It follows the lives of Winston and Julia as they seek to eke out their lives under this oppressive system which is headed by 'Big Brother'. Television screens dominate the story, with constant proclamation of state-sponsored propaganda providing a background to almost every scene. The television screens are two-way, watching as well as imparting information, and they are everywhere – in the home, at work, in public places. Little wonder that the catch-phrase 'Big Brother is watching you' has become a summary of the novel.

The film opens with a scene in which workers are gathered before a large television screen for an indoctrination session, the Two Minutes

Hate. They are whipped up into a frenzy by the scenes that pour forth from the screen and the patriotic narration that accompanies it. The crowd is told that their land, Oceania, is one of peace, harmony and hope. They are the workers, the strivers, the strugglers, who are fighting, bleeding and dying in their struggle against the dark, murdering hordes of Eurasia. The workers are encouraged to shout, in mass hysteria and hatred, the name of the leader of their enemy Eurasia, a man named Emmanuel Goldstein. After this we see the cheering and acclamation by the crowd of Big Brother, lovingly known as 'B'. Patriotic hymns and evocative images pouring from the screen unite the crowd into a heady spirit of nationalism.

Winston Smith works in the Records Department of the Ministry of Truth, where he changes the newspaper reports of the past to reflect the present wishes and policies of the Party. We have already been alerted to this in the opening credits, which declared in ominous fashion: 'Who controls the past controls the future; who controls the present controls the past.' Winston keeps a secret diary in which he records his thoughts and misgivings about life as he experiences it. In the background the omnipresent television proclaims: 'Thought-crime is death.' Winston records in his diary, 'I have committed, even before setting pen to paper, the essential crime that contains all others in itself.' He writes, 'From a dead man, greetings!'

Indoctrination is the regular pattern of life for Winston. He is subjected to it everywhere he goes – as he awakes, at the communal breakfast, at his desk at work. The only place he can find where he manages to escape the watching eye of Big Brother is a small, second-hand shop outside the city of London in which he once bought a diary, and where he now sees a spare bedroom with no television screen. Back in the city Winston keeps catching the eye of another Party member, Julia. She manages to slip him a note which reads, 'I love you. Victory Square.' Clandestine meetings have to be arranged as the state is opposed to loving relationships, to family life. There is even a lecture on the eradication of the orgasm, because of the intimacy involved between people; such relationships carry a loyalty within them that leads to thought-crime. Winston and Julia meet in the countryside where the beauty and freedom of fields and woods contrasts with the grim propaganda-drenched atmosphere of London. Here their love-affair begins. Both know the violation of society's rules that is being committed here. 'I'm corrupt to the core,' says Julia.

The couple rent the bedroom above the shop, where they can be alone together. Julia brings real coffee, bread, milk, sugar and jam – bought on the black-market for they are forbidden items to members of the Party like Winston and Julia. She wears a dress for Winston, abandoning the drab uniform of gray dungarees provided by the state, another small act of defiance which shows her independence. In his diary Winston records, 'There is truth and there is un-truth. Freedom is freedom to say two plus two equals four. If that is allowed, all else follows.' Meanwhile, back at work he continues to re-write the past to make it fit with the present. During another visit to their secluded hide-away, Julia picks up a hundred year-old paperweight. 'What is it?', she asks. Winston answers, 'A little chunk of history that they have forgotten to alter.'

A major political revolution rocks the society of Oceania: Eurasia is now declared an ally and Eastasia is the enemy. This new development requires a further re-writing of history and Winston is busily engaged in this task at his work. He writes in his diary, 'Everything fades into mist. Past is erased, the erasure is forgotten. The lie becomes truth, and then becomes a lie again.'

In bed with Julia he says, 'It's not so much staying alive, but staying human that's important. We must not betray each other. Julia responds, 'It'll mean confessing. We're bound to do that; everyone does. You can't help it.' Winston answers, 'I don't mean confessing. Confessing isn't betrayal. I mean feelings. If they can make me change my feelings, they can stop me from loving you. That would be real betrayal.' This Julia affirms, 'They can't do that … They can torture, they can make you say anything, but they can't make you believe it. They can't get inside you, get to your heart.'

Winston is invited to go to the office of O'Brien, a member of the Inner Party, to see a copy of the 10th. edition of the Newspeak Dictionary. This dictionary is hailed as an achievement, for it has eliminated many words from the language in an attempt to 'cleanse' and 'purify' speech. O'Brien is able to turn off the television screen in his office, something which Winston finds difficult to comprehend since his own life is so governed by the watchful eye of Big Brother. 'A privilege,' explains O'Brien.

In conversation with Winston he explains that there are no agents of resistance in Oceania, even though a list of captured agents has just been read out on the latest propaganda broadcast. This is part of the continuous contradiction that makes up the public information system of Oceania.

O'Brien gives Winston a book to read. Winston discovers it to be a subversive document against state dictatorship. While in bed with Julia he reads from the book: 'The war is not meant to be won, but to go on forever ... to keep the people at starvation level and the structure of society intact.' He says to Julia, 'Julia, there is truth and untruth. To be in a minority of one does not make you mad!' Suddenly a picture hanging on the wall crashes to the floor and reveals a television screen. The police break in and the pair are beaten and separated. Only too late does Winston discover that the shop owner, from whom he had rented the room, was a Party official.

The film now moves to a prison cell and an interrogation room. Winston has been beaten and had his hair shaven off. He is questioned by O'Brien, who tortures him on a rack. Now and again we see images of the fields in the country, suggesting Winston's thoughts travel back to the place where he and Julia first made love. O'Brien tells Winston that reality is in the collective mind of the Party, that two plus two can equal four, or five, or three. Winston, tormented by pain, says that he no longer knows the answers to the questions he is being asked. O'Brien says, 'Noone escapes. We do not destroy the heretic because he resists. We make him our own before we kill him.' He then informs Winston that Julia has betrayed him. Winston is also subjected to torture by electric-shock. As O'Brien inflicts this upon him, he whispers words of indoctrination: 'Power is inflicting pain. Tearing human minds apart and putting them together in new shapes ... No loyalty except to the Party. No love except love of Big Brother. All competing pleasures we will destroy ... The future – a boot stamping on the human face forever!' Back in his cell, Winston continues to see the fields and Julia. O'Brien asks him about his feelings for Big Brother. 'I hate him!' replies Winston. 'It's not enough to obey him. You must love him,' counters O'Brien.

Winston is led to Room 101, where incarcerated prisoners are forced to face their greatest fear. In Winston's case this is a fear of rats, echoing memories of a traumatic event in which he saw rats devouring the dead body of his mother. Rats are placed next to Winston's face and, as he sees again the image of fields and Julia, he shouts out, 'Do it to Julia, and not to me!'

The scene now changes to a cafe where an apparently-brainwashed and subdued Winston meets an equally passive Julia. The ubiquitous television screen announces war with Eurasia; we have come full circle in the endless cycle of deception and nationalist propaganda. After a lethargic conversation the couple say goodbye and Julia leaves. On the television screen we have an image of Winston and hear his all-too familiar confession. In the dust on the table in front of him Winston writes, '2 + 2 = ' – and leaves the answer blank. Propaganda continues with news of yet another victory. 'Wonderful news!' says Winston to the waiter. A picture of Big Brother appears on the screen; Winston turns his back to the screen and says, 'I love you!'

Topics for further thought and discussion
1. 'I think, therefore I am'
A. The motto of the Ministry of Truth is: 'War is Peace. Freedom is slavery. Ignorance is Strength.' In the light of this, why is thinking regarded as a crime? Is the suppression of thought limited to totalitarian regimes, or can it take place in democracies?

B. Why are relationships, family life, and intimacy between people viewed as threats and eradicated? Why does unorthodox loyalty lead to thought-crime? How does 'thought-crime' compare with what Jesus says, for example, in Matthew 5:21-22, 27-28?

C. What is significant about Winston's words: 'Freedom is the freedom to say "two plus two equals four." If that is allowed all else follows.'? What absolutes do we have, outside of the world of politics, that allow us to be free? What light do Jesus' words in John 8:32 shed on this: 'You shall know the truth, and the truth shall set you free'?

D. How far can propaganda go in shaping the mind of a nation? O'Brien tells Winston, 'Reality is the human mind – the collective mind of the Party that is immortal ... No loyalty except loyalty to the Party. No love

except love of Big Brother. All competing pleasures we will destroy ...
The future – a boot stamping on the human face forever.' Yet Winston is
still trying to think for himself, still trying to remember, still imaging. In
Descartes' famous dictum, 'I think, therefore I am.' But is he, in the end,
still Winston Smith or has he simply become another *unperson*?

*2. The difference between the love of a slave and the love of a son or
daughter*
A. What is the nature of adoration of Big Brother within the film? What
motivates it?

B. What is the difference between adulation of the popular figure and the
love of equals within a relationship? What might this suggest about the
true nature of worship? How do we interpret Jesus' citation of
Deuteronomy 6:4-5 in Mark 12:28-33 (and parallels)?

C. When Julia and Winston meet for their clandestine affair they share
real coffee, milk, sugar, bread and jam. Does this symbolize anything
about the love they also share? In what ways might this be seen as an
attempt to break free from the propaganda which fills their lives?

D. What differences can be identified between the adoration of Big
Brother (along with hatred for Goldstein) which is expressed by Winston
and Julia at several places in the film, and their love for each other? Julia
says that the Party cannot make her change her feelings for Winston:
'They can torture, they can make you say anything, but they can't make
you believe it. They can't get inside you, get to your heart.' What does all
this tell us about the nature of love in human relationships?

3. True humanity: being made in the image of God
A. In the final scenes of the film the subdued, passive Winston appears to
say all the right things, yet he still writes '2 + 2 = ' on the table. He also
turns his back to Big Brother when he says 'I love you!' To whom do you
think he says this? Orwell's final lines of the book were: 'He had won the
victory over himself. He loved Big Brother.' Do you think that this is what
the film-makers intended to portray in their ending? Is it ever possible for

our essential humanity to be completely destroyed within fallen people? Is there always an essence remaining of what it means to be 'made in the image of God'?

B. Winston, in resolute hope, declares to O'Brien that the spirit of man will eventually defeat the Party. O'Brien replies to the beaten Winston, as he pulls out one of his rotted teeth, 'You're rotting away ... This is humanity.' Has Winston lost? Is our humanity measured by our outward appearance? (See 2 Corinthians 3:17-18 and 4:1-10 for an interesting passage dealing with some of these issues).

C. Why is it that Julia and Winston act as they do in the Two Minutes Hate as part of the cheering masses in front of the giant television screen images of Big Brother, and yet act in the way that they do when they are alone? What does this indicate about how individuals behave in crowds? Compare this with John 12:12-18 and 19:1-15.

D. O'Brien and Winston Smith are both members of the Party, but why do they have differing attitudes of loyalty to Big Brother? What part do power, wealth and privilege play in the society of Oceania? What parallels might we point to in our modern world? In what ways does Jesus break the stranglehold of power-structures in calling people to discover their true humanity? Cite some examples from the New Testament.

25
Cry Freedom!:
Living with Apartheid

Film details

Cry Freedom! (1987)

Directed by Richard Attenborough.

Starring Kevin Kline as Donald Woods, Denzel Washington as Steve Biko, and Penelope Wilton as Wendy Woods.

Screenplay by John Briley.

BBFC certificate 'PG'.

Duration 157 minutes.

Released on video-cassette and DVD by CIC Films.

The film is based on the books *Biko* and *Asking For Trouble* by Donald Woods (London: Penguin, 1982).

Arising from the film, and about its production, is Richard Attenborough's *Cry Freedom: A Pictorial Record* (London: The Bodley Head, 1987).

Several other books on the life of Steve Biko are also available, including *The Testimony of Steve Biko* edited by Millard Arnold (London: Panther Books, 1979).

Synopsis

The film begins with a scene typical of the impact of the horror that was apartheid in South Africa. It is 24 November 1975, as dawn breaks over the Crossroads squatter camp, and the police launch a search with batons, dogs and tear gas. Men, women and children run in fear as troop-carriers, landrovers and armed policemen run through the camp. In the city of Cape Town the radio news broadcast speaks of the raid as being in the interests of national health and of people voluntarily returning to the protected homelands. Meanwhile the squatter camp is bulldozed and we are left with the image of a cross silhouetted against burning homes.

In his office, Donald Woods, the editor of a progressive newspaper, the *Daily Dispatch*, is discussing Steven Biko and the question of black supremacy, when one of the leaders of the Black Consciousness Movement arrives. Her name is Dr Mamphela Ramphele and she challenges Woods to become better informed and to actually meet Biko before passing judgment upon him and what he stands for. Woods accepts her invitation and meets the 28-year old Biko in a community centre in King William's Town. They discuss Biko's banning order, something of which Woods does not approve. 'Oh, a white liberal!' says Biko as a gentle criticism, 'A white liberal who holds on to his privileges.' Biko takes Woods into the country where he shows him the Zanempilo medical clinic run and staffed by black personnel. For Biko this is an important project for it shows the worth and self-sufficiency of the people. He leaves Woods, who is openly impressed, with another challenge: 'Have you ever been to a black township? We've seen how you live; come see how we live.' The contrast such a challenge implies is brought home vividly, as Woods returns to his luxury home with a swimming pool and a servant's quarters where the family's black maid lives.

Biko proceeds to educate Woods about the life of the black population of South Africa. He shows him the squatter camps, explains the lack of education and its debilitating effects, explains how the separation of families takes place because in order to work one needs a residence permit and the place of work is often far away from the family's place of residence. Biko remarks how it is that blacks, when they see the way that whites live, can only conclude that there must be something wrong and inferior in being black. He says, 'You can beat me, even kill me, but I'm not going to be what you want me to be … We believe in an intelligent God who knew what he was doing when he made the black man and when he made the white man.' This demand for an equality of worth clearly impresses Woods who, when he returns to his newspaper, appoints a black man and a black woman to work on the newspaper reporting black affairs.

At a football match, which in fact serves as a political rally, Biko encourages the crowd to grow in understanding of their worth. He encourages teachers and parents to tell children about black history, black heroes, and black culture. He appeals for people to help build a South

Africa worth living in, where blacks and whites are equal, a country as beautiful as its people. Later, in a courtroom scene, where some of Biko's fellow activists are on trial, he tells the judge that the Black Consciousness Movement is about hope for black people, hope for the country; it is about black humanity and finding a legitimate place for black people in their world.

Biko is arrested for breaking the rules of his banning order and is maltreated by the police, assaulted by Captain de Wet. Failure to make the charges against him stick leads the police to react by breaking into and vandalizing the community centre in King William's town. Incensed by the outrage of this, Woods goes to Pretoria to see Kruger, the Minister of Justice. Here Woods is presented with the Afrikaaner view of things. Kruger tells him about the arrival of the white Afrikaans to South Africa in 1652 and about the Long Trek. He is also reminded about British concentration camps and about the Boer War. 'We did not colonize this country. We built it!' he declares and scathingly asks Woods if he thinks that the white Afrikaaners are simply going to roll over and give it all away. He does, in any event, agree to investigate Woods's complaint about the wrecking of the community centre. However, the investigation turns out to be one of Woods himself, and he is subsequently summoned for withholding the name of the eyewitness to the incident. Woods' maid is harassed in the middle of the night by the police who want to see her documents. Then both the black reporters whom Woods hired to work for the newspaper are arrested. The man, named Mapetla, is dead within a few days, allegedly committing suicide by hanging himself in his police cell.

Biko decides to risk arrest for breaking his banning order by going to speak at a student rally in Capetown. He is arrested by the police at a road block on 18th August 1977 and is taken to jail in Port Elizabeth. On 11th September 1977 the police doctor is called to examine a badly-beaten Biko, who has a severe head injury. Instead of being taken to a local hospital the police insist on taking Biko to a police hospital in Pretoria 700 hundred miles away. He is brutally thrown into the back of a landrover and is driven over rough terrain in the dead of night. Biko dies in police custody in Pretoria on 12th September. The Minister of Justice Kruger tells a meeting of the Afrikaner Nationalist Party that he died after a hunger strike, to the acclaim of the apartheid-supporting crowd.

Woods manages, with the help of Biko's widow Ntsiki, to take photographs of his scarred and battered body. Donald and Wendy Woods are encouraged to attend the funeral as 'brother and sister', and the funeral itself is a great rally for black-consciousness. An oration declares the hope of a South Africa wherein all people will be judged as equal members of God's family. The funeral closes with the singing of a moving African anthem: 'God Bless Africa, raise up her name. Hear our prayers and bless us.'

After the funeral Woods finds himself the object of police harassment; there are threatening telephone calls to Wendy and the house is subjected to gunfire. When Donald tries to leave the country to encourage international pressure for an inquest into the death of Steve Biko he is arrested at the airport and declared a banned person, unable to travel outside of the district of East London for the period of five years. Woods tells one of the policemen, 'The days of a few whites running a black country are over.' He adds that he hopes that the country will then be in the hands of men like Biko.

He begins to write a book about the life and death of Biko. A supportive black clergyman, Father Kani, reminds him that such an act would be treason and that he will have to get out of South Africa in order to publish it. When Donald tells Wendy of his plans she is upset because South Africa is her home, and she wonders if Donald is being selfish in wanting publicity for himself, accusing him of playing God. When their children receive T-shirts bearing Biko's image, impregnated with acid and sent by the security police, Wendy agrees that the book about Biko should be published.

Donald begins to make plans for the whole family to leave the country. With the help of a newspaper colleague and Father Kani a false passport is obtained. Travelling under the name of Father Curran, with his hair suitably dyed, Donald makes plans to travel north by road to Lesotho, and from Lesotho by plane to Botswana. Elaborate plans are made to deceive the ever-vigilant police stationed outside the Woods' house. They use a New Year's Eve celebration as cover for the first stage of the escape. Donald hitches various lifts as far as the Telle River, but the river is too deep to cross by foot and he is forced to pass over Telle Bridge through the South African border post. In Maseru, capital of Lesotho, Donald introduces himself to the British Deputy High Commissioner and asks for political asylum.

Meanwhile, Wendy is gathering up the children and taking them to her parents' home on the route north to Lesotho. She receives a confirming telephone call from Donald to say that he has reached the safety of Lesotho and to tell her to join him there. They too cross Telle Bridge and are rejoined with Donald. The Lesotho Airways, its plane piloted by an Australian and New Zealander crew, agrees to ignore the order against flying over South African air-space and to risk escorting the Woods family to Botswana. The Lesotho government places one of its officials on board as a safeguard and secures United Nations passports for the family. They make the flight without challenge by the South African Air Force jets.

The film ends with a flash-back to June of 1976 and the school strike in Soweto. Woods tells Biko over the telephone, 'They're refusing to study in Afrikaans, refusing to be trained simply as servants to the system. The name "Biko" has been uttered.' In reply to this Biko says, 'It's the beginning of the end, Donald. Change the way people think and things will never be the same again.' This is followed by a scene depicting the slaughter of the children of Soweto by the South African police force; over 700 are killed and over 4,000 wounded. To the sound of the South African hymn, the same one sung at Biko's funeral, and the words 'Descend Holy Spirit', a list of those who have died in police custody in South African jails over the years is run across the screen.

Topics for further thought and discussion
1. Black and white: ebony and ivory
A. What instances are there in the film which demonstrate the power of those who own political propaganda? What does Dr. Ramphele mean when she describes herself as 'the token of your white paternalistic concern'? In what ways is the reporting of Biko's death made to serve political interests?

B. Is it possible to understand the political tensions in South Africa without knowing the history of the nation from an Afrikaaner point of view? Can we fully appreciate the feeling represented by Kruger's potted history of the nation, which he gives to Woods in response to the latter's demand for an unbiased inquiry?

C. Woods sees Biko as a much-needed black leader with whom the whites can talk. In what ways do you think the two central characters understand each other's world? Why is there always a need to understand the other's point of view if there is to be a reconciliation between estranged parties?

D. Biko makes a great deal of the need for black self-worth. When one group so dominates another so as to destroy self-awareness is violence a necessary consequence? Is the feeling of oppression the root of problems in Northern Ireland, tensions in the inner cities, and the cause of persecution along racial, cultural, or religious lines?

E. In the trial scene the judge asks Biko, 'Why do you use the phrase "Black is beautiful"?' Biko replies that it is because black is usually associated with negatives, such as black market and black sheep. 'Why do you call yourselves black?', the judge persists, 'You people are more brown than black.' 'Why do you call yourselves white?' replies Biko, 'You people are more pink than white.' Do you think that 'white' and 'black' are descriptive or derogatory terms?

F. In discussing the school strike in Soweto, Biko says to Woods, 'It's the beginning of the end, Donald. Change the way people think and things will never be the same again.' Is there an answer here for the complex problems of the world? How does the Christian gospel address this issue in terms of describing repentance as a 'renewing of the mind'? (See Romans 12:1-2).

2. Where is God to be found?
A. What is the director trying to say in the opening images of the film, especially by showing the cross silhouetted against the burning ruins of the Crossroads settlement?

B. 'We believe in an intelligent God who knew what He was doing when he made the black man and when he made the white man,' says Biko.

Does apartheid deny the biblical doctrine of creation? What implications does this have for views about mixed-race marriages? Where do we find similar denials in our society?

C. At Biko's funeral the address given looks to a South Africa where all people will be judged as human beings, as equal members of God's family. It speaks of a day when 'the isolation that creates hostility becomes the closeness that creates friendship and love.' In what way might the key to healing the divisions in our communities be found in the radically new community of the people of God (as in Ephesians 2:11-22)? What divisions do we need to deal with within the fellowship of our own church?

D. In discussion over writing a book about Steve Biko's death and leaving South Africa, Wendy Woods accuses her husband of playing God. In reply, Donald says, 'I'm not God. But we know what this country is like now. We can't accept it, and we can't wait for God to change it. We have to do what we can, and this book is what I can do.' What does this say about our role as Christians to be salt and light in the world?

E. Why do you think that Biko risks striking Captain de Wet back while he is in police custody? What does he mean when he says, 'I expect to be treated as you expect to be treated.' How does this scene make you reconsider Jesus' words in Matthew 6:39 and 7:12?

3. Truth and injustice
A. When the police come to interrogate Woods over the witness to the destruction of the community centre they tell him, 'The law is on our side, Mr. Woods.' He replies, 'Yes, well justice is on mine!' What should our response be when we perceive that law and justice are incompatible? Consider Romans 13:1-7 within your discussions.

B. Biko is accused of stirring up violence in the community by means of confrontation. Does confrontation of injustice always lay itself open to this charge?

C. In his last conversation with Woods, Biko says, 'Someday justice will be done. Let us hope that it is not visited on the innocent.' What do you think he means by this? What should we be praying for, now that South Africa has moved into a new era? What form will justice continue to take in a country like South Africa? What form will it take in the United Kingdom? Whose lot in life will be affected and in what way?

D. How did you feel watching the shooting of the schoolchildren in Soweto? What would you have like to have seen done about the incident? Though fully recognizing the considerable differences in the situations, how do you react to some of the incidents in past years involving the police and the security forces in Northern Ireland, and those in more recent years in Afghanistan, Iraq and the Palestinian territories?

E. Biko and Woods both defy their banning orders and both hide illegal documents from the police; Woods even uses a stolen passport and assumes a false identity to escape. When is it right to be untruthful in pursuing the cause of justice?

26
Bridget Jones's Diary: Self-Image and Self-Worth

Film details

Bridget Jones's Diary (2001)
Directed by Sharon Maguire.
Starring Renée Zellweger as Bridget Jones, Colin Firth as Mark Darcy, and Hugh Grant as Daniel Cleaver, plus Jim Broadbent, James Callis, Embeth Davidtz, Shirley Henderson, Gemma Jones, Sally Phillips.
Screenplay by Helen Fielding.
BBFC certificate '15'.
Duration: 95 minutes.
Released on video-cassette and DVD by Miramax Home Entertainment.

The film is based on the book by Helen Fielding, *Bridget Jones's Diary* (London: Picador, 1997).

Synopsis

Bridget Jones is a thirty-something who lives alone in London, works in publishing and is desperate to leave the single ranks and become a 'smug married' like so many of her friends. Avoiding the attempts of her mother (Gemma Jones) to fix her up with an apparently snooty barrister, Mark Darcy (Colin Firth), she starts an office flirtation with her caddish but charming boss, Daniel Cleaver (Hugh Grant). Despite being rather clumsy, and a disastrous public speaker, Bridget (Renée Zellweger) manages to attract admiration from surprising quarters. Bridget's repetitive neuroses about her weight-watching, fag-smoking and message-checking are underplayed, which allows the film to be more pacey and less full of angst than a straight adaptation of the book would have been.

'New Year's Day – my 32nd year of being single. On my own, going to my mother, Brenda's, turkey curry party. She'll be trying to match-make again. This year will be no exception', comments Bridget in a voice-over. 'The Darcys are here. Never get a boyfriend if you look as if you've just wandered out of Auschwitz', says mother. Then, notes Bridget, the question which is dreaded by all singletons: 'How's your love life?' asks one member of the party. 'Your mother's trying to fix you up with a divorcée,' says her father. This divorcée is Mark Darcy. We see from her behaviour at the party that Bridget can't seem to have a 'normal' conversation. She reflects that 'unless something changes in my life my final relationship will be with a bottle of wine'. The answerphone announces: 'You have no new messages.' 'All by myself. Don't want to be all by myself!' is the song on the background soundtrack.

She makes a major decision. 'I decided to take control of myself – start a diary; tell the truth about myself. Will have to lose 20 pounds. Will find nice sensible boyfriend.' Enter her boss, Daniel Cleaver (Hugh Grant). 'I suspect he doesn't fantasize about me' writes Bridget, remembering her dire singing at the office party. There follows mild flirting in the office, discussion with unhelpful friends, and then flirting with Daniel by email. 'Find a nice sensible man': she imagines marriage to Daniel.

'Your whole happiness depends on how you behave on this one social occasion', says one of her friends about a forthcoming book launch. 'First look gorgeous' is the advice. But Bridget once again seems to fall to pieces in conversation when the occasion comes. Mark Darcy turns up and introduces his friend Natasha to Bridget. Bridget's introduction at the book launch is embarrassingly gauche, but she is rescued by Daniel, who takes her out for a meal. Daniel says he knows Mark, explaining that 'He was a mate. Then I made the catastrophic mistake of introducing him to my fiancée.' He says that Mark took her away from Daniel. Daniel wants sex, and Bridget gives in to his advances. 'Weight 131 pounds. Have replaced food with sex. Cigarettes 22, all post-coital.' Bridget asks Daniel how they are going to react to each other at the office. Daniel says, 'It's not exactly a long term relationship.'

Then Bridget notes: 'when one part of your life is OK another part starts to fall apart.' Bridget's mother's marriage is disintegrating. Mother describes this as 'the winter of my life … . nothing of my own … . no life at all.' She has been approached by Julian from the TV Shopping Channel to be his demonstrator. 'He thinks I have got great potential.' Bridget goes to visit her dad and learns that Brenda and Julian are an item. Her father asks her, 'Have you got a boyfriend? A real one?' She tells him about

Daniel, 'He's perfect.' 'So, you're no longer a tragic spinster, but partner of a *bone fide* mini-god,' says father – 'going on a mini-break means true love!'

We move to a scene in a hotel. Mark and Natasha are also there. Bridget and Daniel engage in some childish play to Mark's obvious displeasure. In bed, Bridget asks: 'Do you love me?' – no answer, just sex. Meanwhile the camera pans to the contrast of a wedding taking place in the hotel. Daniel leaves Bridget at the hotel, 'I've got to go back to town … work – an American deal.' Meanwhile Bridget goes to a party, wrongly informed that it is a fancy-dress affair, dressed as a bunny girl. 'Amazing what some men think is attractive', says one partygoer of Bridget. Bridget meets Julian at the party: 'You and your mother could be sisters.' She moves on to find her Dad on his own. Bridget reassures him, 'You love each other. I'm sure it is just a temporary glitch.' Mark expresses his view that Daniel is unsuitable for Bridget.

Bridget goes back to see Daniel at his apartment only to find him with Lara from the New York office. Lara sees Bridget and says: 'I thought you said she was thin.' Understandably upset, Bridget goes back to her flat, where we find her watching *Fatal Attraction* – the scene where Glen Close is finally shot and killed by Michael Douglas. Next day in the office, Bridget tries to be very work-like. Daniel tells Bridget that he feels terrible, and of Lara he says, 'We're two people looking to commit.' He explains to Bridget that he knew Lara in the NY office, and that now they are engaged. Lara in contrast with Bridget is all American and confident.

Bridget muses that she must accept a permanent state of spinsterhood – or drink. 'Instead, I choose vodka,' she says. But then, she decides to go for fitness – books on power for women, exercise and healthy living. She throws away her cigarettes and looks for a new job. She goes for interviews, where she is, again, very gauche. The *Sit up Britain* television programme nevertheless employs her. Bridget has pleasure in telling Daniel that she has a new job in television. Daniel tries to persuade her to stay, but this time she is assertive. Bridget has a piece to present at Lewisham fire-station, for Bonfire Night. She has to wear a mini-skirt and a fireman's helmet and slide down the pole. Seeing the item on TV afterwards, Bridget says of herself, 'Have bottom the size of Brazil – a national laughing stock – daughter of a broken home.'

Next scene is a party made up of couples, including Mark and Natasha, and Bridget on her own. 'Hey Bridget, how's your love life? You ought to get sprogged up!' Then one says: 'Time running out ... offices are full of single girls in their thirties.' Another asks, 'Why are there so many single girls in their thirties, Bridget?', to which Bridget replies, 'Doesn't help that underneath our clothes our entire bodies are covered with scales.'

Mark is kind and supportive. He says, 'I very much enjoyed your Lewisham fire-station report.' But Bridget thinks that he is being sarcastic: 'I feel an idiot most of the time ... I can make a fool of myself all on my own.' Mark speaks honestly to her: 'Despite appearances, I like you very much ... just as you are.' The song on the soundtrack is 'Someone exactly like you.' But the moment is interrupted by Natasha, who snaps her fingers for Mark to come. In conversation with friends Bridget repeats Mark's words as 'Someone exactly like you.' One of them says, 'But this is someone you hate.'

'November 9th – 138 pounds; cigarettes 3; birthday, 33.'

In a TV interview at the High Court – 'Bridget, see if you can get it right this time!' – she is playing the hard-headed journalist ruthlessly committed to the pursuit of the truth (or so she tells herself). But while she is buying sweets the court case concludes. She bumps into Mark. 'Mark, you like me as I really am?' Mark has been defending the man on trial, and agrees to give an interview to Bridget. Success – 'Bridget Jones already a legend!' says her TV boss. 'Oh joy, I'm a broadcasting genius!' cries Bridget.

We move to Bridget celebrating her birthday, cooking dinner for her friends – 'also a genius in the kitchen!' Disaster strikes; she is sprayed with food from the food mixer. Mum phones – Julian is not what she hoped for. Mark turns up to see her, saying 'I came to congratulate the new face of current affairs.' He helps to rescue the disaster of the cooking for the dinner party. Friends turn up. At the table one of Bridget's friends asks, 'Mark, why did your wife leave you?', but there is no answer. At the dinner table a friend makes the toast: 'To Bridget who cannot cook, but who we love just as she is.' 'To Bridget, just as she is,' they all respond.

Then Daniel turns up: 'Darcy, what brings you here?' Daniel says to Bridget, 'I should have guessed; I thought you'd be on your own – what an idiot! I can't stop thinking about you … Bridget, you know me; terrible disaster. Lara dumped me … I've missed you a lot … you're the only one who can save me. I need you.' Bridget replies, 'Why have you come?' Bridget tries to stop Mark leaving, but he goes, insisting 'All right, Cleaver, outside!' Mark hits Daniel twice, then Daniel hits Mark on the head with a dustbin lid. 'Fight! Fight!' cries one of the partygoers happily, 'whose side are we on?' 'Mark's' say Bridget's friends, 'he never dumped Bridget for a naked American … and he said that he liked Bridget just as she is.' Mark finally knocks Daniel out. But all Bridget can say to Mark is 'What is your problem?'.

Bridget accuses Mark of being just like all the rest. Mark replies, 'I've been labouring under a false impression. Very foolish mistake, forgive me', and turns away. Daniel says, 'Let's go back upstairs. We belong together, Jones; me, you and your little skirt. If I can't make it with you, I can't make it with anyone.' To which Bridget replies, 'That's not a good enough offer for me. I'm still looking for something more extraordinary than that.'

'December 25th; weight 140 pounds plus 42 mince pies; alcohol units, oh, 1000s.'

The camera moves from Bridget to father watching mother and Julian in a TV ad. Bridget goes to bed. Mother turns up; Julian was no good – filthy temper. She wants to give it another go with Bridget's dad. 'You used to be in love with me. What do you think?' Father: 'I don't know, it's been very hard [pause] … I'm joking, you daft cow. I just don't work without you.'

The Darcys senior are holding a Ruby Wedding party. 'Mark will be there, still divorced!' Bridget learns from her mother that the breakup between Mark and Daniel came from Mark's finding his own fiancée in bed with Daniel, not the other way round as Daniel had told it. Bridget is now anxious to get to the party to see Mark, but Natasha is also there. Bridget apologizes to Mark and explains the mistake about the story of the fiancée. She tells Mark that she remembers that he said he liked her just as she is – and that she likes him: 'You're a nice man and I like you. If you wanted to pop by some time, that would be nice – more than nice.'

Mark's parents toast themselves and announce that Mark is going to the USA to a senior partnership, and that he is taking with him his bril-

liant partner-in-law, Natasha ... . who is later to be something else in-law!
The toast is: 'To Mark and his Natasha.' Bridget cries out 'No! No!', then
covers her embarrassment: 'Terrible disappointment for England to lose
such a legal brain. Better dash. Another party to go to – single people.'

Bridget returns home and Mark goes to New York. She writes, 'Diary
of Bridget Jones; spinster and lunatic.' Friends then arrive in her flat.
'Have we got the most fantastic surprise ... We're going to take you to
Paris to forget about Mark Darcy ... he's the most dreadful cold fish.' As
they are loading the car to leave, Mark turns up:

> 'Are you ready for Bar Mitzvahs and Christenings?'
>> 'I thought you were in America'.
>> But then I realized that I'd forgotten something back home. I'd for-
> gotten to kiss you goodbye'.
>> 'So you're not going to America? You're staying here?'
>> 'So it would seem'.

She doesn't go to Paris with her friends, but goes into her flat with Mark.
While she is changing, Mark finds Bridget's dairy with uncomplimentary
entries about himself. So he leaves, walking off through the snow. Bridget
realizes he's read the last entry in her diary: 'I hate him, I HATE him!'
She chases after him through the snow, wearing only a pair of pants and a
vest top. She catches up:

> 'I'm so sorry, I didn't mean it. It's only a diary. Everyone knows that
> diaries are full of crap!'
>> 'I knew that, I was just buying you a new one. Time to make a new
> start.'

They embrace. The final song on the soundtracks starts: 'I've been searching a long time for someone exactly like you ... I've been travelling all
around waiting for you to come through ... the best is yet to come ...
someone exactly like you.'

Topics for further thought and discussion

1. Singleness and marriage

A. What does it feel like to be single? Towards the end of the film, the thirty-two year-old Bridget writes in her diary 'The Diary of Bridget Jones – Spinster and Lunatic'. In what ways is her life depicted as an example of the failure of singleness? Who views her singleness in this way?

B. Are offices full of single thirty-somethings, longing to be attached? At a party one of the guests turns to Bridget and says, 'Time is running out. Offices are full of single girls in their thirties.' Another asks, 'Why are there so many single girls in their thirties, Bridget?'. Why do you think this is? Is the situation any different within contemporary churches? Why, or why not? Bridget's answer to this question is cryptic: 'It doesn't help that underneath our clothes we are covered with scales.' What does she mean by this?

C. Is marriage the answer to the perceived anxieties of single women? For you, what is the most poignant or powerful scene in this film depicting what life is like as a single person?

2. Truth-telling and honesty in relationships

A. Bridget sees herself as gauche, overweight, with bad habits, unwanted and useless, and she seems driven to an unhealthy relationship with Daniel because of her negative self-image. What advice would you give to someone who views himself or herself in this way? Jesus says in John 8:32, 'You will know the truth and the truth will set you free.' How might this be applied to Bridget's situation?

B. Bridget fills her diary with the truth as she sees it. She describes how she feels about all the people in her life. In the final scenes of the film we are led to believe that her relationship with Mark Darcy is destroyed when he reads what she has written about him, only to discover that he values truth-telling. Instead of rejecting her he buys her a new diary with which she can record the next year of her life, presumably with him. Is this another indication of what he means when he says, 'I like you just as you are?' How does this compare with what the Christian gospel says about Christ's love of us, just as we are (cf. Rom. 5:7-8)?

C. Bridget Jones' mother and father have a stormy and strained relationship and separate for a time. To what extent are they truthful and honest in their relationship one with another? In what ways do they help us to realize that truth-telling is necessary at every stage in a marriage or relationship? Towards the end of the film Bridget's father Colin uses humour to resolve a potentially volatile confrontation with his estranged wife Pam. Does humour always work in such situations? What is the difference between humour and sarcasm?

3. 'Just as I am' - accepting people for who they are
A. At one point in the film Mark Darcy tells Bridget Jones, 'I like you just as you are.' Do you think that Bridget likes herself 'just as she is'? In what ways does she express dissatisfaction with herself and the direction of her life? How does this contrast with the attitude of Daniel Cleaver, who appears to accept Bridget as she is, and who appears to present himself 'just as he is' when he appeals to her, saying 'You know me, terrible disaster, posh voice and bad character. You're the only one who can save me. I need you.'

B. After her disastrous television broadcast at the Lewisham Fire Station where a shot of her sliding down a fire-pole is aired publicly, Bridget records in her diary, 'Have bottom size of Brazil. National laughing stock.' Examine carefully the entries that Bridget makes in her diary; are any of them positive and affirming of her as a person?

C. The song 'Someone Like You' features a number of times within the film, both as performed by Van Morrison and Dina Carroll. The song includes the lines: 'I've been searching a long time for someone exactly like you … The best is yet to come.' To what extent is this a summary of the theme of hope running throughout the film? How does this compare with the picture of the 'best being saved for the last' in the story of Jesus at Cana (John 2:10).

27
Saving Private Ryan:
The Value of a Single Life

Film details
Saving Private Ryan (1998)
Directed by Steven Spielberg.
Starring Tom Hanks, Tom Sizemore, Edward Burns, Barry Pepper, Adam
Goldberg, Vin Diesel, Giovanni Ribisi, Jeremy Davies, Matt Damon, Ted
Danson, Paul Giamatti.
Screenplay by Robert Rodat.
BBFC classification '15'.
Duration 163 minutes.
Released on DVD by Dreamworks Home Entertainment.

The film won five Oscars for Best Director, Sound, Cinematography,
Sound Effects Editing, and Film Editing.

Synopsis
The film begins with the Stars and Stripes and a family strolling through
a forest of white grave stones in a World War II cemetery. Ryan is upset;
he kneels down in front of a grave, and his family rush to comfort him
before we are transported back to the D-Day invasion and 'Dog Green
Sector, Omaha Beach', 6th June, 1944. The next twenty minutes contain
some of the most violent, brutal and graphic images of war that have ever
been shown in the cinema. Amongst the images we see Captain John
Miller (Tom Hanks) leading his men through the surf and onto the beach,
under a hail of bullets. The soldiers are brutalized by the experience,
demonstrated in their killing of surrendering German troops. With the
beachhead secured we move to a vista of a beach, where bodies are rolled
by a red sea, and amongst the bodies is a soldier, whose backpack carries
the name 'Ryan, S'.

We move to a scene, back in the USA, where typists are writing the
death notices to the bereaved families. One of the supervisors notices

three members of the Ryan family: one killed on Omaha Beach, one on Utah Beach, and one a week earlier in New Guinea. Knowing that there is a fourth member of the family in France, the message goes up to the top of the chain of command, General George C. Marshall (Harve Presnell). Marshall decides on a rescue mission. He is told that such a mission is foolhardy, but drawing on a letter from Abraham Lincoln to Mrs Bixley, who gave all five of her sons as 'a great sacrifice on the altar of freedom,' he says, 'The boy's alive. We're going to send someone to find him and get him the hell out of there.'

Eventually 'the longest day' is over and Miller receives his orders, 'an assignment straight from the top,' to find Ryan (Matt Damon). After parachuting behind enemy lines and becoming separated from his unit, Ryan is now lost somewhere in northern France. Miller draws together a platoon of seven men from the remnant of his command, who will now carry out the seemingly senseless operation of risking their lives to save one. 'We're going on a public relations mission', Miller tells his men.

The platoon is made up of a disparate group of characters including Jackson (Barry Pepper) a country-bred sniper, who prays to Jesus for accuracy, and Mellish (Adam Goldberg) who is a Jew with all-too personal reasons for fighting this war. 'Where's the sense in risking the eight of us to rescue this one?' Miller answers in terms of duty and orders, to which the response comes back: 'Misallocation of resources!'

There are a number of harrowing and bloody scenes of violence, exploring the emotions created by war, before Ryan is encountered. While the men are constantly under threat from the Germans, they are not involved in any key strategic moves that will aid the outcome of the war. But the expedition does allow for the exploration of the feelings and emotions of the characters involved. The commander of one group of soldiers they encounter says to Miller, 'I understand what you are doing. I've got a couple of brothers myself. Get him home.'

After a second of the group is killed in a skirmish with German soldiers, one of the others says: 'I hope mother Ryan is real happy knowing that little Jimmy's life is worth more than two of our guys.' When Ryan is eventually tracked down he is on the front line with a number of comrades guarding a remote, but strategic bridge in the ruins of a bombed village. Miller informs them that he and his men are not the relief column, but are there for Ryan. 'Your brothers have been killed in combat,' says Miller. 'Which one?' asks Ryan. 'All of them,' answers Miller. 'You came to tell me that?' 'No! I've come to take you home.' Ryan, however, refuses to leave his post.

Miller explains that the Army Chief of Staff has given the order and that two of the group have already been killed in fulfilling the mission. 'It doesn't make sense,' says Ryan. 'These are the only brothers I have left, and I'm not leaving them.' A battalion of German soldiers with tanks is steadily approaching and in a bid to complete their mission to save Ryan, Miller's group have to join the efforts to hold the bridge. One of Miller's group says, 'Perhaps we will look back and see that saving Private Ryan was the one decent thing we did ... . And we all earn the right to go home!'

There follows the heroic defence of the bridge. In the process (a sequence of over 40 minutes of the film) almost everyone is killed or wounded with the exception of Ryan. Finally, Miller is fatally wounded as reinforcements arrive. Ryan finds Miller, who says to him, 'James, earn this. Earn it.' Miller dies.

We then move to George Marshall's office, and to a letter: 'Dear Mrs Ryan, it is with profound joy that I write to tell you that James is on his way home ... Nothing can compensate you or other families ...' The film ends in the WWII cemetery again, with an elderly Ryan looking at a white stone bearing the name of Captain John Miller. Ryan says, 'My family are with me today. They wanted to come with me. Every day I think of what you said to me on that bridge. I've tried to live my life the best I could. I hope it was enough. I hope that in your eyes I have earned what all of you have done for me.' Then he turns and speaks to his wife, 'Tell me I've led a good life. Tell me I am a good man.' 'You are,' she says.

Ryan salutes Miller's grave and we fade to the Stars and Stripes.

Topics for further thought and discussion
1. Salvation
A. James Ryan survives and makes it home, yet those who came to rescue him died. Ryan appears as a beardless youth compared with the other rough and ready soldiers, as if to emphasize the incongruity of this

teenage Iowa farm boy in the middle of a war zone. The unspoken question must be: 'What is the value of human life and why is one man worth risking the lives of eight others?' How might this film help us to understand the value of human life?

B. The commander of a group of soldiers that Miller's group encounters says to Miller, 'I understand what you are doing. I've got a couple of brothers myself. Get him home.' When we understand the reality of life and death do we have a *greater* concern for the lives of our close family members? Can we gain further insight from the post-death reaction of the rich man in Jesus' parable, Luke 16:19-31, especially verses 27-28?

C. The rescue group consider that risking the lives of eight men to save one is a 'misallocation of resources.' What is the value of one human life? What answer might the Christian story of the incarnation and cross of Jesus suggest?

2. What is my sacrifice worth?
A. One of the rescue mission comments after the death of one of his buddies, 'I hope mother Ryan is real happy knowing that little Jimmy's life is worth more than two of our guys.' How do you think Ryan's mother might feel, and what would your response be, if you were her?

B. Near the end of the film, as Miller's group join in the defence of the bridge, one of them comments, 'Perhaps we will look back and see that saving Private Ryan was the one decent thing we did ... And we all earn the right to go home.' Do we expect that we will necessarily receive a reward for our sacrificial actions? Do Jesus' words give us the answers we want to hear? Consider the following passages: Mark 10:35-45; Matthew 19:27-30; and Luke 9:57-62.

C. 'We're going on a public relations mission', Miller tells the rescue group. What is the motive behind *our* sacrificial actions? Is our discipleship a life lived for God or for ourselves? Consider Jesus' words in the Sermon on the Mount: Matthew 5:43-6:18.

3. Responding to the sacrifice of others

A. Miller, speaking to Ryan, as he lies dying on the bridge says, 'Earn it!' Ryan ponders on whether he has actually earned the sacrifice of those who died in saving him. At Miller's grave he asks his wife if he has led a life worthy of their sacrifice, 'Have I lived a good life?' What does Ryan mean by a 'good life' and how could he have earned his rescue?

B. Ryan is not only saved from death. Miller's final words suggest that he has a new purpose, he is saved for something. Nicolaus Ludwig von Zinzendorf (AD 1700-1760), who wrote the hymns *Jesus Thy blood and righteousness* and *Jesus still lead on,* was a Saxon nobleman, who studied for the diplomatic service, but who had a profound religious experience through a trip to an art gallery. He was looking at a painting of Jesus crowned with thorns, inscribed with the words: 'This have I done for Thee, what hast thou done for Me?' This led him to build a Christian village, which led to the founding of the Moravian Church. What do we think we are saved from? and for what are we saved? Consider Ephesians 2:8-10 and discuss your own answers.

C. When Ryan is informed of the death of his brothers, and about the rescue mission on which Miller has been sent, he says, 'It doesn't make sense. These are the only brothers I have left [i.e. his comrades in battle], and I'm not leaving them.' Jesus had a clear understanding of who his family were (Mark 3:31-35), while the expert in the law asked Jesus, 'And who is my neighbour?' (Luke 10:29). If being a disciple of Jesus implies living for others, who are our brothers and sisters?

INDEX OF FILMS

1984, 279-85

-A-
Ali, 48
Alien, 14
Amadeus, 251-4
American Beauty, 48, 67
Apocalypse Now, 23
Armageddon, 23

-B-
Babette's Feast, 25
Back to the Future, 137, 151, 162, 207
Becket, ix, 25
Ben Hur, ix, 9, 16
Big Fish, 83-96
Blade Runner, 9, 18, 241-245
Blood Simple, 18, 23
Blue Velvet, 14
Braveheart, x
Breaking the Waves, 25
Bridge Over the River Kwai, ix
Bridges of Madison County, 161
Bridget Jones' Diary, 295-302

-C-
Cape Fear, 18, 23
City of Angels, 20
Color Purple, 271-8
Cool Hand Luke, 13, 26
Crouching Tiger, Hidden Dragon, 55-57
Cry Freedom!, x, 77, 287-94

-D-
Dead Man Walking, 19, 23
Dead Poets Society, 17, 18, 70
Die Hard, 12, 16, 37-8
Dogma, 48
Dune, 23

-E-
E.T., 13
Exorcist, 11
Eyes Wide Shut, 22

-F-
Field of Dreams, 14, 19, 161
Fifth Element, 17
Forrest Gump, 17
Four Weddings and a Funeral, 12
Fugitive, 12

-G-
Gandhi, 255-261
Ghost, 19
Glass Bottom Boat, ix
Godfather, 18, 23, 104, 149
Grand Canyon, x
Greatest Story Ever Told, 26
Green Mile, x, 25
Groundhog Day, 14

-H-
Hulk, 53-55

-I-
Ice Storm, 53
Incredibles, 70
In the Good Old Summertime, 101
Ipcress Files, ix

-J-
Jesus Christ Superstar, 12, 217
Jesus of Nazareth, 217
Jesus of Montreal, 217
JFK, ix
Johnny English, x
John Q, 157, 162

-K-
Kill Bill, 226
Killing Fields, 68, 232, 263-269
King of Kings, 26

-L-
Last Temptation of Christ, 16, 217, 225
Lawrence of Arabia, ix
Life is Beautiful, 18
Life of Brian, 16, 217, 225, 226
Lord of the Rings, 59, 193-205

-M-
Magnificent Seven, 11
Man for all Seasons, ix
Master and Commander, 61, 64, 72, 123-
    135
Man who Sued God, x
Matrix, x, 17, 49-52, 67, 71
Meaning of Life, 11
Minority Report, 19, 137
Miracle Maker, 217
Mission, 59, 65, 73, 75-6, 233-240

-N-
Natural, 161

-O-
One Flew Over the Cuckoo's Nest, 13, 68,
    113-122
Open Water, 163-74
Ordinary People, 14, 15, 18

-P-
Pale Rider, 17
Parenthood, 157, 162
Passion of Joan of Arc, 25
Passion of the Christ, 68, 217-228
Planet of the Apes, 151
Pulp Fiction, 226
Platoon, 23
Pleasantville, 1, 69, 207-216

-R-
Rocky, 13, 14

-S-
Saving Private Ryan, x, 232, 303-7
Schindler's List, 18, 62, 73, 175-91
Sense and Sensibility, 53
Seven, 18
Shawshank Redemption, 17
Shop Around the Corner, 101
Siege, 39-42, 69
Sliding Doors, 19, 59, 69, 137-148
Sophie's Choice, 161
Star Trek, 72
Star Wars, 14, 17, 23, 48, 72
Stigmata, 66

-T-
Tender Mercies, 14
Terminator, 17, 19, 23, 137, 149-162
Thelma and Louise, 11, 19
Truly, Madly, Deeply, 19
Truman Show, 18, 67, 207

-W-
Waterworld, 23
What Dreams May Come, 20
Witness, 247-250

-X-
X-Men 2, 52

-Y-
You've Got Mail, 97-111